Legal Aspects of the
New International Economic Order

Legal Aspects of the
New International Economic Order

edited by Kamal Hossain

Frances Pinter (Publishers) Ltd., London
Nichols Publishing Company, New York

© Centre for Research on the New International Economic Order, 1980

First published in Great Britain in 1980 by
Frances Pinter (Publishers) Limited
5 Dryden Street, London WC2E 9NW

ISBN 0 903804 50 6

Published in the U.S.A. in 1980 by
Nichols Publishing Company
P.O. Box 96, New York, N.Y. 10024

Library of Congress Cataloging in Publication Data

Main entry under title:
Legal aspects of the new international economic order.
    1. International economic relations — Addresses,
essays, lectures.   I. Hossain, Kamal.
K3823.Z9L44   341.7'5   80–12089
ISBN 0–89397–088–3

Typeset by Anne Joshua Associates, Oxford
Printed in Great Britain by A. Wheaton & Co., Exeter

CONTENTS

PART I   GENERAL PRINCIPLES AND THE CHARTER OF ECONOMIC RIGHTS AND DUTIES OF STATES

PART II   TRANSNATIONAL CORPORATIONS AND TRANSFER OF TECHNOLOGY

PART III   LAW OF THE SEA AND THE NIEO

PART IV   PERMANENT SOVEREIGNTY OVER NATURAL RESOURCES

LIST OF CONTRIBUTORS

Dr Samuel K.B. Asante Ghana, Senior Adviser on Legal Matters, UN Centre on Transnational Corporations, Visiting Fellow, Clare Hall, Cambridge, 1978–79.

Professor Brigitte Bollecker-Stern France, Professor of International Law, University of Dijon and University of Paris.

Dr Milan Bulajic Yugoslavia, Legal Adviser, Ministry of Foreign Affairs.

Dr Jorge Castaneda Mexico, Minister of Foreign Affairs.

Mr Subrata Roy Chowdhury India, Senior Advocate, Supreme Court of India, Chairman, ILA Sub-Committee on Regional Implementation of Human Rights.

Dr Hugo Caminos Argentina, Deputy Director (Special Studies) UNCLOS III.

Dr Julio Faundez Chile, Lecturer, School of Law, University of Warwick.

Professor Yash Ghai Kenya, Professor, School of Law, University of Warwick.

Dr Reginald H. Green USA, Professorial Fellow, Institute of Development Studies, Sussex.

Dr Kamal Hossain Bangladesh, Director, Centre for Research on the New International Economic Order.

Dr Eduardo Jimenez de Arechaga Uruguay, Former President, International Court of Justice.

Mrs Elsa Kelly Argentina, Research Associate, Centre for Research on the New International Economic Order; Argentine Foreign Serivce.

Mr Salman Khurshid India, Lecturer in Law, Trinity College, Oxford.

Mr T.T.B. Koh Singapore, Permanent Representative of Singapore to the United Nations.

Dr Maurice Mendelson United Kingdom, Fellow St. John's College, Oxford.

Mr Tawfique Nawaz Bangladesh, Research Associate, Centre for Research on the New International Economic Order.

Judge Shigeru Oda Japan, Judge, International Court of Justice.

Dr Felipe Paolillo Uruguay, Senior Legal Officer UNCLOS III.

Professor Oscar Schachter USA, Professor of Interntional Law, Columbia University.

Professor Enrique Syquia Philippines, President, International Law Association, full Professor of International Law, University of Santo Tomas, the Catholic University of the Philippines.

Dr Hasan S. Zakariya Iraq, UN Inter-Regional Adviser on Petroleum Economics and Legislation.

ACKNOWLEDGEMENTS

Permission received from the respective authors to publish the material included in this volume is gratefully acknowledged.

Some of the material has been presented and/or published elsewhere as indicated below, and is being reproduced with the author's permission:

Eduardo Jimenez de Arechaga, 'State Responsibility for the Nationalization of Foreign-Owned Property', *New York University Journal of International Law and Politics*, Fall 1978.

Samuel K.B. Asante, 'UN Efforts at International Regulation of Transnational Corporations', *Journal of World Trade Law*, January 1979 1979

Samuel K.B. Asante, 'Stability of Contractual Relations in the Transnational Investment Process', *International and Comparative Law Quarterly*, July 1979

Milan Bulajic, 'Legal Aspects of a New International Economic Order', presented at the Madrid Law of the World Conference, September 16-20 1979

Jorge Castaneda, 'The Peaceful Uses of the Oceans and the New Law of the Sea', 29th Pugwash Conference, Mexico City, July 18-23 1979

Enrique Syquia, 'UNCTAD Code and Problems of Transfer of Technology and Restrictive Practices: The Viewpoint of Developing Countries', presented at a symposium at the Centre for Interdisciplinary Research of the University of Bielefeld, July 16-18 1979

H.S. Zakariya, 'Sovereignty over Natural Resources and the Search for a New International Economic Order', *Natural Resources Forum*, January 1980

H.S. Zakariya, 'Changed Circumstances and the Continued Validity of Mineral Development Contracts', *Arab Oil and Gas*, April 1979

PREFACE

This volume is the result of efforts, initiated at the 58th Conference of the International Law Association held in Manila in September 1978. Many at that Conference, including a number of contributors to this volume, shared the perception that proposals for the establishment of a new international economic order bristled with complex legal issues, which merited the serious attention of lawyers. Moved by the conviction that these proposals aimed at restructuring international economic relations and effecting a global redistribution of wealth and power, presented a challenge to legal creativity, the Conference adopted a resolution urging the International Law Association to undertake a study of the Legal Aspects of a New International Economic Order.

The Executive Council of the International Law Association met in London on 18 November 1978 when the above resolution was taken up for discussion. The Council was informed of certain initiatives which had been taken since the Manila Conference towards formulating a work programme on legal aspects of a new international economic order: a meeting had been organised by the Centre for Research on the New International Economic Order, in New York at the UNITAR Conference Room on 19 September 1978, to draw up a list of topics for consideration at a Seminar, to be held in Oxford in March 1979. The Executive Council decided to establish a Working Group to elaborate a work programme and identify the topics which could be taken up for study by the International Law Association. The Working Group, under the Chairmanship of the Editor of this volume, met in St John's College Oxford from 15-17 March 1979 when its members also participated in a Seminar on the Legal Aspects of a New International Economic Order, organised by the Centre for Research on the New International Economic Order.

This volume consists for the most part of papers presented at that seminar. Among the materials added are an introduction in six parts and a number of individual contributions, some of them being edited versions of statements which were part of the verbatim transcript of the proceedings of the Seminar. In this latter category are the contributions made by: Dr Hugo Caminos, Ambassador T. Koh, Dr Maurice Mendelson, Judge Shigeru Oda, Dr Felipe Paolillo and Professor Oscar Schachter.

The Editor would like specially to record his gratitude to the contributors and to the participants at the Seminar.

An expression of gratitude is owed to the President of the International Law Association, Professor Enrique Syquia, to the Chairman of its Executive Council, Lord Wilberforce, and the late Professor D.P. O'Connell, Director of Studies of the Association, for their encouragement and support. The material support extended by UNESCO through the International Law Association, to meet part of the expenses for the holding of the Seminar must be acknowledged with gratitude, as also the support received from the OPEC Special Fund towards preparing this volume for publication.

Sincere appreciation must be recorded of the substantial contributions made towards organising the Seminar by Dr Maurice Mendelson, Fellow of St John's College, Oxford, Mrs Elsa Kelly de Guibourg and Mr Tawfique Nawaz, Research Associates of the Centre, and by Ms Vanessa Hall-Smith, Secretary at the time of the International Law Association. Thanks are due to Hameeda Hossain for editorial assistance and to Mrs Joan Peacock and Mrs Irene Clapson for typing the final manuscript.

Kamal Hossain

Centre for Research on the New International Economic Order
Queen Elizabeth House
Oxford
3 April 1980

INTRODUCTION*

I: GENERAL PRINCIPLES, THE CHARTER OF ECONOMIC RIGHTS AND DUTIES OF STATES, AND THE NIEO

In 1945, fifty-one States founded the United Nations. Its Charter declared sovereign equality to be one of its basic principles, and proclaimed all States sovereign and equal. Since then over a hundred new members have been added. During this period, it has become increasingly clear that while all States are juridically sovereign and equal, some are in fact markedly *more* equal than others.

The economic order created at the end of the Second World War had been built on the principles of equal and non-discriminatory treatment of all countries in matters of trade and economic relations. Here too, experience was to show that 'no matter how valid the principle of the most-favoured nation may be in trade relations among equals, it is not an acceptable and adequate concept for trade among countries with highly unequal economic power'.[1]

While the objective of the establishment of 'a new international economic order' was formally proclaimed at the Non-Aligned Summit in Algiers in 1973, and reiterated in the Declaration on the Establishment of a New International Economic Order adopted in the Sixth Special

---

*The Introduction consists of six parts as follows: Part I: General Principles . . . (Kamal Hossain); Part II: Transnational Corporations (edited version of oral presentation made at the Oxford Seminar by Dr S.K.B. Asante); III: Legal Aspects of Transfer of Technology (Professor Yash Ghai, with section on the Code of Conduct, being an extract from a paper by Professor Enrique Syquia); Part IV: International Trade, Law and the NIEO (Dr R.H. Green); Part V: New Law of the Sea (extract from a paper by Dr Jorge Castaneda, circulated at the 29th Pugwash Conference, Mexico City, July 1979); Part VI: Permanent Sovereignty over Natural Resources (Kamal Hossain).

Session of the UN General Assembly in 1974, grievances with the existing economic order and demands for change began to be articulated by developing countries at least two decades earlier.

The principle of permanent sovereignty over natural resources was asserted in the early fifties in order to justify abrogation, or alteration of terms of concessions, secured by foreign companies, by which they were granted extensive rights to extract petroleum or minerals underlying the territories of host States. These concessions were perceived to be 'inequitable' as being markedly more advantageous to the foreign concessionaire than to the host State, or as having been granted as a result of duress or undue influence.

Growing dissatisfaction was felt by developing countries with the working of the international economic system in general, and that of the rules governing international trade in particular. The legal framework of international trade defined by the General Agreement on Tariffs and Trade, which came into effect in 1948, was seen as producing results which were either injurious or not beneficial to the developing countries – injurious when, for example, GATT allowed an increase in agricultural and other commodity protectionism requested by the developed countries; not beneficial when the reduction of industrial tariffs was concentrated on those products in which developed and not developing countries had comparative advantage.[2] In 1958, the report of a panel of experts (the Haberler Report) stressed that export growth in developing countries was not as rapid as in developed countries, and agreed that this was largely due to import tariffs and other barriers erected by developed countries against goods in which developing countries had particular exporting interests.[3] In the early 1950s the developing countries accounted for 32 per cent of world trade, in 1972 this had been reduced to 17 per cent. If the exports of oil-exporting countries are excluded, some one hundred developing countries accounted only for 10 per cent of world trade.[4]

It thus appeared that the existing economic order, while it worked well for the developed countries, served the developing countries poorly (though today, with developed countries facing recession, growing unemployment and inflation, it may be questioned whether the existing order is adequately serving the interests even of the developed countries).

From 1952 to 1972, the total gross product of the developed market economies rose from $1,250 billion to about $3,070 billion (in 1973 prices), the increment alone ($1,810 billion) being three-and-a-half times the aggregate gross product of the developing countries in 1972 ($520 billion). In terms of per capita real income, the contrast was even greater. Real income in the developed market economies rose by $2,000 per head of population from 1952 to 1972 (valued in 1973 prices) to a figure of about $4,000 in the latter year. The corresponding real per capita income for the developing countries in 1972 was about $300, the increase since 1952 being only $125. As a result of these uneven developments, the global income inequality gap had widened even further. In 1976, the developed market-economy countries, with 20 per cent of the world population, enjoyed about two-thirds of total world income. By contrast, the developing countries — excluding China — with about 50 per cent of world population, received only one-eighth of the total world income.[5]

This widening gap between developed and developing countries is seen to result from the structure of the existing order, which operates in favour of the rich and the powerful. 'The weaknesses of the structure . . . are manifested in each of the major areas of economic relations between developed and developing countries — in the trade in commodities and manufactures, in the transfer of technology, and in the provision of financial resources through the international monetary and financial system.'

The developing countries suffered from the weakness in the markets for their commodity exports. In many of these markets the buyers are concentrated, while the sellers are numerous, widely dispersed and poorly organized. Thus, developing countries receive only a small portion of the ultimate price which is paid for their primary commodities — since they are too weak, or lack resources, to exercise any meaningful control over the processing, shipping and marketing of their primary exports. On one estimate, the final consumers pay over $200 billion (excluding taxes) for the major primary exports (excluding oil), but the producer countries receive back only $30 billion; it is estimated that if developing countries could exercise the same degree of control over their exports as the developed countries do and if they were to get back the same proportion of the final consumer price, their export earnings would be closer to $150 billion.[6] A protective wall of tariff and non-tariff barriers erected by the developed countries impedes the entry of exports of developing countries into the markets of the developed countries.

Other impediments to the expansion of trade and to industrialization of developing countries are presented by restrictive business practices of transnational corporations, particularly restrictions on exports of manufactures produced under licence in developing countries and restrictive conditions attached to the use of modern technology transferred by these companies. Developing countries have to bear a heavy foreign-exchange burden in acquiring technology: the cost of acquisition of foreign technology by them is estimated to be in the region of $3–5 billion, while a rapid expansion in the international market in skills has led to a reverse transfer of technology by the loss of trained manpower by developing countries.[7]

The existing economic order has also worked inequitably for the developing countries so far as financial flows and distribution of international financial resources are concerned. Of the total world increase in official external reserves from 1952 to 1972 of $108 billion, about two-thirds or $70 billion accrued to developed market economies. Developed countries control the creation and distribution of international reserves, through expansion of their own national reserve currencies, and through their decisive control over the International Monetary Fund. Over the decade from 1964 to 1974 the real value of official development assistance from the developed countries (in terms of purchasing power and imports from these countries) actually declined by 3 per cent.[8] The developing countries have thus been compelled to borrow on commercial markets, or resort to suppliers' credits, at high interest rates and relatively short maturities, leading to growth in the external indebtedness of developing countries, from around $9 billion at the end of 1956, to $90 billion in 1972, to around $300 billion in 1979.[9]

Pressures for change in the rules governing international trade led to the concerted efforts of the developing countries bringing about the convening of the United Nations Conference on Trade and Development (UNCTAD) in Geneva in 1964. UNCTAD I in its Final Act set out new general principles, one of its first enunciations being the need for preferential and non-reciprocal economic relationships. Thus general principle eight provided:

> New preferential concessions, both tariff and non-tariff should be made to developing countries as a whole and such preferences should not be extended to developed countries. Developing countries need not extend to developed countries preferential treatment in operation amongst them.

Successive UNCTADs (UNCTAD II – New Delhi, 1968; UNCTAD III – Santiago, 1972; UNCTAD IV – Nairobi, 1976 and UNCTAD V – Manila, 1979) have identified different areas of international economic relations where changes were perceived to be needed if the objectives of development and other legitimate interests of the developing countries were to be realized. In UNCTAD III, President Echeverria of Mexico proposed that a Charter of Economic Rights and Duties of States be formulated to 'reinforce the precarious legal foundations of the international economy . . . removing economic co-operation from the realm of good will and rooting it in the field of law by transferring consecrated principles of solidarity among men to the sphere of relations among nations.'

In UNCTAD III it was decided to undertake the formulation of a Charter which would spell out the basic norms on which a more equitable international economic order could be built. The successful collective action of OPEC members in achieving an upward adjustment of oil prices in 1973 gave an added impetus to the developing countries' demand for fundamental changes in international economic relations. The Declaration on the Establishment of a New International Economic Order adopted at the Sixth Special Session of the UN General Assembly in May 1974 drew together the different proposals for changes which had been urged by developing countries in different international forums, and the UN General Assembly proceeded in December 1974 to adopt the Charter of Economic Rights and Duties of States.

The Charter of Economic Rights and Duties of States

The Charter of Economic Rights and Duties of States was adopted on 12 December 1974 by a roll-call vote of 120 in favour, 6 against (Belgium, Denmark, Federal Republic of Germany, Luxembourg, United Kingdom, United States) with 10 abstentions (Austria, Canada, France, Ireland, Israel, Italy, Japan, Netherlands, Norway and Spain). The UN General Assembly while adopting the Charter characterized it as 'an effective instrument towards the establishment of a new system of international economic relations based on equity, sovereign equality, and interdependence of the interests of developed and developing countries'.

The Charter was conceived of as 'a kind of basic code' containing fundamental principles in different spheres of international economic relations. Among the areas covered are: international trade, transnational corporations, nationalization, international economic co-operation, development of natural resources, industrialization, transfer of technology, and exploitation of the resources of the seabed. The fundamental principles which are set out in the Charter are: equity, sovereign equality, interdependence, common interest and co-operation among all States, permanent sovereignty over natural resources and the common heritage of mankind. These principles are invoked to support certain basic positions, which reflect the principal concerns of the developing countries. Developing countries, being weak, seek the protection of the law to protect themselves from coercion by the powerful. They would also like the law to operate as it has done in certain constitutional systems by way of affirmative action and reverse discrimination to secure equal opportunity. This is seen as a way of giving substance to the principle of sovereign equality of States, so that the majority of States which have been *less* equal than the powerful minority may progressively improve their position relative to the latter.

A proper appreciation and assessment of the structure and provisions of the Charter must begin with the recognition of its character as an instrument of change to give effect to a strategy for the re-distribution of wealth and power. Its Preamble declares that 'it is a fundamental purpose of the Charter *to promote* the establishment of the new international economic order', and speaks of 'the urgent need to evolve a substantially improved system of international economic relations.' It takes cognizance of an international community which is made up of *developed* and *developing* countries, and recognizes that the existing structure of international economic relations works to the disadvantage of developing countries and impedes their development. It, therefore, urges 'the advancement of *more rational* and *equitable* international economic relations . . . the strengthening of the economic independence of developing countries' and the need for 'promotion by the entire international community of economic and social progress of all countries, specially developing countries'.

The substantive provisions of the Charter are contained in four chapters – Chapter I: Framework of International Economic Relations; Chapter II: Economic Rights and Duties of States; Chapter III: Common Responsibility towards the International Community, and Chapter IV: Final Provisions. The Charter, upon analysis, appears to be a compendium of established principles and rules of international law as well as broad principles which bear a strong resemblance to provisions which are contained in constitutional documents as 'Directive Principles of Policy' and operate as signposts to be followed in the making of legislation or the exercise of state power. Thus, Chapter I while setting out fifteen fundamental principles which shall govern economic, political and 'other' relations among States, embraces not only such established principles of international law as sovereignty, territorial integrity and political independence, sovereign equality of all States, non-aggression and non-intervention, but at the same time enumerates such principles as mutual and equitable benefit, remedying of injustices that have been brought about by force and promotion of international social justice. The latter set of principles can be distinguished from the former in that while the former are established norms, with clearly understood connotations, directed at preserving the status quo, the latter are principles whose application in specific situations raises complex juridical issues, and are manifestly principles directed at changing the status quo.

A similar mix of established norms and 'directive principles' is found throughout the Charter. Thus, Chapter II sets out rights, based on the fundamental and established principle of State sovereignty, such as the sovereign right of each State to choose its own political, economic, social and cultural system, without outside interference, coercion or threat (Article 1), permanent sovereignty over natural resources, and the right to regulate and exercise authority over foreign investment within its national jurisdiction (Article 2), the right to form producers' associations (Article 5), the right to participate in sub-regional, regional and inter-regional co-operation (Article 12). At the same time, it contains a number of provisions which prescribe 'the duty to co-operate *to promote*' a variety of objectives, such as 'facilitating more rational and equitable international economic relations' (Article 8), strengthening and con-tinuously improving 'the efficiency of international organizations in implementing measures to stimulate the general economic progress of all countries' (Article 11), 'promoting a steady and increasing liberalization of world trade' (Article 14) and 'the achievement of general and complete disarmament under effective international control' (Article 15). There are further directive principles, which, for example, urge developing countries 'to promote expansion of their mutual trade' (Article 21), and developed countries 'to grant generalized, preferential, non-reciprocal and non-discriminatory treatment to developing countries in those fields of international economic co-operation *where it may be feasible*'. The determination of the scope of a duty, couched in such terms as 'a duty to co-operate to promote', and more specially, where it is qualified by words such as 'where it may be feasible', raises complex issues. They call for analysis and elucidation, based on an appreciation of the eco-nomic implications of particular courses of action, which may be called for if the obligations created by such provisions are to be fulfilled.

The fact that the Charter has been designed as an instrument of change means that the principles embodied in it must undergo progressive develop-ment through implementation and application to specific situations. This is expressly recognized in Article 34 of the Charter, which provides that an item would be inserted in the agenda of the General Assembly at its Thirtieth Session (1980) and thereafter on the agenda of every fifth session for 'a systematic and comprehensive consideration of the implementation of the Charter, covering both progress achieved and any improvements and additions which might become necessary'. It is provided that such consideration should take into account the evolution of all the economic, social, legal and other factors related to the principles upon which the Charter is based and on its purpose.

The New International Legal Order

The papers published in this volume reflect views which are being increasingly articulated in different international forums that the existing international economic order, and the legal framework within which the current international economic order operates, no longer satisfy the legitimate expectations of the overwhelming majority of States and their peoples. Whereas in the sixties this perception was more widely held by developing countries, today it is a perception shared also by representatives of the industrialized countries. The need for change is thus almost universally recognized — for a new international legal order in which some of the existing rules are to be changed, and new rules are to be created in areas where no rules have hitherto existed, for new regulatory frameworks to be formulated and for new institutional and decision-making arrangements and procedures to be established. Thus, proposals for a change of existing rules and for creation of new rules are under active consideration in the Third United Nations Conference on the Law of the Sea. New regulatory frameworks are being elaborated — an International Code of Conduct on Transfer of Technology is under negotiation in UNCTAD and a Code of Conduct on Transnational Corporations is being formulated by the United Nations Commission on Transnational Corporations. Proposals for amendments to GATT have been urged, as to the Paris Convention on Patents. The Charter reiterates the right of *all* States to participate fully and effectively in the international decision-making process in the solution of world economic, financial and monetary problems and recognizes that this would require recourse not only to existing but *evolving* rules. National and regional legislation are being designed to improve the terms on which technology may be acquired by developing countries. New types of natural resource development arrangements to give effect to the principle of permanent sovereignty over natural resources are being devised.

It is through such changes in the legal framework within which international economic relations are conducted that progress is likely to be made towards the establishment of the new international economic order. The proposals for change raise complex issues. They call for innovation and ingenuity in devising instruments and mechanisms at the international, regional and national levels, and for an imaginative application of legal techniques and legal analysis, all of which present a challenge to legal creativity.

The papers in this volume have sought to identify the legal issues and problems raised in specific areas, which are currently under active consideration in different international forums. The introductory notes (which cover the following areas: Code of Conduct on Transnational Corporations, International Transfer of Technology, International Trade, the New Law of the Sea and Permanent Sovereignty over Natural Resources) seek to survey the issues and provide background and perspective for a consideration of the problems discussed in the papers.

II: CODE OF CONDUCT ON TRANSNATIONAL CORPORATIONS

The concern about operations of transnational corporations felt by developing countries has been reflected in their demand for international regulation of these operations. Among the matters that have caused concern are practices that militate against the interest of the host governments. Many of these result from the fact that a large part of the transactions of such corporations are 'within the group', that is, with their own affiliates. The Declaration on the Establishment of a New International Economic Order (Para. 4(g)) declares that the right to control transnational corporations is one of the fundamental principles of the new order:

> The new international economic order should be founded on full respect for the following principles:
>
> . . .
>
> (g) Regulation and supervision of the activities of transnational corporations by taking measures in the interest of the national economies of the countries where such transnational corporations operate on the basis of the full sovereignty of those countries.

The Programme of Action adopted in the Sixth Special Session dedicated a whole section (Section V) to 'Regulation and Control over the Activities of Transnational Corporations'. It urged that 'all efforts should be made to formulate, adopt and implement an international code of conduct for transnational corporations' in order:

> (a) To prevent interference in the internal affairs of the countries where they operate and their collaboration with racist regimes and colonial administrations;
> (b) To regulate their activities in host countries, to eliminate restrictive business practices and to conform to the national development plans and objectives of developing countries, and in this context facilitate, as necessary, the review and revision of previously concluded arrangements;

(c) To bring about assistance, transfer of technology and management skills to developing countries on equitable and favourable terms;
(d) To regulate the repatriation of the profits accruing from their operations, taking into account the legitimate interests of all parties concerned;
(e) To promote reinvestment of their profits in developing countries.

In the same vein, the Charter of Economic Rights and Duties of States affirms (Chapter II, Art. 2, 2(a), (b)) that:

Each State has the right:

(a) To regulate and exercise authority over foreign investment within its national jurisdiction in accordance with its laws and regulations and in conformity with its national objectives and priorities. No State shall be compelled to grant preferential treatment to foreign investment;
(b) To regulate and supervise the activities of transnational corporations within its national jurisdiction and take measures to ensure that such activities comply with its laws, rules and regulations and conform with its economic and social policies. Transnational corporations shall not intervene in the internal affairs of a host State. Every State should, with full regard for its sovereign rights, co-operate with other States in the exercise of the right set forth in this subparagraph.

Within the United Nations system, a concrete step taken in this area was the initiation in 1972 of a study on transnational enterprises by a 'Group of Eminent Persons'. Their Report in 1974 recommended the establishment of a Commission on Transnational Corporations. The United Nations Commission on Transnational Corporations was set up in 1975, as was the United Nations Centre on Transnational Corporations. The Centre was entrusted with the task of research and data collection, and of assisting developing countries in dealing with transnational corporations.

The Commission in its meeting in March 1975 decided that 'among the various tasks it would undertake in the next four years priority would be assigned to the formulation of the Code of Conduct', and proceeded to establish an Intergovernmental Working Group on the Code of Conduct.

Since 1977, the *ad hoc* Intergovernmental Working Group, constituted by the Commission on Transnational Corporations has been engaged in the formulation of a Code of Conduct. The Working Group proceeded by defining the general areas and topics, to be included in a possible Code of Conduct. The first negotiations in the Group were with regard to what topics should be included. This task was entrusted to the Chairman, who produced an annotated version of a series of topics. An important question at that stage was whose conduct was to be affected by this Code of Conduct, that is, whose conduct was going to be regulated. The developing countries took the view that it was the conduct of transnational corporations. The developed countries, however, insisted that it was meaningless from their point of view to have any code of conduct merely confined to the regulation of transnational corporations, without prescribing some general standards of conduct to be observed by governments in their treatment of transnational corporations. It was therefore agreed that the Code would have two basic parts: the first part dealing with the regulation of transnational corporations; the second part setting up standards of conduct to be observed by governments in their treatment of transnational corporations.

This concession by developing countries was to affect their entire strategy through the negotiations, because the developing countries themselves had reservations about the Code being binding in view of a part being incorporated in it which purported to lay down standards to be observed by governments.

Another issue which had emerged was the question of definition. What sort of entities were to be regarded as transnational corporations for the purposes of the Code? This issue was shelved, as it was found to be a rather sensitive one. The definition of TNCs became a major political issue because the Socialist countries would not agree that their trading organizations could be classified as transnational organizations. They did not want them to be put on the same sort of level as Western transnationals. So the definition question has not been touched yet. A third issue which was broached in the early stages, and then remained postponed until its recent re-introduction into the agenda for discussion, is the legal nature of the Code and the modalities for the implementation of the Code.

Having defined the topics to be included in the Code, the Members of the Commission discussed in several sessions the broad principles and began to formulate the foundations of the norms or the standards to be included in such a Code. The reason why countries thought that it would be premature to determine the legal nature of the Code was, it would appear because they wanted to have a better appreciation of what the substantive provisions of the Code would be before committing themselves to whether it should be a binding or a non-binding Code. After these discussions, the Commission asked the United Nations Centre on Transnational Corporations to prepare a paper on transnational corporations, formulating some general standards, which could be the basis for further discussions. Tentative general propositions were formulated by the Chairman based on previous discussions, setting out certain broad norms. The first part dealing with the regulation of transnational corporations has three main sections. The first section deals with the general and political norms, the second with economic, financial and social issues and the third with disclosure of information. These are thre three basic elements. The second part dealing with the treatment of transnational corporations has also three basic elements: (a) the general treatment of transnational corporations by countries within which they operate, (b) nationalization and compensation, and (c) jurisdiction. There is a third part on intergovernmental co-operation.

In the first section of the first part which deals with the general and political issues, among the standards of general and political significance which are set out, are the following:

1. Transnational corporations should respect the national sovereignty of the countries in which they operate and the exercise by each State of its right to full permanent sovereignty over the wealth and resources within his territory;

2. Transnational corporations are required to observe the laws and regulations and commercial practices in the countries in which they operate and respect the right of each such State to regulate and supervise the activities of transnational corporations;

3. Transnational corporations are required to promote the economic goals and developmental objectives of their host countries;

4. Transnational corporations should, as all parties to contracts freely entered into, respect and adhere to such contracts. In the absence of contractual clauses providing for review or renegotiation transnational corporations should respond positively to requests for review or renegotiation of contracts concluded with governments or governmental agencies in circumstances marked by duress or clear inequality between the parties, or where the conditions upon which such a contract was based have fundamentally changed, causing thereby unforeseen major distortions in the relations between the parties and thus rendering the contract unfair or oppressive to either of the parties. With the aim of ensuring fairness to all parties concerned, review or renegotiation of such a situation should be dealt with in accordance with applicable legal principles and generally recognized legal practices.

This proposition, as might have been anticipated, was resisted by the developed countries. They maintained the position that renegotiation or review of contracts should be an exception to the established principle of *pacta sunt servanda* and should not itself be formulated as a standard. In the event, the formulation which was adopted was a compromise.

Other matters covered by the first part were respect for human rights and fundamental freedoms, non-interference with internal political affairs and non-interference with intergovernmental relations. The second section of the first part deals with economic, financial and social matters. It sets out certain broad principles relating to such matters as ownership and control, balance of payments, taxation, transfer pricing, consumer protection and environmental protection. The third section deals with disclosure of information, and is given a prominent place in the Code of Conduct.

The second part of the Code deals with the treatment of transnational corporations by governments. It consists of three sections: (a) the general treatment of transnational corporations by home and host countries, (b) nationalization and compensation and (c) jurisdiction. Among the prescriptions in the first section are the following:

1. Transnational corporations should be treated by their host countries in a fair and equitable manner consistent with the interests of all concerned and in accordance with national laws, regulations and practices as well as international norms and contractual obligations which have freely been assumed;
2. Transnational corporations should be treated by their home countries in a way that recognizes the rights of host countries to regulate the activities of transnational corporations.

Also included are the standards of non-discrimination and fair treatment. Improper use of transnational corporations by countries as instruments for the attainment of foreign policy objectives is prohibited. Another prescription addressed to the home countries enjoins them to ensure that action taken toward other countries in support of the interests of transnational corporations remained within the bounds established by international norms concerning normal diplomatic representation and the submission of international legal claims. Their action should not amount to the exercise of economic or political pressure.

The second section deals with nationalization and compensation, and reflects the age-old controversies. The developing countries assert that they have the right to nationalize and that the standard of compensation is referable to national law; no international law standards are recognized.

If any dispute should arise from such an exercise of sovereignty, the dispute should be resolved in accordance with the national judicial or arbitral procedures. This is opposed by the developed countries. They assert that nationalization gives rise to the duty to pay prompt, effective and adequate compensation. They do not deny the right to nationalize, but insist that the right to nationalize as well as the duty to pay compensation are referable to international law. As to settlement of disputes, they press for international arbitration or adjudication.

The Chairman's formulation on nationalization and compensation was as follows:

> In the exercise of their sovereignty, States have the right acting in their sovereignty interests to nationalize property in their territory. Fair and equitable treatment of Transnational Corporations by the countries in which they operate include payment of just compensation in the event of nationalization or other taking of their property. Such Government action being undertaken under due process of law in accordance with national laws, regulations and administrative practices without discrimination between enterprises in comparable situations and with full regard to international obligations and contractual undertakings to which States have freely subscribed.

The third section of the second part deals with jurisdiction. It provides that transnational corporations are subject to the jurisdiction of the countries in which they operate. Disputes between a State and a transnational corporation which are not amicably settled between the parties are subject to the jurisdiction of the Courts and other authorities of that State and are to be submitted to them except for disputes which the State has agreed to settle by arbitration or other method of dispute settlement. It then deals with conflict of jurisdiction, an important matter as far as transnational corporations are concerned. Where the exercise of jurisdiction over transnational corporations by more than one State may lead to conflicts of jurisdiction, adoption is urged by the States concerned of mutually acceptable principles and procedures bilaterally or multilaterally for the avoidance of conflict or settlement of such conflicts on the basis of respect for the interests of the States concerned and their mutual obligations, as this would serve to improve the relations among States and between States and transnational corporations.

This part of the Code also deals with the mechanisms for inter-governmental control. It describes norms for inter-governmental co-operation in matters relating to the activities of transnational corporations and also in the implementation of the Code. Governments are required to co-operate on a bilateral as well as a multilateral basis with a view to encouraging positive contributions that transnational corporations can make to economic and social progress and to resolve difficulties to which the operations of transnational corporations may give rise.

III LEGAL ASPECTS OF TRANSFER OF TECHNOLOGY

The importance of technology for development can scarcely be exaggerated. The disparities in the technological capabilities of the rich and poor countries is not merely a reflection of their inequality but an important cause of it. As long as the industrialized countries retain their superiority in technological resources over the poor countries, so long are they likely to retain their hold over the process of economic and social change in the latter countries. This point is better appreciated in the industrialized countries than in the developing world, as is evident from the resources the former is willing to commit to the development of new technological capability, compared to the efforts of the latter.

While it is vital that developing countries establish the ability to generate their own autonomous advances in technological development, it is nevertheless true that their technological capacity would be enhanced by a systematic assimilation of the inventions and processes already in use in industrialized countries. The transfer of technology is thus important. The international regime is concerned with matters of transnational transfers, rather than with domestic generation of technology, and it is not surprising that lawyers have concentrated attention on the former.

The law has played an important part in the preservation of rights in technology as well as in the transfer of technology. A number of legal rules operate at the domestic and international levels which bear upon the establishment and safeguarding of these rights and which also define the parameters within which transfers take place. Of particular importance are the laws about patents in municipal systems, profoundly affected as they are by the international conventions on the subject, the Paris Union. These rules provide for fundamental rights in industrial property on the basis of which dealings in technology are made through various forms of contractual arrangements. The specific terms on which the transfers take place are embodied in contractual arrangements. Patents legislation protects the rights of the patent holder, and the protection can extend over large parts of the globe. The institution of contract enables the holder of patent or other know-how to exact harsh terms from the other party, which nevertheless enjoys the sanction of the law. As a result, there has been a considerable degree of criticism of the system of protection of patents and rights stemming from them, and of the 'freedom' of contract which enables unequal transactions to be concluded.

There have been debates for years in North America and Europe over the merits of patent protection, and criticism over the monopoly rights that are implicit in such protection. There has also been considerable disquiet about the harsh or restrictive terms on which technology may be transferred, and many legal systems have established rules to prevent the abuse of patent rights and have outlawed various forms of discriminatory and restrictive covenants, qualifying in important ways the freedom of contract. However, support for patent protection and the freedom of contract are not lacking. Patents are presented as property and thus sacrosanct, while the freedom to deal in rights over it is defended as an essential attribute of property or ownership. Thus the debate about patents and contract is obscured by a not inconsiderable amount of ideology and mystification.

It may be that the unfairness with which the law is seen to operate in technology transactions has resulted in an excessive concern with the law and has tended to over-emphasize its importance, and perhaps, unjustifiably to ascribe technological backwardness to the restrictions which hedge the use of patents. The patent system compels the disclosure of a vast store of scientific and technical knowledge, which passes in the course of time into public domain, and thus ceases to be private property. This store of knowledge which is potentially very valuable to the poorer countries, is available to them without charge. Yet few of these countries have established systems to exploit this knowledge and assimilate it into their industrial organization. Vast sums of money are paid for knowledge which has already lost patent protection. Numerous studies show that little attempt is made to search out the most appropriate technology, and to obtain it from the least expensive source. The reform of the legal provisions alone will not remedy these deficiencies.

Patents

The existing system of patents is based on a tight interlocking between international instruments and national legislation. The most important of the former is the Paris Convention (Union) established in 1884, and subsequently modified from time to time. About ninety countries are members, in relation to whom the Convention takes precedence over national regulation. The Convention thus prescribes the policy choices of these countries in several important respects. How seriously this restricts policy choices at the national level is a matter for controversy. The critics of the Paris Convention argue that it is suffused with the theory of patent protection; that it defines in great detail and with particular specificity the rights of the patent holders, and that it does so at the expense of the public interest. Its strongest supporters are transnational corporations. The supporters of the Convention argue that many choices are left to the member States, as to the definition of a patent, as to what products are patentable, as to the length of protection. International regulation of this kind is necessary to encourage inventiveness, and its transfer from one country to another. The fact that so many developing countries have signed the Convention must, they argue, mean that they perceive that their interests are better served by adherence to it than by remaining outside. (Its opponents attribute this result to the heavy sales efforts of WIPO, backed up by the vast resources of the transnational corporations, and not to any objective assessment of the costs and benefits of membership.)

It would be true to say that the international community has accepted the criticism that in several important respects, the Convention does not protect the interests of the developing countries. Thus it is not merely UNCTAD which has attacked the Convention; it has also been accepted by WIPO, the bastion of the protection of industrial property, that all is not well, so that in 1980 it will convene a world conference on the revision of the Convention to accommodate the interests of the developing countries — the first such review in its nearly hundred-year history.

The UNCTAD Report on the Revision of the Paris Convention[10] proposed that any revision of that Convention should take into account the following elements:

(a) It should recognize explicitly the right of a member State to adopt any legislative measure deemed necessary to prevent the non-working of patents and other abuses emerging from the patentee's exclusive rights. The recourse to any one of these measures should not be conditional upon, or conditioned by, the prior or simultaneous use of any of the other measures.

(b) It should not include restrictions on the national legislation with regard to the effect of importations of a patented product, nor obligations in relation to the rights concerning importation deriving from a process patent.

(c) The priority period should be reduced. At the same time, the possibility should be explored of granting preferential treatment with regard to its duration for inventions originating in developing countries.

(d) The priority right should not apply against third parties that have in good faith started the exploitation of the invention concerned. Moreover, as a measure of preferential treatment, applicants of developing countries should not be prevented from the use of their inventions when they have in good faith filed an application during the priority period.

(e) There should be an obligation on the applicant for a patent who claims priority rights to indicate the results of the application in other countries to the relevant authorities. There should also be provision for the compulsory exchange of information among patent offices of all orders passed by administrative and judicial authorities with regard to the granting and validity of a patent. Such a provision should be incorporated to enable the competent authorities to pass orders similar, when the same legal or factual circumstances apply, to those passed in the country where another patent was applied for or granted.

(f) The Convention should recognize the possibility of measuring the duration of patents claiming priority from the date of the first filing.

(g) Developing countries should be encouraged to design certain types of patents for which only their own nationals would be eligible and whose purpose would be to encourage domestic inventions, innovations and adaptation. The principle of non-reciprocal preferential treatment for developing countries should be expressly accepted.

These amendments will do much to remedy the one-sidedness of the Convention. They do not impose any positive obligations on the patent holder, but they would enable a developing country to take remedial action and to ameliorate the monopolistic and protectionist tendencies of patent rights, and thus lead to the greater genuine exploitation of technical knowledge. Whether these desirable results will necessarily follow is difficult to tell, and the varied experiences of those countries which have not joined the Paris Union must caution us against exaggerating the impact of the legal freedom to make forays into foreign technological information. This leads us to a consideration of major legal issues in the transfer of technology which arise from the contractual arrangements for it.

Contractual Arrangements

It is said that one important reason why rights in industrial property are valued is that they provide the basis for dealing in it, especially in the form of licensing agreements. The Paris Convention envisages such agreements, and indeed as we have seen, provides for compulsory licensing under certain contingencies. The criticism from the point of the developing countries (which are overwhelmingly the major purchasers of knowledge under such contracts) is that licensing agreements contain a large number of restrictive covenants, which have serious adverse effects upon the ability of these countries to take full advantage of such knowledge and thus inhibits their growth, penetration of foreign markets, the adaptation of technology, the localization of staff, protection of their foreign reserves, etc. The Paris Convention has nothing to prohibit such restrictive terms, and indeed many proponents of the Convention are willing to justify these terms on the basis that they represent sound commercial assessments and decisions of the holders of patents. There is a growing international recognition that there is a problem here, if not yet a consensus on what is undesirable and on the remedial steps. Since legal systems based on notions of the free and competitive market, especially in the United States and Western Europe, have had to grapple with similar problems at the domestic level, certain analogies as to what is undesirable and as to the remedies can be drawn, which the home countries of transnational corporations would find difficult to resist. It is equally difficult to resist the internationalization of these analogies, for the American anti-trust legislation, which deals, *inter alia*, with restrictive business practices, has been applied to the overseas operations of American-based transnationals while the West European states in the EEC (and previously EFTA), have been working their way towards a regional framework of prohibition and regulation of restrictive business practices.

A further impetus to international efforts at regulation has come from the more general concern with the power of transnational corporations, which are the main perpetrators of such practices. Thus Codes of Conduct have been or are being drawn up by various institutions – the OECD, the International Chamber of Commerce, UN Centre on Transnational Corporations etc. The discussion of the problem is best pursued through an examination of UNCTAD's efforts to secure agreement on an international instrument to regulate such practices. UNCTAD's work on the Code of Conduct on the Transfer of Technology began several years ago, but picked up momentum in the mid-seventies, and is now seen as an essential part of the efforts to restructure the international economic order. It has led to intensive and wide-ranging debate among the OECD countries and the Group of 77, and has, in its tortuous way, helped to clarify various issues in the contractual transfer of technology.

Code of Conduct on Transfer of Technology

The latest Draft International Code of Conduct on the Transfer of Technology, prepared by the UNCTAD Secretariat, as at the adjournment of the first resumed session of the United Nations Conference on 9 March 1979, consists of a preamble and ten chapters. Although there are complete texts and full agreement on some chapters, there are still major outstanding issues that remain unresolved.[11]

To understand the viewpoint of the developing countries (Group of 77, but now increased to 119) on these unresolved issues, one must keep in view their underlying principle formulated thus:

> In view of the crucial importance of technology to the economic and industrial growth and development of countries, the Group of 77 reaffirms that the basic aims in the negotiation on the code of conduct on the transfer of technology are to eliminate restrictive and unfair practices affecting their technological transactions and to strengthen their national technological capacities in order to accelerate the process of their technological transformation and development while increasing the international flow of all forms of technology under favourable terms.[12]

The major unresolved issue is the legal character of the code. The Group of 77 has consistently maintained 'that an internationally legally binding instrument is the only form capable of effectively regulating the transfer of technology'.[13] This position was reiterated in the Group of 77 Draft Resolution submitted at UNCTAD V which '*Requests* the resumed second session of the United Nations Conference to adopt a universally applicable code in the form of a legally binding instrument.'[14] As explained in its Arusha Programme: 'The Group of 77 reaffirms the need to adopt a legally binding code of conduct as one of the key instruments which will contribute to the establishment of the New International Economic Order.'[15] While previously, Group D (the socialist countries of Eastern Europe including Mongolia) did not have a definite stand on this issue,[16] in its Draft Resolution submitted at UNCTAD V it recommended that the 'Code should be legally binding'.[17]

This position however is opposed by Group B (the developed countries) which insists that the code should not be legally binding but should only be a 'code of conduct consisting of guidelines for the international transfer of technology';[18] although this position was later expanded by adding the clause 'with an effective international institutional machinery'.[19]

A second outstanding unresolved issue is the concept of 'international' transfer of technology which will govern the scope of application of the Code. Although all groups are agreed that the Code applies 'to international transfer of technology transactions which occur when technology is transferred across national boundaries between the supplying party and the acquiring party',[20] the Group of 77, joined by Group D but opposed by Group B, would also include the situation

> when a transfer of technology transaction is entered into between parties which do not reside or are not established in the same country, as well as between parties which are resident of or established in the same country, if at least one party is a branch, subsidiary or affiliate or is otherwise directly or indirectly controlled by a foreign entity and the technology transferred has not been developed in the technology-acquiring country by the supplying party, or when it otherwise acts as an intermediary in the transfer of foreign-owned technology.[21]

This is reiterated in the Group of 77 Draft Resolution at UNCTAD V;[22] and explained in its *Arusha Programme*:

> The Group of 77 maintains that all international transfer of technology transactions must be within the scope of application of the Code, and that such transactions occur either when the parties are from different countries or when they are located in the acquiring country if one of the parties is either owned or controlled by a foreign entity in accordance with the relevant national legislation.

> The Code must be applicable in transactions or arrangements between parent enterprises and their subsidiaries in the acquiring country, or between subsidiaries or affiliates of the same enterprise wherever they are located.[23]

A third outstanding unresolved issue is the scope of the practices to be restricted by the Code. The Group of 77 insists on a wide coverage and would 'avoid practices which restrain trade or adversely affect the international flow of technology, particularly as such practices hinder the economic and technological development of acquiring countries.'[24] This is also reiterated in the Group of 77 Draft Resolution submitted at UNCTAD V.[25] As explained in its *Arusha Programme*, 'The Group of 77 affirms that the aim of the chapter on restrictive practices must be to eliminate practices which have an adverse effect on the social and economic development of countries, and particularly of developing countries.'[26] For this reason, the Group of 77 would title the chapter on restrictive practices in a broad way as 'The Regulation of Practices and

Arrangements Involving the Transfer of Technology.'[27] This is, however, opposed by Group B which would restrict these practices only to those which actually restrict competition, and would therefore add the word 'unreasonable' to qualify some of the enumerated practices, and would title the chapter as 'Restrictive Business Practices.'[28]

A fourth outstanding unresolved issue is the question of the applicable law and the settlement of disputes. The different Groups presented their respective proposals, but due to the wide divergence, no composite text could be produced for the Draft Code.[29] The proposal made by the Group of 77[30] would make the law of the acquiring country 'applicable to matters relating to public policy (order public) and to sovereignty' and 'to questions of characterization'; and for the settlement of disputes arising therefrom the jurisdiction shall be vested in 'the courts and other tribunals of the technology-acquiring country'. As to matters of private interest, the applicable law is that 'which has a direct, effective and permanent relationship with the transaction'; and the proper forum 'must have a direct, effective, and permanent relationship with the contract'; although recourse to arbitration is recognized.[31] This position is reiterated in the Group of 77 Draft Resolution submitted at UNCTAD V.[32] As explained in its *Arusha Programme*:

> The Group of 77 considers that the law applicable to transfer of technology transactions must be the code of conduct and the law of the acquiring country, particularly with respect to issues involving public policy. Moreover, public policy issues, as determined under the law of the technology acquiring State, should normally be decided by national courts and tribunals of the technology acquiring State. Arbitration is recognized as a means of the settlement of disputes if the manner of selection of arbitrators and the procedure is of a type which will be fair and equitable, and if the code and national law provided for under the provisions of the code is the law applied by the arbitrator.[33]

This is opposed by Group B whose position is that 'the parties to a technology transfer agreement may freely choose the law governing the formation, validity, performance and interpretation of the agreement'; and 'the courts before which disputes relating to the agreement shall be tried'; and that 'the parties should also be freely permitted to choose arbitration or other third-party procedures'.[34]

The debates about the legal character of the instrument are instructive. They raise questions as to the commitment of the OECD countries to effective regulation in this area. It also shows that the bulk of industrial property is owned by transnational corporations (and this fact is indeed used by the OECD countries to argue that the instrument cannot be legally binding, since such corporations are not members of the international system of states). For these, among other reasons, the international regulation of the contractual terms of the transfer of technology will suffer from deficiencies of enforcement, unless there is a massive change in the attitude of the OECD countries and agreement on a supranational enforcement body, such as the EEC Commission.

National and Regional Regulation

There is scope, however, for the weaknesses of the international regulation to be made up to an extent by national and regional laws and practices. Just as the strength of the Paris Convention stems not only from its own provisions, but from its influence on, and underpinning by, national legislation, developing countries should use the Code (and the hoped for revisions of the Paris Convention) to adopt national and regional legislation and administrative practices), giving effect to the principles underlying the Code. Efforts at these levels are underway and it can indeed be argued that the impetus for the Code came from certain regional and national exercises on the regulation of technology transfer.

These international, regional and national efforts at establishing a new legal standards and instruments, will achieve little by themselves. They may open up certain channels for the flow of technology, and they may make certain forms of obvious exploitation more difficult to carry through. They will not by themselves change the unequal relationship between transnational corporations and business or public institutions in the Third World. The new rules may redefine the parameters within which commercial negotiations take place; they are not a substitute for such negotiations, and the poor preparation and negotiating skills of representatives of Third World country institutions may well help to ensure that the costs and burdens to it of technology transfer are merely shifted from one part of the contract to another. At the regional level, success will depend on unity and a sense of common purpose.

Few of the new rules or proposals will by themselves generate new flows of technology. It is hard enough to regulate the negative aspects of international transfers; it is considerably more difficult to generate new flows or to cultivate new capacity in the poorer countries to assimilate and produce technology. Legal provisions are likely at best to be facilitative.

IV   INTERNATIONAL TRADE, LAW AND THE NIEO[35]

Law does not figure prominently among the disciplines perceived as serving or facilitating progress toward NIEO. Nowhere is this truer than in respect to overall trade institutions and structures. Lawyers are involved but either as diplomats rather than as legal professionals or as 'translators' to cobble up formal texts to reflect (or distort) agreed positions.

This is not a satisfactory situation for several reasons:

1. Lawyers do approach negotiations with a perception that there are usually both common and conflicting interests and with a preference for reaching an agreed position by dialogue and compromise rather than rushing into arbitral or judicial dispute resolution. Both the perception and the preference are relevant to international trade structure and institution negotiations.
2. Knowing the present legal position — including present rights and powers — is important for Third World negotiators. Unfortunately such knowledge is by no means always present.
3. To make a fully effective contribution, a lawyer needs to know the present and desired substantive position (in respect to Multilateral Trade Negotiations or 'safeguards' clauses or whatever topic is to hand) and to be brought into consideration of what changes to seek before and during negotiations not after they are concluded. A lawyer is no more plausibly viewed as a translator than an economist or an ambassador.

GATT — Foundations and History

The General Agreement on Tariffs and Trade was created and has operated as a mechanism and a forum for reducing barriers (particularly tariff barriers) to trade. Founded in the late 1940s, it has always been most concerned with North–North trade but has adopted a number (the cynical might say a rag bag) of provisions limiting obligations on and giving preferences to peripheral economies. That these actually redress certain built-in biases against the periphery is very doubtful, but they do represent a certain possibility of negotiated gains and favourable legal instruments in the GATT forum.

On paper GATT is controlled by a governing body of all its members — a majority of whom are Third World States. In practice, its 'most favoured nation' (a cut in tariff against one State being generalized to all States) approach and immensely lengthy negotiating rounds greatly limit the reality of participation for all except the Big Three (United States, Japan, EEC).

Given that an immediate problem confronting many Third World economies is the rise of selective discrimination by First World States against their exports (especially of manufactures), the legal nature and potential value of GATT's anti-barrier raising and anti-discrimination provisions need reconsideration by the periphery. They are potential tactical weapons for the Group of 77 even if the appropriate strategic path to NIEO presumably includes their modification toward a more managed and less 'free' market-dominated international trading system.

The Tokyo Round and the New Protectionism

Free trade is on the defensive. An extended family of 'agreements' (e.g. in textiles), 'reference prices' (e.g. in steel), cartels (e.g. in artificial fibres), 'voluntary quotas' (e.g. in electrical goods) are steadily eroding access and carrying forward the banner of the New Protectionism. There are real dangers of North–South and North–North trade was reminiscent of the 1920s and 1930s.

This pattern is quite clear in the main legal innovations (or disagreements) of the Tokyo Round:

1. A series of complex Codes on non-tariff discrimination apparently designed to protect North–North trade from new barriers but so formulated as to escape general GATT surveillance and probably to exclude most Third World States;
2. A disagreed dialogue on 'safeguard' clauses (against import surges), 'adjustment' (to allow removal of temporary restrictions), 'selectivity' (to make it easier to discriminate against highly competitive economies with little retaliatory power) — a dialogue in which the EEC took a hard neo-Mercantilist line and the Group of 77 (or at least those who participated) a combined defense of free trade and demand for GATT monitoring of 'safeguards' and 'adjustment' position;
3. A somewhat hidden dialogue on 'graduation' (from 'developing' status — subject to less duties as to reciprocity and able to use certain access concessions — to developed status with full reciprocity duties and no Generalized Scheme of Preferences rights) with the Group of 77 tending to stonewall (perhaps unwisely) and the Big Three moving to an armtwisting exercise to win bilateral concessions from individual peripheral economies.

Some Legal Issues

Even this brief sketch suggests a number of issues in respect to which lawyers' contributions are — or should be — critical:

1. What access rights do the Group of 77's members have under GATT now and how could they be used more effectively?
2. Can 'selective safeguards' be challenged in GATT violation review bodies and, if so, can findings be enforced?
3. How can a safeguards/adjustment package meeting the real First World concerns about sudden, disruptive imports but also meeing the Group of 77 States' need to preserve and expand access for their manufactured exports be formulated?
4. What role could enforceable GATT monitoring and adjudication of 'safeguards' and 'adjustment' (called for at the Manila UNCTAD and late in the Tokyo Round) play?
5. How can the Codes be revised to be accessible to — rather than likely to discriminate against — Group of 77 members?
6. What medium-term changes could allow GATT to move towards a form of trade management that would be equitable and trade expanding, rather than a code word for unilateral, industrial-economy protectionism?

GATT, MTN and Other Legal Issues

The legal aspects of trade which circle around GATT and the MTN interact with other areas in which NIEO requires a New International Legal Order. Two such areas are contract law and TNC law.

Contract law is still rather close to *caveat emptor* (let the buyer beware), at least when the buyer is smaller and/or less well informed than, and in a different country to, the seller. Indeed contract law poses problems nationally, but these are exacerbated in centre–periphery transactions.

Two doctrines now widely used in some capitalist economies — 'unforeseeable contingency' and 'unjust enrichment' (*rebus sic stantibus*) — would appear to deserve attention. They could both be used domestically (and within contracts) by Third World States and, potentially, brought into the range of accepted international legal concepts (as, for example, 'permanent sovereignty over natural resources').

In addition, however, new legal thinking is needed on how the obligations of the seller (especially in large construction or complete plant sale operations) can be defined and backed up by enforceable penalty provisions. In too many cases cost escalation is *de facto* at the seller's choice, deadlines and rated capacities are backed by derisory penalty clauses, most of the critical damage resulting from late or non-functioning units is simply not covered at all on the basis of a rather archaic 'too distant' doctrine.

TNC law involves at least five clusters of issues. Firstly, restrictive business practices. Secondly, adequate disclosure of relevant data on group (whole TNC) as well as local subsidiary/affiliate operations. Thirdly, regulations controlling the cost and the effectiveness of knowledge sales ('transfer of technology'). Fourthly, control of intra-firm transactions which are across national boundaries ('transfer pricing'). Fifthly, overall regulation of the activities of TNCs in host countries to ensure that they are subject to national economic sovereignty at least in legal form, and the potential for its increasing implementation.

These issues are being discussed — and, perhaps, negotiated — in several forums (UNCTAD, World Intellectual Property Organization, UN Transnational Commission). They all appear to lack an adequate legal input, an adequate interaction with other trade issues. (For example, given transfer pricing, more access via GATT or better commodity prices via the Integrated Commodities Programme — when and if achieved — may benefit TNCs much more than their host countries' economies.) Above all they lack an integrated legal examination of the range of trade and trade-related issues either from a narrowly technical and procedural or a more substantive, change-oriented and interdisciplinary approach.

V: THE NEW LAW OF THE SEA

Since the beginning of the 1970s, a large-scale reform of the entire Law of the Sea has been initiated. In 1970 a world-wide conference was convened for this purpose and a preparatory committee set up, which completed its work in 1973, but without succeeding in drawing up a generally acceptable project which could serve as a basis for the work of the conference. The latter began to tackle its major tasks in 1974 in Caracas. Many lengthy sessions have been held and still the work has not been completed. Nevertheless, general aspects of the Law of the Sea are at an advanced stage of negotiation: one might even say that there now exists a general consensus on many aspects of the new Law of the Sea. But basic agreement is still lacking on the question of the exploitation of the seabed beyond national jurisdictions.

This monumental effort on the part of the international community was the result of a series of new factors: mainly, the advances in the technology for exploiting the living resources of the sea and of hydro-carbons at greater depths, as well as the possibility of extracting and processing in the near future the abundant and extremely valuable minerals lying on seabeds in the form of polimetallic nodules containing a con-siderable proportion of precious metals such as nickel, copper and manga-nese, the exploitation of which is increasingly difficult and costly on land, either because of the exhaustion of certain reserves or because of the greater cost of exploiting existing resources.

The revolutionary change in the Law of the Sea was not basically occasioned by causes to do with the military use of the seas, although there was one important factor of this nature which did indeed exercise an important influence on the agreement of all States that a general revision should be undertaken. This was the following factor: towards the end of the 1960s and at the beginning of the 1970s, a clear tendency to extend territorial waters became evident, resulting, among other causes, from the failure of the 1958 and 1960 conferences to establish a maxi-mum limit on the width of territorial waters. Faced with this tendency, the great sea powers, above all the United States and the Soviet Union, drew attention to the need to provide some measure of satisfaction to coastal States, in particular, developing countries, in what concerns the exploitation of living resources near the coasts, and the exploitation of hydrocarbons; but at the same time, as compensation for accepting an extended working jurisdiction for the exploitation of resources which favoured coastal States, the powers wanted to obtain a basic agreement limiting territorial waters to twelve miles, and also guaranteeing almost *unrestricted* passage through straits. These powers argued that if terri-torial waters were increased from three to twelve miles, a great number of straits in the world — more than a hundred — would cease to be in high seas and would fall within the jurisdiction of territorial limits of coastal States. For this reason, they asked for a ruling which would guaran-tee freedom of navigation for all vessels, be they military or not, through straits. In fact it is most doubtful whether at that period the ruling of a maximum width of three miles for territorial waters was still considered to be in force, since many States regarded it as accepted custom for them to fix their territorial waters up to twelve miles. Certainly, the passage through straits, whatever the ruling on the width of territorial waters, represented a problem since it could considerably restrict freedom of navigation of the world's oceans, owing to the problems arising from the question of straits.

Finally, it was agreed that the conference should in the future study the reforms necessary in all the traditional aspects of the Law of the Sea, including a new chapter on the exploitation of mineral resources in the seabed beyond national jurisdictions, because the delimitation of those facing the continental shelves of coastal States constituted a very serious problem.

As has been stated, the preparatory committee and later, the conference itself, have been working since 1971 on the drawing-up of a comprehensive world-wide treaty dealing with all these aspects. In some matters, the changes have been radical. Perhaps the most important innovation arising from the Conference is the so-called exclusive economic zone, up to 200 miles from the coast and starting from the twelve miles of territorial waters. Although as yet the treaty is not open to signature, it has been informally agreed, after arduous negotiations, that within this zone coastal States should have sovereign rights over all resources, living and non-living, in the sea, and on or under the seabed. This agreement has important consequences for the prevention of sea pollution, for scientific research, and also for the question of the placement of all types of installations, artificial islands and structures within the exclusive economic zone or which could be anchored on the continental shelf of a coastal State, even if it extended beyond the 200 miles.

This exclusive economic zone implies a delicate balance of power between the coastal State and the other States. The basic principle is that the former should not exercise sovereignty on its own account over the precise area of the exclusive economic zone, but only over its resources for purposes of exploration and exploitation. Therefore, the rest of the traditional freedoms remain in force within the economic zone for the other States: basically, freedom of navigation, of communication, of laying underwater cables and pipelines and of flight passage. It has been finally accepted, after much effort, that we are dealing with a zone which has a special system of rules, *sui generis*, that reconcile the rights of coastal States with those of other States, as has been shown. Naturally, this fact is of great importance as far as the military aspects of the use of the seas is concerned. Both in the first version of the basic negotiating document, drawn up in 1975, and known as the Single Text, and in a second version of 1976 known as the Revised Single Text — worked out by the President of the conference's Plenary Commission, and which did not constitute official texts of a treaty plan but merely texts drawn up for negotiating purposes — the other States were granted freedom of navigation and all those traditional practices recognized by international law, concerning navigation and communication. In the face of the maritime powers' desire for greater clarity, in a third version of the basic negotiating text, drawn up in 1977 and called the Composite Negotiating Text, the said formula was altered to expound more precisely the practices — including military ones — relating to navigation, which were claimed for the other States and which could not, therefore, be violated by coastal States. Article 58 of the said Composite Text stipulates that, subject to the relevant provisions of the present convention, the other States shall enjoy freedom of navigation and flight passage, of laying underwater cables and pipelines, 'and of other uses of the sea internationally recognized as legitimate, related to the said freedoms, such as those linked to the functioning of ships, aeroplanes, underwater cables and pipelines, and which are compatible with the remaining provisions of the present convention'. Thus, all the freedoms of navigation, even when it is a question of military aspects, are guaranteed in favour of the other States.

As regards the right of passage through straits, a special system of rules was agreed upon, contained in Articles 38 and 45 of the Composite Text, in which it is established as a basic premise that all ships and aeroplanes shall have the right of passage in transit, which shall not be impeded, to apply to the straits used for international navigation between one area of the high seas or one exclusive economic zone, and another area of the high seas or exclusive economic zone. The said right of transit passage applies, with few limitations, both to military vessels and to other ships. This system of rules is more favourable to the remaining States than that of friendly passage within territorial waters.

As for the third aspect, which could have military implications for the system of rules of the economic zone, it was agreed after full debate that the coastal State should have jurisdiction to establish and utilize artificial islands, installations and structures (Article 56). Article 60 of the same Composite Text laid down that 'within the exclusive economic zone, the coastal State shall have the exclusive right to construct, and likewise to authorize and establish rules for the construction, exploitation and utilization in the said zone of (a) artificial islands; (b) installations and structures for the ends envisaged in Article 56 and for the purposes of an economic nature (this refers to the exploitation of live and inanimate resources by the coastal States within the economic zone); (c) installations and structures which may impede the exercise of the rights of the coastal States within the zone.'

This system of rules was the subject of lengthy and problematic discussion, negotiation and agreements. The coastal States, above all those of Latin America, were particularly emphatic on the need to ban military uses by other States within the economic zone. As will be appreciated, Article 60 does not prohibit the erection or installation of other types of structures or installations beyond those specifically mentioned in it, so the inference is understood that certain kinds of installation not listed here, and which could have a military purpose, are permitted. The essential point of this system of rules and of the agreement was that the coastal States accepted this formulation on the basis that the erection of artificial islands inside the economic zone without the consent of the coastal State should be expressly forbidden.

Since the drawing up of the Composite Text in 1977 up to the present date, the negotiations have actively proceeded and comprehensive agreements have been reached on some special matters. Nevertheless, general and uniform progress on all fronts has not been made, as would have befitted a general revision of the whole of the Composite Text to produce a new revised version. In the eighth meeting held in Geneva in spring 1977 sufficient progress was finally made for the President of the Conference, in conjunction with the Presidents of the three main Plenary Commissions, to be entrusted with the preparation of a new revised text. Therefore, in the meantime, they are subject to all sorts of attempts to modify them, by those members who were not in line with the general agreements reached on particular topics. This creates a situation of flux and instability.

Finally, in the revised version of the Integrated Text, which has been the basis for the negotiations in New York in the summer of 1979, basic agreements were incorporated for which there exists a very broad consensus on three matters concerning the general Law of the Sea:

1. The very difficult question of the access of countries with no coast and geographically at disadvantage, to the exploitation of an equitable share of the surplus of living resources within the economic zones of States in the same region or subregion;

2. The question of the peaceful resolution of controversies for which a generally accepted formula was thought to be obligatory reconciliation in order to settle disputes which might arise on the exercise of the sovereign rights of coastal States related to the exploitation of living resources within their economic zone. In this way, abuses on the part of the coastal States could be prevented, while at the same time upholding the principle that it is a question of sovereign rights being exercised by them which cannot be subject to the decision of an obligatory demand alien to their own will;

3. Finally, agreement was at last reached on the outer limit of the continental shelf, beyond 200 miles. In this matter, a combination was accepted of the so-called Irish formula which put foward certain geographical and geomorphological criteria (distance from the foot

of the continental slope and density of the deposits and sediments), with a Soviet proposal to establish a maximum limit beyond which the exercise of sovereign rights by the coastal State over its continental shelf ceases.

Concerning the system of rules for the seabed, although no agreement was reached which has the definite backing of all the groups of States, considerable progress was made. In the proposals drawn up by the Presidents of the three work groups as a basis for negotiation, the positions of the industrial States and of the developing countries are much closer on some of the following matters: restrictions on underwater production so as not to excessively damage the land producers of the same metals; on the transfer of technology to the Authority itself and to the developing countries by companies or States to which contracts have been granted; on the conditions of exploitation and the manner in which contracts should be awarded by the Authority and surveillance of their operation; on difficult financial arrangements, in particular with regard to taxes, royalties and other forms of finance of the international Authority; and on the conference for revision which should take place twenty-five years after commercial operations for mineral extraction begin. It is possible, though not certain, that on these new bases a definite agreement could be reached on all questions still pending.

In the Eighth Session two attempts were made to modify the balance achieved on two questions with obvious military implications. The Soviet proposal on maximum delimitation of the continental shelf contained a second point which proved totally unacceptable to the coastal States. It was suggested that, further than 200 miles from the coast, but on the continental shelf, the setting-up of artificial islands should not be subject to the consent of the coastal State. In the proposal, it was added that such artificial islands would be for peaceful uses, but owing to the difficulty of verifying this point, many delegates objected precisely on the grounds that such artificial islands built on the continental shelf of a coastal State, although beyond 200 miles, might be used for military purposes.

The second proposal which was also rejected by a solid majority was put forward by the United States and concerned scientific research. On this question it has been agreed, as is evident in the Composite Text, that scientific research carried out on the continental shelf and within the economic zone was subject to rules of consent by the coastal State, even when the latter ought not normally to refuse when it was a question of scientific research with no bearing on the exploitation of resources, and not involving the use of explosives, or such other conditions. The new American proposals sought to establish another dual system of rules regarding the continental shelves. Further than 200 miles from the coast, scientific research on the shelf ought only to be subject to a ruling of notification and not of consent by coastal States. As has been pointed out, this proposal, which to a certain extent concurred with the Soviet suggestion, although dealing with a different matter, was also rejected and neither will be incorporated into the new Revised Composite Text. Again, in the case of the American proposal, one of the reasons why the coastal States objected to it was the possibility that such research might be concerned with military uses.

The attitude adopted by the group of coastal States and, in fact, by the great majority of the participants in the Conference, is in harmony with a proposal put forward in Caracas in 1974 by thirty-two countries, concerning the continental shelves. The said proposal was initially presented solely by Mexico, but on its third revision it was sponsored, as already mentioned, by thirty-two countries. It proposed the following:

> No State shall have the right to construct, maintain, place or put into operation in the continental shelf of another state, or on top of the same, installations or military devices, or installations for any other purpose, without the consent of the coastal State.

This proposal has not been withdrawn. It is hard to predict what its fate will be in the last phase of negotiations, when the States are able to present formal amendments to an official text. Perhaps it will not obtain the necessary majority to be passed, particularly in view of the words 'or installations for any other purposes', since this contradicts the system of rules already described which appears in Articles 56 and 60. But in any case, it seems reasonable to predict that it will be difficult for any other proposal to succeed, such as the Soviet one already mentioned, which tends to permit installations on the continental shelf of other States, even if further than 200 miles from the coast, or which, like the American proposal, permits scientific research on that part of the shelf, without the consent of the coastal State.

V: PERMANENT SOVEREIGNTY OVER NATURAL RESOURCES

The principle of permanent sovereignty over natural resources emerged in the early fifties as the process of decolonization got underway, and newly-independent States felt it necessary to re-appraise and alter 'inequitable' legal arrangements, in the form of concessions, inherited from the colonial period, under which foreign investors (mostly transnational corporations with their headquarters in the metropolitan country) were exploiting their natural resources. While permanent sovereignty over natural resources is now recognized as a fundamental principle of international law, the definition of its precise scope and implications remains a juristic task of some importance. This is not only because it is a principle that is undergoing progressive development, but also because it continues to be a seminal source from which rules can be derived to safeguard the interests of developing countries in relation to the utilization of their natural resources.

The principle of permanent sovereignty over natural resources has been enunciated and re-affirmed in a series of resolutions of the United Nations General Assembly, culminating in its incorporation in the Charter of Economic Rights and Duties of States (adopted by UN General Assembly resolution 3281 (XXXI) in December 1974). As early as 1952 it was recognized in UN General Assembly resolution 626 (VII) of 21 December 1952 that 'the right of peoples to use and exploit their natural wealth and resources is inherent in their sovereignty'. The draft Human Rights Covenants proposed by the Human Rights Commission in January 1955 affirmed, in paragraph 3 of Article 1, that:

> The right of peoples to self-determination shall also include permanent sovereignty over their natural wealth and resources. In no case may a people be deprived of its own means of subsistence on the grounds of any right that may be claimed by other states.

The text proposed by the Human Rights Commission was modified by the Third Committee of the UN General Assembly, so that a 'right' was incorporated in the first Article of the UN Covenants on Human Rights in the following terms:

> The peoples may, for their own ends, freely dispose of their natural wealth and resources without prejudice to any obligations arising out of international economic co-operation based up to the principle of mutual benefit and international law. In no case may a people be deprived of its own means of subsistence.

UN General Assembly resolution 1314 (XIII) of 12 December 1958 established a Commission on Permanent Sovereignty over Natural Resources 'to conduct a full survey of the status of permanent sovereignty over natural wealth and resources as a basic constituent of the right of self determination' and resolution 1515 (XV) of 15 December 1960 recommended that 'the sovereign right of every State to dispose of its wealth and natural resources be respected'. The work of the Commission culminated in the adoption of resolution 1803 (XVII), regarded as one of the landmark resolutions, in the form of a Declaration on Permanent Sovereignty over Natural Resources. The Declaration, after reiterating that 'the sovereign right of every State to dispose of its natural wealth and resources should be respected', and recognizing 'the inalienable right of all States freely to dispose of their natural wealth and resources in accordance with their national interest', sets out its substantative provisions in eight paragraphs.

To assess the significance of the Declaration it has to be appreciated that, having been negotiated within the United Nations framework, it represented an attempt to reconcile the competing, and in some respects conflicting, interests of *capital-importing* developing countries — the owners of the natural resources — and *capital-exporting* developed countries — the home countries of the foreign investors, holding concessions or other rights to exploit those resources.

For developing countries the principle of permanent sovereignty was important because it provided a basis on which they could claim to alter 'inequitable' legal arrangements under which foreign investors enjoyed rights to exploit natural resources found within their territories. Such alteration could be effected through an exercise of (a) the right to nationalize, that is, to acquire the rights enjoyed by the foreign investor or (b) the right to alter certain terms of the arrangements (or to repudiate an agreement entered into with the foreign investor).

The Declaration also provided guidelines on the basis of which developing countries proceeded to establish new legal frameworks for natural resources' development which are a manifest improvement on the old framework of traditional concessions. Under the traditional concessions, the State was a mere tax-collector receiving certain modest financial payments, while the ownership of the minerals or other resources stood transferred to the foreign investor as did control over operations; thus, all critical decisions, such as those relating to the pace and extent of exploration and development and policies relating to production, pricing and marketing were left to be determined by the concessionaire.

The new frameworks have not only ensured more substantial financial payments, but have reserved for the State ownership of the resources, and incorporated mechanisms which are aimed at developing national capabilities and securing effective control over operations.

For the developed countries and transnational corporations engaged in natural resource development, the new developments are seen as reducing

their freedom of action (that is freedom from control by host governments over their operations), and as threatening the stability of contractual arrangements. They retain a preference for arrangements in
which host governments seek to maximize financial returns rather than
control over operations. They also assert the importance of maintaining
stability of contractual relations and in case of nationalization, of paying
to the affected party prompt, adequate and effective compensation.

The Right to Nationalize and the Duty to Pay Compensation

The affirmation of 'the right of peoples to use and exploit their natural
resources' in the 1952 resolution emerged from discussions, on a draft
resolution introduced by Uruguay urging member States to respect the
right of a State to nationalize its natural resources. The 1952 resolution
and subsequent resolutions on Permanent Sovereignty over Natural Resources recognized that the right to nationalize natural resources was
inherent in the sovereignty of a State and thus rejected the view that
nationalization was incompatible with the rules of international law,
as was canvassed, for example, when the validity of the Iranian Nationalization Law, enacted in 1951, was challenged in different municipal courts.
It is noteworthy that two of the courts where this matter was raised,
the High Court of Tokyo and the Civil Court of Rome expressly referred
to the 1952 resolution in support of their conclusion upholding the
validity of the Iranian Nationalization Law.[36]

An issue relating to nationalization which remained a source of controversy was the scope and extent of the duty of the nationalizing State
to compensate those whose rights were nationalized. The following propositions summarize the position in international law as it existed immediately before the adoption of the Charter of Economic Rights and
Duties of States:[37]

1. A considerable number of States held the position that nationalization
could only take place on prompt payment of adequate and effective
compensation;
2. Neither the principle of 'acquired rights' nor that of 'national treatment'
provide reliable guidance;
3. The majority of States in practice accept the principle of compensation,
but not necessarily on the basis of the adequate, effective and prompt
'formula';
4. Where major natural resources are concerned, considerations of principles reinforced by the Declaration of 1962 militate against the 'adequate,
effective and prompt' formula.

The 1962 Declaration, in paragraph 4, provided for payment, of *appropriate* compensation in accordance with rules in force in the State taking such measures in the exercise of its sovereignty and '*in accordance with international law*'. It further provided that:

> In any case where the question of compensation gave rise to a controversy, the national jurisdiction of the State taking such measures should be exhausted. However upon agreement by sovereign States and other parties concerned, settlement of the dispute should be made through arbitration or international adjudication.

These provisions of the 1962 Declaration substantially met the requirements of the developed countries and led critics of the Declaration to describe it as 'a charter for foreign investment'.

The Charter of Economic Rights and Duties of States ('the Charter') adopted in 1974 formulated the duty to compensate in terms, which on the face of it were more in line with what the developing countries had been pressing for. Thus, Article 2 of the Charter after declaring that 'Every State has and shall freely exercise full permanent sovereignty including possession, use and disposal over all its wealth, natural resources and other economic activities', spelt out the scope of the duty to compensate in the following terms:

> In case of nationalization, expropriation or transfer of ownership of foreign properties appropriate compensation should be paid by the State adopting such measures, taking into account its relevant laws and regulations and all circumstances that the State considers pertinent. In any case where the question of compensation gives rise to a controversy, it shall be settled under the domestic laws of the nationalizing State and by its tribunals, unless it is freely and mutually agreed by all States concerned that other peaceful means be sought on the basis of the sovereign equality of States and in accordance with the principle of free choice of means.

The Charter thus effected significant changes in respect of the mode of determination of compensation, and the mode of settlement of disputes relating to the question of compensation. The provision in the 1962 Declaration that compensation should be in *accordance with international law* was strongly supported by developed countries since they construed it to mean that in the event of nationalization, compensation would be 'prompt adequate and effective', even though the Declaration did not so provide in express terms. Article 2 (2c) of the Charter, however, excludes all references to *international law*. It provides for determination of compensation by the State 'taking into account its relevant (national) laws and regulations and all circumstances that the State considers pertinent.' No provision in the Charter elicited such strong opposition from the developed countries as did those of Article 2 relating to compensation. The view has been expressed that if the developing countries had not pressed for such a 'strong' formulation of Article 2, there might have been more positive support for the Charter as a whole from developed countries. It is noteworthy that despite the strong formulation relating to compensation in the Charter, the actual State practice (of developing countries) shows that in the overwhelming majority of cases compensation has in fact been paid upon nationalization. The actual quantum has more often than not been settled by negotiation, and provisions have been made for deferred payment or payment in instalments.

The principle of Permanent Sovereignty over Natural Resources can, however, be said to have affected the question of quantum of compensation in one important respect. Since this principle re-affirmed that the right to nationalize was inherent in the sovereignty of a State, it could no longer be maintained that nationalization constituted an international delict or tort for which damages (which would imply full restitution) could be claimed. It has been persuasively argued that as 'damages' can no longer be the basis of compensation,[38] a more acceptable basis may be found in the principle of unjust enrichment.

The Right to Repudiate/Modify Arrangements Incompatible with the Principle of Permanent Sovereignty

The principle of Permanent Sovereignty as elaborated in the 1962 Declaration embodies a number of criteria by reference to which the compatibility with that principle of legal arrangements for exploitation of natural resources may be tested. These include the following:

1. The exercise of the right must be in the interest of national development and the well-being of the people of the State concerned (paragraph 1);
2. Legal arrangements for exploration, development and disposition of natural resources must be in conformity with rules and conditions which the peoples and nations freely consider to be necessary and desirable (paragraph 2);
3. The capital imported and earnings on the capital shall be governed by the terms of the arrangement, by the national legislation in force, and by international law. The profits derived must be shared in the proportions freely agreed upon in each case care being taken to ensure that

there is no impairment, for any reason, of the State's sovereignty over its natural wealth and resources (paragraph 3);

4. The legal arrangements between the foreign investor and the host government shall be such 'as to further independent national development and shall be based upon respect for the sovereignty over their natural wealth and resources' (paragraph 6);

5. Only those foreign investment agreements shall be observed in good faith which are freely entered into (paragraph 8 — it may be noted that there is no similar provision in Article 2 of the Charter).

There is, therefore, a substantial basis for the view that a legal arrangement for the development of mineral or other natural resources can be repudiated, or be sought to be modified, at the instance of the host government, if it can be shown that the arrangement is incompatible with the principle of Permanent Sovereignty over Natural Resources. It has even been suggested that this principle has the status of *jus cogens* is that, a rule of customary international law of an over-riding character so that if a treaty or an agreement is in conflict with that principle, such a treaty or agreement would be void.[39]

The criteria enunciated in the 1962 Declaration underline at least three basic requirements which must be met in order for a legal arrangement to be regarded as being compatible with the principle of permanent sovereignty, namely:

1. It must be in the interest of national development and well-being of the people of the State concerned;
2. It must be in accordance with the national legislation in force;
3. It must be *freely* entered into.

The first criterion may prove to be difficult to apply in cases where there is scope for honest difference of opinion about whether a particular arrangement is conducive to national development and the well-being of people or not. Its application, however, would present little difficulty where a manifestly disadvantageous agreement had been entered into, as for example, in a State where oil is newly discovered, the government agency concerned either in ignorance or due to being unduly influenced by bribery or other forms of illegal inducements, agreed to sell oil at $10 per barrel at a time when the price was over $30 per barrel. Such an agreement, it is submitted, would be voidable at the instance of the State.

The second criterion — that is, compatibility with national legislation — should be easier to apply and enforce. A basic question, however, which arises here is the extent to which contractual provisions can be altered by subsequent legislation. It has been cogently argued that a legal mechanism by which Permanent Sovereignty over Natural Resources can be secured is through exercise of legislative powers to modify natural resource development arrangements in order to effect such modifications or adjustment of contractual terms as may be warranted by changed circumstances. It is a distinctive feature of contractual arrangements relating to natural resource development that they are of long duration — twenty-five to thirty years — during which important changes can take place which may invalidate the original commercial assumptions on which the arrangement had been based. Thus, for example, it would be difficult to insist on the continued validity of a set of financial or fiscal provisions, formulated on the assumption that the price of oil produced would be around $3 a barrel, when in fact the price rises to over $12 per barrel.

It is instructive to consider different national responses to this problem. In Canada, the legal mechanism developed to deal with this problem is 'a clause in oil agreements requiring the oil company to accept as binding all legislative and regulatory changes which may be enacted or promulgated from time to time in the future.'[40] Thus, the Alberta Mines and Minerals Act was amended in 1962, to change the term of renewal of existing leases to ten years (in place of twenty-one years). It was also provided that existing twenty-one year leases would be brought to an end after ten years if the lessee had not drilled and gained production. In Britain and Norway, in 1975, a new tax was imposed so as to appropriate a substantial part of the 'windfall profits' which were being earned by the oil companies as a result of the unanticipated increase in oil prices which began to take place in 1973. Such alterations, even if they deprived the party affected of a benefit previously enjoyed, did not entitle him to compensation, since the original agreement had expressly subjected the terms and conditions to modification by subsequent legislation.

The third criterion that the agreement must be one which is freely entered into, *prima facie*, suggests that agreements entered into in favour of a metropolitan country (or its nationals) when it was the ruling power over a territory would be voidable on the ground that they were not freely entered into. A newly independent state can thus relieve itself of the burden of one-sided or onerous concessions granted during the period when it was under colonial administration.

It is submitted, however, that the criterion requiring an agreement to be 'freely' entered into can equally be applied to agreements entered into by an independent government, if the giving of 'free consent' is understood in the sense in which it is understood in the jurisprudence relating to formation of contracts. 'Free consent' in that context is understood as consent which is not caused by *coercion, undue influence, fraud, misrepresentation* or *mistake*. Thus, any natural resource development agreement would be void (or voidable) on the ground that it was not freely entered into if it can be shown that the consent of the State was obtained through coercion, undue influence, fraud, misrepresentation or mistake. It may even be argued that given the fact that in the case of such arrangements, the foreign investor has a much higher degree of expertise and possesses much greater information than the government with which he is dealing that there is a duty on the part of the foreign investor to make a full disclosure of all material facts; in other words that it is a situation where *uberimmae fides* is required so that if the foreign investor fails to disclose a material fact which is later discovered, and which if known might have deterred the government from entering into the agreement, then the agreement would be voidable at the option of the State.

Since the adoption of the 1962 Declaration, natural resources development arrangements, in particular relating to petroleum and hard minerals have been subjected to extensive review. States have invoked the principle of permanent sovereignty over natural resources to repudiate agreements or to alter certain terms which were regarded as incompatible with the principle.[41]

New Legal Frameworks for Natural Resource Development

The principle of permanent sovereignty over natural resources as elaborated in the 1962 Declaration, contains certain guidelines on the basis of which new types of arrangements for development of natural resources have been developed. Paragraph 6 of this Declaration provides that international co-operation for development of natural resources in developing countries, whether in the form of public or private capital foreign investment, should be such as to further their independent national development and should be based upon respect for permanent sovereignty over their natural resources.

UN General Assembly resolution 2518 (XVI) in 1966 while reaffirming 'the inalienable right of all countries to exercise permanent sovereignty over their natural resources in the interest of their national development', and that 'the United Nations should undertake a maximum concerted effort to channel its activities so as to enable all countries to exercise that right fully' goes on to state 'that such an effort should help in achieving the maximum possible development of the natural resources of the developing countries and *in strengthening their ability to undertake this development themselves*'. OPEC in its Declaratory Statement of Petroleum

Policy in 1968 reflected the same orientation and spelt out the principles underlying the new types of arrangements for petroleum development, thus:

> Member Governments shall endeavour, as far as feasible, to explore for and develop their hydrocarbon resources directly. The capital, specialists and the promotion of marketing outlets required for such direct development may be complemented when necessary from alternate sources on a commercial basis.
>
> However, when a Member Government is not capable of developing its hydrocarbon resources directly, it may enter into contracts of various types, to be defined in its legislation but subject to the present principles, with outside operators for a reasonable remuneration, taking into account the degree of risk involved. Under such arrangements, the Government shall seek to retain the greatest measure possible of participation in and control over operations . . . Where provision for governmental participation in the ownership of the concession-holding company under any of the petroleum contracts has not been made, the Government may acquire a reasonable participation on the grounds of the principle of changing circumstances . . .

The signposts provided by the Declaration, and later by the OPEC resolution, have led to the evolution of new types of arrangements which from the host State's point of view marked significant improvements over the traditional concessions, under which the State granted rights over vast expanses of territory, for long durations, reserving for itself only a modest financial payment.

The fifties and the sixties witnessed the development of different types of joint ventures in particular in the field of petroleum development. Both equity joint ventures and what were called contractual joint ventures (or 'joint structures') were widely adopted. The latter half of the sixties produced service contracts and a type of joint venture which was described as a 'production sharing contract'. While under concessions, ownership of the petroleum or mineral resource effectively stood transferred to the concessionaire, under equity joint ventures these were owned in common, while under contractual joint ventures and production sharing contracts each party owned its portion of the resource.

Under the equity joint ventures and joint structures, powers of management were exercised jointly, often through joint management committees, in which the host government (or national oil company) and the foreign investors were equally represented. Under production sharing contracts, powers of management were exclusively vested in the national oil company and the foreign contractor exercised only those powers as were delegated to it by the national oil company.

The third generation of agreements are service contracts where ownership of the resources, including the disposition of the oil produced is retained exclusively by the State, and the foreign investor provides only 'technical, commercial and financial services' for which he is entitled to a fee, in cash or in kind (or a combination of both). Under these contracts, powers of management remained vested in the national oil company. The new types of arrangements thus underline the importance of such national objectives as retaining ownership over resources, securing control over operations through retaining powers of management and the developing of national capabilities, over and above maximization of financial returns to the State.

For it is increasingly appreciated that ultimately it is mainly through development of national capabilities to undertake and conduct operations that a State can expect effectively to exercise its sovereignty over natural resources.

NOTES AND REFERENCES

1 R. Prebisch, the first Secretary-General of UNCTAD cited in J.F. Dorsey, 'Preferential Treatment: A New Standard for International Economic Relations', *Harvard International Law Journal*, Vol. XVIII (1977), p. 109 at p. 113.

2 B. Gosovic, *UNCTAD: Conflict and Compromise* (Leiden: Sijthoff, 1971), p. 12.

3 Ibid., p. 14.

4 M. Perez Guerrero, 'Opportunity in the Present Crisis', in K. Huq, *Equality of Opportunity within and among Nations* (New York/London: Praeger, 1977) p. 28.

5 *New Directions and New Structures for Trade and Development*, Report by the Secretary-General of UNCTAD, to UNCTAD IV (New York: United Nations, 1977), (UNCTAD IV Report), p. 8.

6 M. Huq, *The Poverty Curtain* (New York: Columbia University Press, 1976), p. 160.

7 UNCTAD IV Report, p. 10.

8 Ibid.

9 Ibid., also *North–South: A Programme for Survival* (Brandt Commission Report), p. 238.

10 TD/B/C.6/AC.3/2, 28 June 1977.

11 TD/237/Add.I, 12 April 1979, p. 5, para. II. 17 (a).

12 *Arusha Programme for Collective Self-Reliance and Framework for Negotiations*, 12–16 February 1979, 77/MM (IV) /21,TD/236,p.61, item 13 (a), para. 1.

13 TD/CODE TOT/1 Add. 1, 25 July 1978, Annex I, para. 8 of Preamble; TD/CODE TD/CODE TOT/14, 28 March 1979, p. 2, para. 12.

14 TD(V)/NG.V/CRP. 1, 12 May 1979, para. 2.

15   *Arusha Programme*, p. 63, para. 10.
16   TD/CODE TOT/1/Add.1, 25 July 1978, Annex III, concluding phrase of the Preamble.
17   TD(V) /NG.V/CPR.7, 14 May 1979, para. 5(b).
18   TD/CODE TOT/1/Add.1, 25 July 1978, Annex II, concluding phrase of the Preamble; TD/CODE TOT/14, 28 March 1979, p. 2, para. 12.
19   TD(V) /NG.V/CRP.19, 24 May 1979, para. 1.
20   TD/CODE TOT/14, 28 March 1979, p. 4, para. 4.
21   Ibid.
22   TD(V) /NG.V/CRP. 1, 12 May 1979, para. 1 (a).
23   *Arusha Programme*, pp. 62–3, paras. 5 and 6.
24   TD/CODE TOT/14, 28 March 1979, p. 11, sec. A.
25   TD(V) /NG.V/CRP. 1, 12 May 1979, para. 1 (c).
26   *Arusha Programme*, p. 63, para. 7.
27   TD/CODE TOT/14, 28 March 1979, p. 11.
28   Ibid., p. 11, et seq.
29   TD/CODE TOT/14, 28 March 1979, p. 30.
30   Ibid., Appendix B, part 1.
31   Ibid., paras. A1, A3, B1, B2.
32   TD(V) /NG.V/CRP. 1, 12 May 1979, para. 1 (e).
33   *Arusha Programme*, para. 9.
34   TD/CODE TOT/14, 28 March 1979, Appendix B, Part 3, paras. 7.1, 7.4.
35   A paper entitled 'Access for Exports, The New Protectionism and All GATT: Notes Towards Negotiable Proposals' by Dr R.H. Green was presented at the Oxford Seminar but it is not included in this volume as it has been published in Arjun Sengupta, ed., *Commodities, Finance and Trade: Issues in North–South Negotiations* (London: Frances Pinter, 1980), pp. 215–34.
36   *Anglo-Iranian Oil Col. Ltd. v. Idemitsu K.K.K., International Law Reports*, Vol. 20 (1953), p. 305 at p. 313; *Anglo-Iranian Oil Col. Ltd. vs. S.U.P.O.R., International Law Reports*, Vol. 22 (1955), p. 23 at p. 40.
37   These and related propositions are set out in Brownlie, *Principles of International Law* (Oxford: Clarendon Presss, 1973), pp. 527–8.
38   See Chapter 17, E. Jimenez de Arechaga, 'Application of the Rules of State Responsibility to the Nationalization of Foreign-owned Property'; W. Friedmann, 'Social Conflict and Foreign Investment', in American Society of International Law, *Proceedings* (1963), p. 126.
39   Brownlie, *Principles of International Law*, p. 500.
40   A. Thompson, 'Sovereignty and Natural Resources — A Study of Canadian Petroleum Legislation', *Valparaiso University Law Review* (1967), p. 284 at p. 290.
41   M.A. Mughraby, *Permanent Sovereignty over Oil Resources* (Beirut: Middle East Research and Publishing Centre, 1966), and K. Hossain, *Law and Policy in Petroleum Development* (London: Frances Pinter, 1979), esp. Ch. IV.

Part I

GENERAL PRINCIPLES AND THE CHARTER OF ECONOMIC RIGHTS AND DUTIES OF STATES

I   Legal Aspects of a New International Economic Order[1]

Milan Bulajic*

The contemporary world is in the process of creating a new global system in general and a new international economic order in particular. The colonial system which prevailed for several centuries in an area extending over 80 per cent of the surface of the earth and encompassing 75 per cent of the world population has collapsed. The inhabitants of more than one hundred developing countries continue to live in conditions of economic instability and face a continuing struggle against neocolonial oppression. The gap between the developed and the developing countries continues to widen further within a system established at a time when the majority of countries were not independent. The new international economic order represents an ordered process for decolonization in the economic sector, a necessary prerequisite to world peace.

The new international economic order cannot be established on the foundation of the old international legal system, 'law of the civilized nations'. It is not a question of 'revolutionary' destruction of existing international economic law but rather a gradual substantive evolution and adjustment to new realities. The non-aligned world, consisting mainly of developing countries, does not have at its disposal the same economic capacity in the struggle for their rights, as do the industrially developed countries. Under these circumstances, a new international law of economic development would raise the principles of non-alignment to the level of international legal norms, binding upon all states, developed and developing, in the interest of all.

The founders of the United Nations Organization have expressed determination based on the principles of the Atlantic Charter, 'to employ

*Ministry of Foreign Affairs, Yugoslavia.

international machinery for the promotion of the economic and social advancement of all peoples'. The UN Charter provides: 'With a view to the creation of conditions of stability and well being which are necessary for peaceful and friendly relations among nations based on respect for the principles of equal rights and self-determination of peoples, the United Nations shall promote: a. higher standards of living, full employment. . .'.[2]

The final act of the Havana Charter was signed on 24 March 1948 by fifty-three states but was never put into force, the International Trade Organization never becoming reality. Instead, we have the temporary General Agreement on Tariffs and Trade (GATT), now over thirty years old and embodying newest 'Tokyo Round' adaptations. The UNCTAD Secretary General is proposing to update the Havana Charter by a new international economic convention.[3]

The first call for an NIEO was made in connection with the question of permanent sovereignty over natural resources. It was in 1952 when a certain developing country (Chile) raised this question during the debate on the Draft International Covenant on Human Rights.[4] It was in the context of the debate on the right of self-determination that the economic, social and political aspects of this right were invoked. The debate, which started in the Human Rights Commission, continued unabated for ten years in various forums of the United Nations until it culminated in the landmark resolution on 14 December 1962.[5]

The United Nations Conference on Trade and Development (UNCTAD) adopted in Santiago de Chile in 1972 a decision on the urgent '*establishment of generally acceptable norms* for a systematic restructuring of international economic relations', proceeding from the recognition that 'until the implementation of a charter on the protection of rights of all states, in particular of developing countries, it will not be possible to establish a more equitable order and more stable world'.[6]

At the Fourth Conference of non-aligned countries held in Algiers 5–10 September 1973, a recommendation was adopted to the effect that the UN General Assembly should give priority to drafting a Charter of Economic Rights and Duties of States that should reflect 'the economic aspirations of States engaged in the struggle for promoting their own development, as well as the aspirations of the international community as a whole'.[7]

Acting on these recommendations, the Sixth Special Session of the UN General Assembly adopted the Declaration of the Establishment of a New International Economic Order.[8] The twenty-ninth regular session of the UN General Assembly adopted the Charter of Economic Rights and Duties of States on 12 December 1974, as the *'first step in the codification and progressive development of this matter'*.[9]

While formulating the fundamental attitudes towards the NIEO, the heads of states of the eighty-five non-aligned countries participating at the Fifth Conference held in Colombo in August 1976, worked with the conviction that the 'establishment of the NIEO calls for courageous initiatives, new concrete and global solutions'. This is contrary to the slow reforms and improvisations aimed at solving the present-day economic problems, 'the basic goal of the NIEO being the establishment of a balance in international economic relations based on justice, co-operation and respect for human dignity'.

The UN Commission on International Trade Law (UNCITRAL), acting on the basis of the General Assembly resolutions[10] and on the recommendation of the Asian-African Legal Consultative Committee,[11] decided to establish the Working Group on legal implications of the NIEO.[12] This decision was confirmed by the UN General Assembly at its thirty-third regular session.[13]

The International Law Association at its 58th Conference in Manila on 2 September 1978 adopted an initiative at the recommendation of a Yugoslav branch to establish a standing committee on the legal aspects of an NIEO. On the basis of the report of an *ad hoc* working group, the ILA Executive Council passed the initiative on 12 May 1979. On the agenda of the Ninth Conference of the Law of the World in Madrid 16–21 September 1979, the subject of legal aspects of an NIEO is included. In the provisional agenda of the thirty-fourth regular session of the UN General Assembly is included the item, 'Consolidation and progressive development of the principles and norms of international economic law relating to the legal aspects of the new international economic order'.[14]

Arguments to the effect that it is too early to examine international legal aspects of the NIEO fail to take into account the fact that in progress are negotiations and formulations of international conventions and codes of conduct which either regulate or prejudice the questions relating to the basic assumptions of the NIEO. It is not a matter of codification and progressive development of abstract principles and norms of the NIEO, but of incorporating and harmonizing current international negotiations with the basic conception of the NIEO: the Common Fund and international commodity agreements, the evolution of agreed principles to promote long-term industrial adjustment in developed countries, the international code of conduct on the transfer of technology, the set of rules and principles on restrictive business practices, the code of conduct of transnational corporations, the revision of the Paris convention on protection of industrial property, a reformed international monetary system and an effective system of international financial co-operation for development are necessary to support and promote the structural changes that are required.

In the report of the Secretary General of UNCTAD to the Fifth Conference, it was emphasized that because of 'the close interrelationship that exists between trade flows and flows of money and finance, the rules and principles governing these two sets of flows need to be mutually supportive, and directed to the same basic objectives. The provision of a general legal basis for differential and more favourable treatment for developing countries in their trade with developing countries is now overdue'. There is, in other words, need for a further evolution of the rules in order to incorporate the principle of preference for developing countries as an integral part of them, rather than as an exception.

Special attention was drawn to the fact that the existing rules ignore a major, and growing, part of world trade, namely, the intra-firm and related-party transactions of transnational corporations.

The expansion of this trade in recent years has greatly widened the scope of discrimination among different countries with regard to their participation in international trade. The trade of developing countries, in particular, has become substantially affected by the restrictive business practices used by transnational corporations, as well as by decisions taken by these corporations on the basis of their global interests which affect the location of production facilities as well as the volume and pattern of trade flows.

In sum, it would appear that the existing rules and principles governing international trade have become largely outmoded and increasingly ineffective, and are in need of review, revision and extension. The objectives of such revision and extension would need to go beyond those of the commercial policy provisions of the Havana Charter, which were essentially to provide an international legal framework for freely competitive markets, albeit with adequate safeguards for national employment and balance-of-payments interests. What is now required is a reformulation of the trading rules so that they operate to promote the development of the third world while, at the same time, taking into account the new development in the world economy.

A reformulated set of trading rules, to be effective, will need to be supported and complemented by internationally agreed principles relating to the impact of domestic economic policies on trade in general, and on the trade of developing countries in particular.

The UNCTAD Secretary General concluded that,

> this raises the question of the desirability of negotiating on a universal basis, *a new international economic convention* which would embody mutually consistent principles and rules covering all the various policy aspects mentioned above, i.e., the revised trading rules and related principles concerning domestic economic policies, the operations of transnational corporations, restrictive business practices, and trade and economic relations between developing countries and socialist countries. Such a comprehensive economic convention, which would constitute, in effect, a new and updated version of the Havana Charter, could also usefully include general principles for the conclusion of international commodity agreements and arrangements.

A new economic convention on the lines proposed should take fully into account the relevant provision of the Charter of Economic Rights and Duties of States, as well as those of General Assembly decisions on the establishment of a new international economic order.[15]

THE UNITED NATIONS CHARTER OF ECONOMIC
RIGHTS AND DUTIES OF STATES

The United Nations General Assembly on 12 December 1974, adopted the resolution containing the Charter of Economic Rights and Duties of States '*as the first step in the codification and development*' of the norms 'for the development of international economic relations on a just and equitable basis'.[16] The General Assembly solemnly declared 'that it is a fundamental purpose of the present Charter to promote the establishment of the new international economic order, based on equity, sovereign equality, interdependence, common interest and co-operation among all States, irrespective of their economic and political systems.'[17]

While the Declaration and the Programme on the establishment of the new international economic order were adopted without voting, with reserves of the industrialized developed countries, the voting on the Charter was: 120 States in favour, 6 against, and 10 abstentions.[18]

The drafting of the Charter had begun before the formal proclamation of the NIEO, on the initiative of President Alvarez of Mexico, the formulate an instrument to serve as a 'firm legal footing' for international economy:[19]

We must strengthen the precarious legal foundations of the international economy. A just order and a stable world will not be possible until we create obligations and rights which protect the weaker States. Let us take economic co-operation out of the realm of goodwill and put it into the realm of law.

The Charter is founded, *inter alia*, on

the need to establish and maintain a just and equitable economic and social order through the achievement of more rational and equitable international economic relations and the encouragement of structural changes in the world economy; the creation of conditions which permit the further expansion of trade and intensification of economic co-operation among all nations; the strengthening of the economic independence of developing countries and the establishment and promotion of international economic relations, taking into account the agreed differences in development of the developing countries and their specific needs.

The Charter provides that

Every State has the sovereign and inalienable right to choose its economic system as well as its political, social and cultural systems in accordance with the will of its people, without outside interference, coercion or threat in any form whatsoever.

Every State has and shall freely exercise full permanent sovereignty, including possession, use, and disposal over all its wealth, natural resources and economic activities. [Each State has the right] to regulate and supervise the activities and transnational corporations within its national jurisdiction and to take measures to insure that such activities comply with its laws, rules and regulations and conform with its economic and social policies.

International co-operation for development is the shared goal and common duty of all States.

With a view to accelerating the economic growth of developing countries and bridging the economic gap between developed and developing countries, developed countries should grant generalized preferential, non-reciprocal and non-discriminatory treatment to developing countries in those fields of international economic co-operation where it may be feasible.

Close relationship between the Charter of Economic Rights and Duties of States and the Charter of the United Nations Organization is expressed in Article 33: 'Nothing in the present Charter shall be construed as impairing or derogating from the provisions of the Charter of the United Nations or actions taken in pursuance thereof.' 'In their interpretation and application, the provisions of the present Charter are interrelated and each provision should be construed in the context of the other provisions.'

The last, 34th Article stipulates that

an item on the Charter of Economic Rights and Duties of States shall be included in the agenda of the General Assembly at its thirtieth session, and thereafter on the agenda of every fifth session. In this way a systematic and comprehensive consideration of the implementation of the Charter, covering both progress achieved and any improvements and additions which might become necessary, would be carried out and appropriate measures recommended. Such consideration should take into account the evolution of all the economic, social, legal and other factors related to the principles upon which the present Charter is based and on its purposes.

The first fifth session and the second step in the codification of international law of development comes in 1980 at the thirty-fifth regular session of the UN General Assembly.

THE COMMON HERITAGE OF MANKIND

The World Peace Through Law 1967 Conference passed a resolution recommending that the UN General Assembly should proclaim that the resources of the seabed beyond the national jurisdiction belong to the United Nations. The UN General Assembly on 18 December 1967 adopted unanimously a resolution[20] recognizing 'the common interest of mankind in the seabed and the ocean floor', and an attitude was set forth stating that 'the use and exploitation of the seabed and oceans' should be exercised 'in the interest of preserving international peace and security and for the benefit of all mankind'. A year later the General Assembly adopted a resolution[21] reiterating the conviction that explorations and exploitation of the seabed must be 'exercised for the benefit of mankind as a whole irrespective of the geographical position of States, taking into account particular interests and needs of developing countries', 'under an international regime including appropriate international machinery'. By its resolution of 18 December 1970,[22] the UN General Assembly solemnly proclaimed that the seabed beyond the limits of national juris-diction and its resources are 'the common heritage of mankind'.[23]

The fundamental problem of the contemporary law of the sea which is in the process of being created is, from the viewpoint of the NIEO, the question of a powerful international machinery for the management of the 'common heritage of mankind' on the seabed and subsoil beyond national jurisdiction. That is why developing countries have insisted that an international authority over the seabed, as an 'agent of mankind' would have the exclusive jurisdiction over all the area concerning the extraction of minerals from the seabed, explorations, processing and selling.

But what was left out of the great new concept of the common heritage of mankind after unilateral proclamations of the exclusive economic zone of 200 nautical miles, was the original idea of developing Latin American countries.[24]

The exclusive economic zone comprises one third of the oceans and contains 90 per cent of the living resources (fish, petroleum and natural gas). A large number of developing countries do not have a coastline, or are situated at a small coastal sea. According to the data provided by the Trilateral Commission almost half (46 per cent) of the exclusive economic zone belongs to the developed countries, which represents less than a fourth of the world population. A little more than half is owned by the developing countries, accounting for three-fourths of the world population.[25] The industrially developed countries are capable of protecting and exploiting their enormous areas of the sea and subsoil entirely, which is not the situation with the developing countries.

Many of the developing countries without coast (land-locked) or those with an unfavourable geographical position gained nothing. It led to the first great division of the non-aligned developing countries. Approximately sixty states were excluded from areas where they had previously enjoyed the right of fishing.

Never in the whole history of mankind have such a small number of states gained so much: out of 34 million square miles, covered by the exclusive economic zone, 13 million is shared by some ten countries. The United States of America got the most — 2,222,000 sq. miles, the area equal to the continental United States; Canada acquired 1,370,000; Japan 1,126,000; and Norway 59,000. The representative of New Zealand stated that his country acquired by the exclusive economic zone, an area of the sea and subsoil fourteen times larger than its continental territory.[26] Iraq lost the area that its fishermen exploited for centuries.

We should be reminded that the Charter of Economic Rights and Duties of States provided:

> The seabed and ocean floor and the subsoil thereof, beyond the limits of national jurisdiction, as well as the resources of the area, are the common heritage of mankind, [and that] all States shall ensure that the exploration of the area and exploitation of its resources are carried out exclusively for peaceful purposes and that the benefits derived therefrom are shared equitably by all States, taking into account the particular interests and needs of developing countries; an international regime applying to the area and its resources and including appropriate international machinery to give effect to its provisions shall be established by an international treaty of a universal character, generally agreed upon.[27]

THE ROLE OF INTERNATIONAL PROTECTION OF INDUSTRIAL PROPERTY AND NEGOTIATIONS OF AN INTERNATIONAL CODE OF CONDUCT IN THE TRANSFER OF TECHNOLOGY

It is a misconception that the revision of the Paris convention on protection of industrial property could be in the interest of the developing countries, less 'a significant contribution towards the establishment of the NIEO', for the simple reason that the developing countries do not have industrial property needing protection.[28] The industrial property system is an instrument of the institution of monopolist control over the creation and application of the technological knowledge in the development of developing countries. The United Nations study demonstrated that the existing system of industrial property represents a legal instrument for the preservation of the existing relations between industrially developed and developing countries in industrial economic relations and an obstacle to the establishment of the NIEO.[29]

The developing countries in 1974 initiated the revision of the Paris convention for the protection of industrial property with the objective of adapting it to the interests of development. The Declaration of the objectives of the revision 'in the interest of developing countries' was adopted,[30] and the United Nations conference was scheduled for 1980. Judging from the results of the negotiations, the real purpose of the revision is the legalization of the existing situation, to make the Paris convention deceptively more attractive for a number of developing countries that are not parties to the Paris convention.

Serious problems emanating from the transfer of technology into the developing countries, analyzed in the UNCTAD study, show that restrictive clauses are found in over 90 per cent of the licensing contracts, and that they seriously impede the economic and technological advancement of the enterprises for the developing countries which are using the licenses. The examination of a sample of 2,000 contracts for the transfer of technology concluded that in ten developing countries, disastrous results have been found. According to them, restrictive clauses are found in 99 per cent of the contracts in Peru, 97 per cent in Mexico, 93 per cent in Chile, 43 per cent in India, etc.

Activity concerning the creation of new legal rules with regard to the international code of conduct in the transfer of technology was begun by the United Nations in 1961.[31] After many years of negotiations under the auspices of the UNCTAD, the UN General Assembly of 1977 adopted a resolution convening a United Nations conference for the negotiations and adoption of an international code of conduct in the transfer of technology.[32] The conference could not agree on the basic issues — the protection of industrial property through the code, the scope of application and applicable law, the control of restrictive business practices in the transfer of technology,[33] the treatment of transfer of technology in the relations with transnational corporations, the legal nature of the code, etc.

The demand by the Group of 77 for a legally binding code has been strained to the edge of confrontation between developed and developing countries, on the expense of watering down the rules and principles by provisions of the 'rules of reason'. The legal requirements have become political slogans, in the final analysis, counterproductive to the real interests of the developing countries.

Thus, the question of the proper strategical course for the developing countries concerning the international regulation of the transfer of technology is raised. The re-examination should start with the facts that around 90 per cent of the transfer of technology is performed among the industrially developed countries, only 10 per cent remaining between developed and developing countries, and the minimum among the developing countries. The struggle for a universally applied code of conduct means the battle for changing the rules of the behaviour among the developed countries as well. The competing interests of industrially developed countries on the world market makes difficult a universally applied compromise in the interest of developing countries.

Aspiring for the universally applied norms, the developing countries should undertake parallel negotiations by establishing a code of conduct between developed and developing countries in order to elaborate universal preferential norms of conduct. The developing countries should turn to themselves, to adopt a code of conduct in their mutual relations. For this the consensus with the developed countries is not needed. It will strengthen the position in defending the interests of development during the process of negotiations of a new international economic law in the framework of the NIEO. The draft of the Group of 77 of the code of conduct in the transfer of technology could serve as a basis. The industrially developed countries themselves are giving examples of how to protect the interest of the regional groups (the European Patent), the Andean Pact offering good examples for the developing countries. Through national legislation, then account could be taken of the specific needs, interest, and differences between developing countries.

PRINCIPLES AND RULES ON RESTRICTIVE BUSINESS PRACTICES (ANTIMONOPOLISM)

The elaboration of a study of restrictive business practices (RBPs) of private enterprises from the developed countries, with the particular emphasis being put on the effect of such practices on the export interests of the developing countries, was initiated by the UNCTAD II decision on 27 March 1968.[34] The UNCTAD III put most weight on restrictive business practices by transnational corporations having adverse effect on the trade and development of the developing countries. The task of formulating model law or laws to assist developing countries in devising their own legislation was given. The UNCTAD IV established the Third Ad Hoc Group of Experts and requested states to undertake joint measures on the national, regional and international level aimed at the elimination of certain RBPs.[35] The UN General Assembly decided on 20 December 1978 to convene in the period between September 1979 and April 1980, under the auspices of the UNCTAD, a UN Conference on Restrictive Business Practices to negotiate a set of multilaterally agreed equitable principles and rules for the control of RBPs having adverse effects on international trade, particularly that of developing countries, and on the economic development of those countries, 'including a decision on the legal character of the principles and rules'.[36]

At the closing meeting of the Sixth Session of the Third Ad Hoc Group of Experts at the UN Conference on 27 April 1979, the most important and basic issues of the Set of Principles and Rules on RBPs remained unresolved: differential treatment for enterprises of developing countries; the inclusion of RBPs occurring in the relations between the various entities constituting transnational corporations; exceptions to the application of the principles and rules; the legally binding nature of the principles and rules; the role of UNCTAD in implementing and monitoring the principles and rules, etc. And yet, the Fourth Ministerial Meeting of the Group of 77, held in Arusha (Tanzania), requested the Secretary-General of UNCTAD to convene the Conference on RBPs at an earlier date, in the latter part of 1979.[37]

The Set of Principles and Rules on RBPs in the context of the NIEO should be devised in the interest of development. Group B of the developed countries achieved a 'compromise' to include among the objectives in agreed text 'the creation, encouragement and protection of competition' and 'control of the concentration of capital and/or economic power'.[38] It is not difficult to foresee the position of developing countries in competition on the world and domestic market. The interests of development may require concentration of capital and economic power.

Instead of differential treatment for enterprises of developing countries, Group B proposed that special attention should be paid to the needs of small and medium-sized enterprises irrespective of their location. The Group of 77 took a strong position that small and medium-sized enterprises in developed countries operate in a completely different economic situation and accordingly cannot claim differential treatment. The conclusion is apparent — without preferential treatment of the developing countries, any Set of Principles and Rules on RBPs does not make sense, becoming counterproductive to the interests of developing countries.

One of the basic controversies between developed and developing countries is the question of the application of principles and rules on RBPs for the transactions between parent-companies and subsidiaries of transnational corporations. On this point Group B takes a strong uncompromised negative position, except for the case of the abuse of a dominant position on a market having adverse effect on the competition outside those enterprises. A spokesman of the Group of 77 pointed out that as much as 50 per cent of world trade could be between related entities of transnational corporations, and to exclude control over such transactions from the scope of the principles and rules would seriously impair the value of the instrument.[39]

Again, universal application of principles and rules on RBPs is not possible. In the control of RBPs in the developing and in the industrially developed countries, the same approach cannot be taken because the reasons for controlling RBPs are not the same in the developing countries as they are in developed countries. Given the varied structures and levels of economic and social development in developing countries, there is an urgent need to accelerate their industrial development and raise their living standards. The equalization of domestic and international monopolism is against the interests of developing countries and serves the international capital and transnational corporations. The principle of equality among the economically unequal, in this case, means legalization of inequality.

MODEL LAWS TO ASSIST DEVELOPING COUNTRIES IN DEVISING APPROPRIATE LEGISLATION

UNCTAD IV recommended elaboration of a model law or laws on restrictive business practices 'in order to assist developing countries in devising appropriate legislation'.[40] Draft international code of conduct on the transfer of technology contains the chapter, 'National regulation of transfer of technology'.[41] Even the World Intellectual Property Organization worked out a model law 'in the interest of developing countries'. Thus, we are witnessing the new phenomenon of international 'transfer of law'.

The elaboration of the model laws should be viewed primarily as a form of co-operation among developing countries in an area of mutual interest, on the basis of collective self-reliance of developing countries. They should take into account a wide diversity of economic, political and social structures in levels of economic development among developing countries in order to achieve a measure of harmony in the approaches of these countries to the question of restrictive business practices, ultimately facilitating the establishment of regional and sub-regional economic integration arrangements. Above all, the model law should reflect the specific situation and needs of a developing country.

The first draft of a model law or laws on RBPs to assist developing countries in devising appropriate legislation[42] worked out by UNCTAD Secretariat was not based primarily on the protection of development but, as a draft set of principles and rules for the control of RBPs, on 'the creation, encouragement and protection of competition', and 'control of the concentration of capital and/or economic power to protect social welfare and the interests of consumers.'[43] This kind of a model law could have been worked out by OECD.

The UNCTAD Secretariat put forward the dilemma whether the model law or laws 'should be universal in application or applicable only to developing countries'. If they are to be universal in application, the model law or laws could be viewed as a negotiable instrument, *inter alia*, to assist in the implementation of the principles and rules. On the other hand, if this is not to be the case, then the model law or laws would become essentially a matter for developing countries and for decision by them.

In negotiating the Set of Principles and Rules, the Third Ad Hoc Group of Experts agreed that 'all States should provide necessary information and experience to UNCTAD in this connection'.[44] The Group of 77 decisively answered this dilemma, taking a strong position that the laws of developed countries could only provide limited assistance, since such laws necessarily reflected the relatively higher levels of economic and social development and greater market power of these countries and their own social and economic objectives.[45] 'Any model law on restricted business practices to be elaborated in UNCTAD would be only a model made by experts of developing countries to assist in formulation of their national legislation.'[46]

CODE OF CONDUCT FOR TRANSNATIONAL CORPORATIONS

In drawing up the Programme of Action on the establishment of an NIEO, the General Assembly emphasized that 'all efforts should be made to formulate, adopt and implement an international code of conduct for transnational corporations' in order:

(a) To prevent interference in the internal affairs of the countries where they operate and their collaboration with racist regimes and colonial administrators;

(b) To regulate their activities in host countries, to eliminate restrictive business practices and to conform to the national development plans and objectives of developing countries; and in this context facilitate, as necessary, the review and revision of previously concluded arrangements;

(c) To bring about assistance, transfer of technology and management skills to developing countries on equitable and favourable terms;

(d) To regulate the repatriation of the profits accruing from their operations, taking into account the legitimate interest of all parties concerned;

(e) To promote reinvestment of their profits in developing countries.[47]

On the basis of the report of the Group of Eminent Persons from 1974,[48] a United Nations Commission was established with the task of conducting research on the influence of transnational corporations on development. The UN Commission on TNCs then established the Intergovernmental Working Group for drafting the Code of Conduct for TNCs.[49]

A crucial issue that emerged during the early stages of the Working Group's deliberations was whether the code of conduct should be addressed exclusively to TNCs or whether it should encompass the treatment of TNCs by governments. The developing countries at first insisted that the only issue before the Working Group was the regulation of the conduct of TNCs and that the conduct of governments was outside the purview of the code. This position was strongly resisted by the developed countries who ultimately succeeded in bringing the treatment of TNCs by governments within the purview of the code.

Within the list of the basic principles for the Code of Conduct there are 'competition and restrictive business practices' (item 5) and 'the transfer of technology' (item 6). But there is no intercourse between the activities of the Intergovernmental Group of Experts on an International Code of Conduct on Transfer of Technology and the Third Ad Hoc Group of Experts on Restrictive Business Practices, to prepare proposals and recommendations for the formulation of a set of multilaterally agreed equitable principles and rules for the control of such practices (both within the UNCTAD). The outcome of the UN Conference on an International Code of Conduct on the Transfer of Technology, the UN Conference on a Set of Principles and Rules on RBPs and the UN Conference on the Revision of the Paris Convention for the Protection of Industrial Property will prejudice the fate of the Code of Conduct for TNCs and the further work on the Charter of Economic Rights and Duties of States.

When in equilibrium, the management of the international economic system is limited to assuring that the rules of the game are observed. For a number of reasons, this task may be entrusted to multilateral organizations each specializing in one of the distinct albeit interrelated components of the system, namely, trade payments and finance. On the other hand, when the system experiences strains of fundamental disequilibrium this largely compartmentalized approach to the management of the international economy bears a number of risks. Since the various elements of the trading are closely intertwined (monetary and financial systems) the success of changes in the rules and procedures in one area will depend on complementary measures and changes in the other area. Changes in the rules and procedures adopted separately in the several spheres should, in the final analysis, be regarded as part of a co-ordinated overall settlement of the tensions in the international economy. It is in the nature of the case that some elements of that settlement will appeal most to some countries, other elements to others. There is a danger that if each measure were acted upon by itself, countries might feel free to accept or reject the various component parts one by one instead of taking a view of the entire settlement as a whole. This in turn could lead to an unbalanced outcome.[50]

A NEW NOTION OF INTERNATIONAL LAW IN THE PROCESS OF THE ESTABLISHMENT OF THE NIEO

In the Declaration of the Heads of States of Governments of the Non-aligned Countries of Colombo, it was stated that the 'establishment of the NIEO demands courageous initiatives, new concrete and global solutions', which is 'contrary to slow reforms and improvisations having the solution of today's economic problems as the aim.' The NIEO demands not only new international economic law, but a new method of its codification too.

The Charter of Economic Rights and Duties of States has introduced certain norms or rules which some of the developed countries consider as fundamental departures from the traditional rules of international law, accordingly contending that the Charter is a non-binding instrument with no legal force. On the other hand, the developing countries consider the Charter a legally binding instrument imposing rights and obligations on the States, the basic source to be found in Article 56 of the UN Charter. The Charter is regarded by a large majority of the members of the United Nations as a development of legal norms for the development of international relations on a just and equitable basis, providing 'primary evidence and guidance for all nations of international legal norms governing international economic relations'. 'A new era in the international law of economic co-operation has arrived.'[51]

A new approach is needed to the theory of obligation in international law. The purpose of this new approach is to make the emerging concept of consensus rather than the traditional concept of consent as the basis of obligation of the international community. If the international society is to function effectively, it requires a limited legislative authority to translate an overriding consensus among the States into rules of order and norms of obligation despite opposition of one or more sovereign states. Accordingly a quasi-legislative competence is attributed to the General Assembly resolutions of a constituent pattern.[52]

'For these reasons, the Charter was considered to be part of a changing process, without any time-limit, to which new contributions would be made little by little. For this reason it contains machinery to provide for its review and adaptation to new conditions as circumstances require.'[53] The opposition by certain developed countries 'raises a serious question as to the legal significance of the Charter'[54] but 'it does show the course that future legal development will take in this area'; that 'the Charter may evidence what States regard international custom to be', and that the provisions of the Charter 'may acquire meaning both as the view of sources of international law changes and as they may be incorporated in practice'. 'It is possible to argue that the provisions of the Charter have become a part of customary international law in as much as they are regarded as binding by a large number of States.'[55]

> Actually, in the international legal system, a distinction between 'binding' and 'non-binding' norms, when possible to delineate, will be seen to be rather shady. . . In the international process, the forces that converge to impinge upon and constrain states to behave one way or another are broader than the narrow consideration of legality and include the moral, the political, the social and the economic aspects. Thus, that a norm is or is not strictly juridical is not a conclusive criterion for its propensity to affect state practice. Indeed, strictly juridical norms may and often do yield to these other ingredients of the international legal process. Moreover, in the case of an entire instrument with multiple and varied provisions, it will usually mean very little to ask in some formal and technical sense whether it is 'binding'. Many of its provisions may, unlike others and irrespective of the formal status of the instrument itself, have the force of law. This is especially so as states are wont to cast negative votes against the entire instrument on the basis of isolated offending provisions . . . It is in this sense that the Charter sets a new frontier in international economic relations.[56]

The establishment of the NIEO requires fundamental changes in the notion of international law. The principle of economic equality of States demands a new approach, correcting it to include preferential treatment for the developing countries. The most favoured-nation clause cannot be applied in the relations between the industrially developed and developing countries.[57] International law concerning human rights denotes a new phase connected with economic development.[58]

The new international law of economic development is emerging.[59] The optimal objective of creating new universal norms, binding upon all states, should be paralleled with codes of conduct regulating the relations between the developed and developing countries. This negotiating process should be added in the future with the adoption of codes of conduct among developing countries. In this way the international law will consolidate the unity of developing countries in protection of the interests of development. The adoption of the common attitude of developing countries, for example, that only two or three restrictive clauses will not b : accepted in contracts with the industrially developed countries, will be of great importance. The national legislation of the developing countries could have a special place in the new international law of development.

INSTITUTIONAL CRISIS IN THE PROCESS OF CODIFICATION
OF PRINCIPLES AND RULES OF NIEO

In the context of intensive considerations of the institutional matter of the United Nations Organization no attention was given to the institutional problems in the process of codification of principles and rules of the NIEO, of the new international law of economic development and of the increased needs for the codification and progressive development of contemporary international law. That fact, in a way, demonstrates the diminishing roles of law and lawyers in contemporary international relations, when the necessities for law and lawyers are apparent in the establishment of the NIEO.

The existing organs of the United Nations — the International Law Commission and the Commission on International Trade Law, the way they are now organized, cannot fulfill the enlarging tasks of the codification and development of the new international economic law. The International Law Commission is limited by the composition of one expert from each of the twenty-five States. The Commission on International Trade Law (UNCITRAL) is restricted to being a technical-legal body confined to the field of international private law.

The codification and development of the principles and rules concerning new international economic relations (NIEO) has been performed by a number of different organs and organizations of the United Nations.[60] There are more and more intergovernmental groups of experts charged with drafting codes of conduct. That system has its undeniable advantages in engaging experts from appropriate fields with a particular mandate. Their drafts are being subject to the diplomatic conferences of state representatives with full powers.

There are, however, many questions of common and fundamental interest, which cut across all the international legal instruments. Every particular international legal instrument should be approached taking as the base one common criterion — the NIEO. In order to ensure creation of a consistent body of international economic law, a 'Clearing House' is needed.

An institutional solution of this problem, without proliferation and creation of new bodies within the United Nations, lies in changing the role and mandate of the UNCITRAL. The delegations of member States can be adapted to the needs of the 'Formulating Agency', both in their number and professional knowledge, in order to establish as many working groups and bodies as necessary. Instead of duplicating the work in the International Institute for the Unification of Private Law and the Hague Conferences on international private law, UNCITRAL can now consider the long experience and expertise of these completed conferences.

In its future activities, UNCITRAL should concentrate on its role as 'Co-ordinating Agency'. The co-ordinating role in the codification and development of norms of international trade law is one of the fundamental functions of UNCITRAL, contained in its original mandate.[61] Because this function was fully neglected during the first ten years of its activity, at its eleventh session, the Commission devoted special attention to this question and unanimously decided, considering a new long-term programme of work,

> to consult where appropriate, with other international organizations and bodies within and outside the United Nations System on their programme of work, to the extent that such programmes relate to legal work carried out by UNCITRAL in the field of international trade and are especially relevant to the new international economic order, and to formulate, for the Commission's consideration, recommendations as to the degree of co-ordination that would be required for a rational programme of work in the area at issue.[62]

Accordingly, taking into account its new role and programme of work, the Commission could change its name to the United Nations Commission on International Economic Law (UNCIEL). That would have an impact on the trend of the codification and development of the new international law in general, and on the international law of development (NIEO) in particular.

The alternative is the establishment of a new, third commission of the United Nations for the Codification and Development of International Economic Law. One of the possibilities is, in accordance with the UNCTAD IV decision, the establishment of 'an appropriate mechanism' for the realization of the goals of the Action Programme for the establishment of the NIEO and the implementation of Article 34 of the Charter of Economic Rights and Duties of States.[63] On the basis of this decision, a United Nations commission on Economic Rights and Duties of States may be created, as an organ of the UN Economic and Social Council, relying on the Secretariat of UNCTAD whose reports, through the Board of Trade and Development and ECOSOC, would be considered by the UN General Assembly.

During the discussions in the Sixth Committee of the UN General Assembly on the item 'Review of the Multilateral Treaty-Making Process', several delegations suggested that more substantive legal work should be undertaken within the Sixth Committee. In the opinion of Erik Suy, the Legal Advisor to the UN Secretary General, 'there are several good reasons for endorsing this idea. For example, diplomatic conferences never have the universal attendance of a General Assembly session.' Also, new states generally lack the resources for participating in all or even most of the conferences which are called into being to codify or progressively develop international law. Sessions of the General Assembly provide better opportunities for a fuller participation and hence for producing texts which have the support of more States.

> While nowadays, most States and delegations tend to consider the purely procedural discussions held in the Sixth Committee as a waste of energy, the involvement of the Sixth Committee in the substance of the law-making will undoubtedly increase its prestige. International conventions are being discussed and adopted on a regular basis in other fora of the General Assembly (e.g. in the Third Committee) mostly without the Legal Committee being involved. The growing tendency is to create special committees for the preparation of international treaties. This tends to leave the Sixth Committee with little choice other than to consider the reports of such committees. Substantive decisions would generally appear to deal merely with either the extension of such a committee's mandate or the recommendations that a diplomatic conference be convened. Such functions involve mostly the financial implications, the place and date of the conference, the question of languages, etc. This it is submitted, is not suitable to the competence and even the dignity of the Sixth Committee.[64]

These 'unfinished reflections' which are widely aired in several fora inside and outside the United Nations indicate a growing awareness that international law-making has become a very complex phenomenon in modern international society, and that the time is ripe to review the processes in order to improve them.

NOTES AND REFERENCES

1   At the Seventh Conference on the Law of the World, sponsored by the World Peace Through Law Center, a work paper, 'The United Nations Charter of Economic Rights and Duties of States', was presented by S. Azadon Tiewul (Washington, D.C., 12–17 October 1975).
2   Charter of the United Nations, Article 55.
3   UNCTAD V, Evaluation of the world trade and economic situation and consideration of issues, policies and appropriate measures to facilitate structural changes in the international economy — Report by the UNCTAD Secretariat, TD/224.
4   Eighth Session of the Human Rights Commission.
5   Hassan S. Zakariya, see Chap. 16.
6   UNCTAD resolution 45 (III) of 18 May 1972.
7   Conference of Heads of State or Governments of Non-aligned Countries.
8   UN General Assembly resolution 3201 (S–VI), UN doc. A/9559.
9   UN General Assembly resolution 3281 (XXIX).
10   UN General Assembly resolution 3494 (XXX), 31/99, 32/145 and 33/92.
11   XIX Session, Doha (Qatar), 23 January 1978.
12   XI Session, New York, 14 June 1978.
13   UN General Assembly resolution 33/92.
14   UN doc. A/34/50, 15 February 1979, decision 33/424 of 16 December 1978.
15   UNCTAD Secretariat, doc. TD/224, pp. 19–21.
16   A/RES/3281 (XXIX), 2315th plenary meeting, 12 December 1974.
17   Charter of Economic Rights and Duties of States — Preamble.
18   The negative votes: Belgium, Denmark, Germany (FDR), Luxembourg, the United Kingdom and the United States; abstaining were Austria, Canada, France, Ireland, Israel, Italy, Japan, the Netherlands, Norway and Spain.
19   Summary of Address, UNCTAD Proceedings, 3rd Sess., UN doc. TD/108, Vol. 1A, Part 1 at 184 /1972; *UN XI Monthly Chronicle* 4 (No. 9, May 1972).
20   UN General Assembly resolution 2340 (XXII).
21   UN General Assembly resolution 2467 A (XXIII) of 21 December 1968.
22   Principles governing the seabed and oceanfloor, and the subsoil thereof, beyond the limits of national jurisdiction, UN General Assembly resolution 2749 (XXV).
23   That 'the seabed and ocean floor beyond the limits of national jurisdiction are the common heritage of mankind'.
24   This concept of 'Patrimonial Sea' originated in Latin America, it was included into the Declaration of Santo Domingo of 9 June 1972 by fifteen Latin American states.
25   The Trilateral Commission, *A New Regime for the Oceans*, pp. 5 and 6.
26   In his speech at the Asian-African Legal Consultative Committee, on its nineteenth session in Doha (Qatar), of 20 January 1978.
27   Article 29.

28   From the aggregate fund of 3.5 million patents, citizens of the developing countries own only about 35,000 or 1 per cent. Patents owned by mixed companies and subsidiaries of transnational corporations in developing countries have been included in that number.

29   *The Role of the Patent System in the Transfer of Technology to Developing Countries*, UNCTAD doc. TD/B/AC.11/19/Rev. 1.

30   At the second meeting of the Committee of Experts of the World Organization for Industrial Property, 15–22 December 1975.

31   UN General Assembly resolution 1713 (XVI).

32   UN General Assembly resolution 32/188 – held in Geneva from 10 October till 16 November 1978, from 26 February till 10 March 1979.

33   At the beginning of the negotiations the Group of 77 identified some forty kinds of restrictive business practices, during the negotiations the number was brought down to twenty, till at the end of the UN Conference only three less important provisions were agreed upon.

34   UNCTAD resolution 25 (II), 78th plenary meeting.

35   UNCTAD resolution 96 (IV), 145th plenary meeting, 31 May 1976.

36   UN General Assembly resolution 33/153, 20 December 1978.

37   Arusha Programme for Collective Self-Reliance and Framework for Negotiations, UNCTAD V, TD/236, p. 46.

38   Report of the Third Ad Hoc Group of Experts on Restrictive Business Practices on its fifth session, TD/B/C.6/AC.6/18, p. 7.

39   It has been pointed out that OECD *Guidelines for Multinational Enterprises* (para. 8) applies to different entities within multinational corporations.

40   UNCTAD resolution 96 (IV), part III(f), of 31 May 1976.

41   TD/CODE TOT/14, 28 March 2979, p. 9.

42   TD/B/C.2/AC.6/16 and Corr. L, for the first draft.

43   Report by the UNCTAD Secretariat, TD/231, 8 January 1979, p. 17--18.

44   TD/B/C.2/AC.6/18, p. 17.

45   TD/B/C.2/AC.6/10, p. 15.

46   Arusha Programme, TD/236 77/MM/IV/21, p. 47.

47   *Programme of Action on the Establishment of a NIEO*, Resolution 3202 (S–VI) of 1 May 1974.

48   UN doc. E/5500/Rev. 1, ST/ESA/6; 'Multinational Corporations in World Development' (E.73.II.A.11, ST/ECA/190); 'The Impact of Multinational Corporations on Development and on International Relations' (UN. doc. E/5500, of 1 November 1974).

49   UN General Assembly resolution 1913, par. 4.

50   Report by the UNCTAD Secretariat 'Policy issues in the fields of trade, finance and money, and their relationship to structural changes at the global level', TD/225, 11 April 1979, p. 6.

51   Robin C.A. White, 'A New International Economic Order', (1975), 24 *Int. and Contemporary Law Quarterly* 542, also see 543.

52   Richard A. Falk, 'On the Quasi-Legislative Competence of the General Assembly (1966), *American Journal of International Law*, Vol. 60, pp. 782, 783.

53   Rabasa of Mexico, UN doc. A/PV.2315 at 67–70 (1974).

54   J. Dubitzky, 'The General Assembly's International Economics', *Harvard International Law Journal*, Vol. 18, pp. 674–6.

55   Subrata Roy Chowdhury, see Chap. 3.

56   S. Azadon Tiewul, 'The United Nations Charter of Economic Rights and Duties of States', *Journal of International Law and Economics*, Vol. 10, p. 687.

57   Commission du droit international, A/CN.4/309 and Add. 1.

58 See the resolution of the 58th International Law Association Conference, Manila, 2 September 1978.

59 Colloque international — Droit international et développement, Alger 11–14 Octobre 1976; Oscar Schachter, 'The Evolving International Law of Development', *Columbia Journal of Transnational Law*, Vol. 15 (1976), No. 1, p. 1–16, etc.

60 In the UN General Assembly through the Sixth (Legal) Committee or directly; in the International Law Commission, UNCITRAL, GATT — international trade and customs; UNCTAD — carriage of goods by sea, transfer of technology, principles and rules on RBPs, model law or laws; Commission on TNCs; WIPO — industrial and intellectual property; IMCO — maritime law; ICAO — civil aviation; ILO — labour law; UNIDROIT — the Hague conferences on international private law, etc.

61 UN General Assembly resolution 2205 (XXI) of 17 December 1966.

62 UN doc. A/CN.9/149 of 4 May 1978; *Report of the United Nations Commission on International Trade Law* on the work of its eleventh session, 30 May–16 June 1978, General Assembly, Official Records: thirty-third session, Supplement No. 17, A/33/17, pp. 44–5.

63 UNCTAD resolution No. 90 (IV) of 30 May 1976; UN General Assembly resolutions 3202 (S.VI), 3281 (XXIX), 3486 (XXX) and 3506 (XXX); ECOSOC resolution No. 1911 (LVII) and 2027 (LXI), 4 August 1976.

64 Erik Suy, *Innovations in International Law-Making Processes*, 1 December 1977.

2 The Legal Character of Emerging Norms Relating to the New International Economic Order: Some Comments

*Brigitte Bollecker-Stern**

Order is an ambiguous notion. In its present form, the New International Economic Order (NIEO), the first general formulation of which can be found in the Declaration and the Programme of Action on the New International Economic Order adopted by the Sixth Special Session of the General Assembly of the United Nations, in a Resolution dated 1 May 1974, represents an unresolved ambiguity. This ambiguity exists as far as its *content*, as well as its *legal binding force* is concerned.

As to the *content* of the NIEO, one may question if the NIEO is an attempt to construct a *new* order based on a new international division of labour and implying an effective redistribution of global wealth and global economic power, or is it a new *order* designed to correct the worst excesses and most visible inequities resulting from the breakdown of the existing international economic order, but without in any way modifying its essential foundations? In other words, is it a 'new system of international economic relations based on equality and the common interest of all countries', as propounded in the Charter of Algiers of 1973, or is it a mere replastering of the old order? The question is crucial to any appreciation of the NIEO, although it is not our main concern here.

Scepticism concerning the reality and depth of the changes implicit in the NIEO is legitimate. The developed market economies only reluctantly accepted the concept of an NIEO, in the aftermath of the petroleum crisis of 1973, also called the 'economic Bandung', and only when the old order was no longer working well. As UN Secretary-General Waldheim declared in 1975: 'the charge against that order in the past is that it worked well for the affluent and against the poor. It cannot now even be said to work well for the rich. This is an additional incentive

*University of Dijon and University of Paris.

for evolving an NIEO.' The socialist countries, while paying lip service to its stated goal have concentrated adroitly on removing themselves from the mainstream of the development dialectic because of their declared policy of non-concern towards under-development, considered as a consequence of capitalism and colonialism. The developing countries are, of course, the main protagonists of the NIEO, but often the commitment to change among certain elites of these countries is suspect. Despite various misgivings in many countries, however, the NIEO has taken hold in the consciousness of the international community and the necessity for some change is accepted. The question is what kind of change?

The nature of the NIEO as an emerging, inchoate order is underlined by the use of the indefinite article in both the Declaration and in the Programme of Action. Without agreement on the content of the NIEO the concept remains precarious and even if the desirability of establishing an NIEO is accepted, there is nevertheless a real danger that it will become merely another addition to the United Nations development vocabulary, a lexicon already replete with the slogans of thirty years' struggle to achieve 'international co-operation in solving international problems of an economic . . . character.'

In fact, the NIEO is the most recent manifestation of the ideology of development, already rooted in the Charter of the United Nations. This ideology of development, has taken and is taking its shape through a vast network of resolutions, declarations, strategies, programmes and institutions.

And here appears the ambiguity of the NIEO as far as its *legal binding force* is concerned. Assuming that the political will to elaborate a New International Economic Order exists, it remains a challenging test to convert it into legal obligations: this raises the *problem of the legal character of emerging norms relating to the New International Economic Order.*

In 1972, in a speech he made during the third session of UNCTAD in Santiago de Chile, President Echeverria insisted on the necessity to convert the hopes of the one side into legal obligations of the other, when he declared: 'It is necessary to take co-operation out of the realm of good will to crystallize it in the field of Law'. Such crystallization appears difficult, especially as the principles of the NIEO have mainly been elaborated through resolutions of different international organizations of the United Nations system, which have no binding force, even if they might have some legal value. This remark gives an idea of the complexity of the norms hierarchy in international law and shows the necessity to examine more closely the different sources of international law in order to ascertain the legal value of the different international documents related to the NIEO. But at the same time, it has to be stressed that not only international legal texts, but very different types of instruments could contribute towards the establishment of the NIEO: of course, most instruments will be purely international, their legal value depending on the means of elaboration; but there are also national texts that will contribute to the implementation of the principles of the NIEO: a place has also to be made for instruments which are closely linked to the concrete coming into existence of the NIEO, that is the international contracts, as well as transnational contracts between a State — most often a developing State — and a company — most often a company incorporated in a developed State — whose legal characterization is controversial.

The birth of the concept of NIEO has been brought about mainly through international documents, although not always through international legal instruments. International law is based on the consent of its subjects — states and international organizations. More precisely, if the consent of the subject is necessary for a rule to come into existence, it is not sufficient. For a rule of international law to emerge, there must be an encounter of consents. These consents can be given tacitly as in the case of an international custom, or expressly as in the case of a treaty. They might also be given by the States through the channel of an international organization as in the case of a resolution. Traditionally, however, according to Article 38 of the Statute of the ICJ, custom and treaty are the main sources of international law, while resolutions of international organizations have no binding force. They are not able to bring into existence, by themselves, a new rule of international law. But the real part played by *resolutions* of international organizations in the creation of new principles and rules of international law, and especially in the field of the NIEO, is much more complex and might even be more important than the part played by the traditional sources. As a matter of fact, resolutions can constitute a very flexible instrument for the progressive development of international law. On their face, they definitely have no binding force, and cannot have in the present state of international law: this apparent handicap can prove to be an advantage, as it often permits an easier adoption of some resolutions, thus leading States to become reconciled to certain emerging principles, this process being not foreign to the creation of international custom. Even if they do not contribute to the emergence of new customary rules of international law, resolutions, by their permissive value, might put aside, for the States that have voted them existing customs: if the resolution does not oblige the States to consider its content as binding, it permits the States to do so, and by doing so, to contest for themselves the value of the former rule. The resolution, therefore, intervenes at two different levels, which in fact interfere, in the creation of international law: by its integration in a customary process, as just seen; but also by itself, if conditions are such as to give the resolution a legal efficiency approaching the legal value of an international convention. The mere fact that States often express reservations, as in treaties, strengthens the impression that resolutions play a not negligible role in the shaping of international law. If the political will of enforcement exists, a resolution can have as much legal effectiveness as a treaty. What then are the elements to be taken into account in the appraisal of the probable legal effects of a resolution?

Much will depend, of course, on the conditions of adoption: the more representative of all groups composing the international community, the majority, the closer the resolution will be to being regarded as an instrument of binding force. This means that if a resolution is adopted even unanimously by an international organization representing only one group of States, for example the non-aligned or the European countries, or if it is adopted by a majority representing only one group of countries in a general international organization like the United Nations, the resolution is liable to have less legal effect than if the same resolution were adopted by a majority representing all groups in the same United Nations. For example, Resolution 1803 on permanent sovereignty over natural resources adopted by a very large majority representing developed States — both capitalist and socialist — and developing States can probably be said to have the effect of a binding instrument; the same certainly does not hold true for the Charter of Algiers adopted by the non-aligned in 1973, or for the Charter of Economic Rights and Duties, adopted in the United Nations, which although it was adopted by a very large majority did not receive the consent of the industrialized States. Depending on the extent and the composition of the majority, and on the framework in which it is adopted, a resolution can be said to have merely political effects, or to be an instrument having legal effects, or to be an instrument of agreement and co-operation.

Likewise, the more precise the content of the resolution, the more likely it is to have legal consequences: this is true whether the resolution has a concrete content — creation of an organ, statement of a programme or of a strategy, or if it is purely abstract — declaration of principles. For example, the First Decade of Development stated very vague aims and provided for quite imprecise measures in order to foster development; in the face of its partial failure, the Second Decade was accompanied by a strategy providing for a whole series of very precise actions to be taken by the different States, the developed as well as the developing ones, and by the international organizations.

Also, the means of enforcement, which are specified, tell much about the probable translation of the resolution into legal reality: especially, it is important whether action has to be taken only by the organization which enacted the resolution, in which case it is quite likely to be enforced; but if action is required from the States, this results in a more complex situation. Besides, the existence of a mechanism of control is also quite relevant: its existence gives more chances to the resolution to be enforced than its absence. Here again, the example of the two Decades for Development is interesting. As the first one was not accompanied by measures of assessment of its results, the second one provided for 'appropriate arrangements . . . to follow closely the improvements accomplished in the carrying into effect of the ends and goals of the Decade, to determine in which fields the progress was inadequate, and to recommend positive measures, including, if necessary, new goals and policies'.

Conditions of adoption, content, and means of enforcement, constitute a bundle of factors to be taken into account to appraise the legal value of a resolution. This analysis leads to the conclusion that if in strict theory, a resolution never has a binding force, in practice its effect can be the same as if it had such binding force. And in fact, as already mentioned, resolutions play an outstanding role in international economic law. For example, the reversal of the long-standing international norms of reciprocity and non-discrimination that prevailed in international economic relations, was obtained through a series of 'non-binding' resolutions. At the first UNCTAD, General Principle Eight, which called in a very general way for the application of the principle of non-reciprocity, without any measures of implementation, was adopted by the vote solely of the developing countries. It is undeniable that applying the criteria suggested above, such a resolution is basically a political instrument, intended to exert pressure on the developed countries. Between 1964 and 1968 countless resolutions concerning the problem were adopted in different forums, tending towards a crystallization of new rules. It ended up by the adoption, during UNCTAD II, of Resolution 21 (II) which stated agreement 'in favour of the establishment of a mutually acceptable system of generalised non-reciprocal and non-discriminatory preferences', established a Special Committee to elaborate more precisely the consequences of the adoption of such a system, and was unanimously approved. It is certain that this second resolution appproaches very much the legal binding value of a convention, and this was eventually proved by its later enforcement through the concrete adoption of generalized preferences schemes, first by the EEC in 1971 and ultimately by the USA in 1976.

If the concept of NIEO has mainly been shaped by resolutions of international organizations, the traditional sources of international law — custom and treaty — have also contributed to its development. Moreover, they play an important role, especially treaty, in the concrete implementation of the new order. Custom and treaty are not *inter se* in a hierarchical situation. No source supersedes automatically the other, each contributes on the same footing to the creation of binding rules of international law. But this means that a custom can make a treaty fall in abeyance, at least through a process extending over a certain length of time; and more importantly, that a treaty can instantly override a principle, even an important principle, of customary law. It is against the consequences of such a situation, that the developing countries tried to make reference to certain peremptory rules known as *jus cogens*. The developing countries felt the need to refer to a corpus of imperative principles that could never be set aside by treaty, because they were conscious of their weakness when they entered for example in a bilateral treaty with developed countries, and they were afraid of being compelled to lose through a conventional provision, the benefit of a customary rule that protected them. This concept of *jus cogens* has been defined by the Vienna Conference of 1969 on the law of treaties which states that 'the peremptory rules of international law are rules accepted and recognized by the whole international community of States, as norms to which no derogation is permitted and which can only be modified by new norms of general international law'. The *jus cogens*, whose origin can be conventional or customary, therefore contains norms that can never be put aside by the will of some States. Although the boundaries of the concept are quite difficult to ascertain, it is agreed that some rules are undoubtedly part of the *jus cogens*: among them, the principle of permanent sovereignty over natural resources, and therefore the *jus cogens* has certainly links with the NIEO.

Among the principles of the NIEO can certainly be found numerous *customary principles and norms*, that result from a general practice considered as being binding: the rule concerning indemnification in case of nationalization of foreign goods, although not quite ascertained to-day, certainly has a customary origin. It must be noticed, however, that contrary to the traditional customary rule, which was essentially emerging out of the practice of States, nowadays customary law creation cannot be separated from the action of international organizations, as seen before.

In general the statements of the customary rules will be found in international or arbitral decisions.

But *treaties* are liable to play a more important role than custom in the concrete implementation of the NIEO, as they can provide for much more precise and detailed action. Many different types of international conventions will contribute to the setting up of the NIEO: multilateral conventions, like the Lomé Convention concluded between the EEC and forty-six African, Pacific and Caribbean States in 1975; multilateral conventions concluded under the auspices of an international organization, like the IRDB Convention on the settlement of disputes adopted in 1975; bilateral conventions between two States, like treaties of commerce or co-operation, 'umbrella agreements'; bilateral conventions between a State and an international organization, like a lending agreement between a State and the IMF; bilateral or multilateral conventions between international organizations, for example to organize their co-operation in a development programme, and so on. It must be noticed here that the type of dialectical analysis formerly made in order to appraise the legal value of a resolution, can also, and must also, be made for international conventions. Although the treaty is formally binding, and the resolution formally recommendatory, it is necessary to go beyond this formal approach to assess their ultimate legal signification. The treaty will often remain a dead letter, when the very same conditions, whose presence give the resolution a quasi-binding force, are absent. Thus, the conditions of adoption can show that the treaty is a true agreement, or on the contrary, hides very diverging views, its content can be so vague as to be almost unenforceable, it can provide for measures of control or not. Of course, this gives indications on the practical effects of the treaty, it has no bearing on its binding value, which remains uncontested: this compulsory character is sometimes resented by the developing countries, which feel that they can be compelled (by economic necessity) to enter into unequal international treaties with developed countries, which stabilizes and stiffens power relations that they strive to modify. To mitigate this inconvenience, several devices can be used: among them, the conclusion of treaties for a determined period of time, with the inclusion of a renegotiation clause: for example, the Lomé Convention was adopted for a five-year time period, and it should be renegotiated in 1980.

Resolutions, customary rules, treaties, all these concur to give to the economic order its new outlines, in the international sphere. But the NIEO is of no use, if it does not penetrate the national economic reality of States. Many national instruments draw the conclusions of the NIEO on the national economic level: acts of the legislator like codes of investments or law of nationalization; acts of the executive like decrees of agreement as priority enterprise; acts of the judiciary; acts of public enterprises or organisms. Of course, from a legal point of view, all these national instruments are 'mere facts' in international law (*Chorzow Factory case*, 1927). But their role in the final implementation of the NIEO is crucial.

As is also crucial the role played by *transnational contracts*: these contractual relations between a subject of international law and a subject of a national legal order can be of several types: contracts of production — concession, participation, association, joint-venture, service contracts among which the production-sharing contracts; contracts of sale — sale of goods, of licences, 'key in hands' contracts, 'product in hands' contracts, 'market in hands' contracts; service contracts like contracts of technical assistance, of formation, of transportation, of loan and so on. But they all raise the same political and legal question of the law applicable to them, of the legal order to which they are to be submitted. The question has far-reaching political connotations. For a long time, these contracts were unquestionably ruled by the national law of a State. The Permanent Court of International Justice declared in 1929 that 'every contract, which is not a contract between States, acting as subjects of international law, is based on a national legislation' (*Serbian Loans* case, Series A No. 20–1, p. 41). This position was confirmed, *a contrario*, by the ICJ, when it declared that a contract between a State and a foreign corporation was not an international treaty submitted to international law (*Anglo-Iranian* case 1951). But the submission of these contracts to the national law of the State entering into them did not meet with the approval of developed countries, which feared legislative or administrative or even judicial interference with them. Therefore, different attempts were made to have these transnational contracts depend from another legal order than the State party's legal order: either to a legal order *sui generis*, a sort of transnational legal order, based on generally accepted principles of law, or to no legal order at all, but to the sole autonomy of will of the contractors, or to international law. All these solutions were deemed acceptable by developed States, either because generally accepted principles of law or international law, in whose genesis they played a determining role were protective of their interests, or because the principle of the autonomy of will is always in favour of the party having the strongest bargaining power. But, by the same token, all these attempts of denationalization of transnational contracts were more and more violently and openly opposed by the developing States. It might well be that with the evolution of the general principles of law, especially as a result of the emergence of certain principles of *jus cogens*, and with the quick evolution of international law, which takes more and more into account the long neglected interests of developing countries, the submission of these type of contracts to the general principles of law or to international law, could become admissible to developing countries and therefore constitute a good compromise. For the moment, however the situation is not ripe for such a move, and the developing States show very strong hostility to any denationalization of these contracts, as results for example from the Charter of Economic Rights and Duties of the States.

Other contracts are liable to play a role in the reshaping of the international economy, that is contracts between private entities originating from two different States, usually a developing State and a developed State. There should be no question in submitting these contracts to a national law, generally the law of the State where the realization of the contract takes place. If these contracts, these '*international contracts*', as well as the so-called transnational contracts, enter into a State's jurisdiction, attempts are made to enact on the international level, some general rules applicable to all those contracts which have an impact on development processes in the form of codes of conduct: code of conduct for the transfer of technology, code of conduct on multinational corporations. While these are being shaped, discussions go on about their place in the legal system: in fact, their legal value will depend on all the factors mentioned above: type of instrument, conditions of adoption, content, measures of control.

So far, we have concentrated our attention on the formal aspects and the formal changes that, in our opinion, are going on in the field of the sources of international law, and especially of international economic law. But more generally, and as a concluding remark, one can say that the role played by international law in the overall shaping of international relations, has completely changed. Law can have very different relations to reality, it can adopt very different positions in front of unequal situations: law can *disregard* reality and treat equally unequal situations giving thus its sanction to existing inequalities: law can take into account reality to *reinforce* it and transpose the existing unequal situations in the legal sphere, by the establishment of parallel legal inequalities. International law, until recently, combined these two approaches towards reality. But law can also take reality into account not by reinforcing it, but by *correcting* it. International law, nowadays, has a tendency to adopt more and more frequently this last approach: therefore most traditional concepts of international law have undergone some significant changes:

the change of meaning of the concept of sovereignty provides a very relevant example.

While sovereignty was for a long time, and until recently, only a legal sovereignty, it has become now — that is since the Second World War and especially since decolonization, which can be analysed as the translation into reality of legal sovereignty — also an economic sovereignty. This evolution was brought about by the establishment that legal sovereignty did not suffice to give a State the mastery over its existence: and while States acceded to international existence, that is to sovereignty, the neo-colonial economic relations they entered into with developed countries — either their former metropoles or other States — wove around them a network of constraints so tied as to empty of all its meaning their newly acquired sovereignty. Sovereignty did not suffice. The economic problems were there to remind us of that fact. A new dimension had thus to be added to sovereignty to give it its true meaning: the economic dimension. The mere fact that the central problem today is the establishment of a new international *economic* order, and not merely a new system of international relations, shows a new awareness of the primordial importance of economics in the evolution of society. And quite naturally, many of the general principles which are at the root of the NIEO have an economic dimension: this is true of the principle of the participation of all States in the resolution of the world's economic problems, the right of each state to adopt its own economic system, and of course, of the very central notion of the NIEO, the permanent sovereignty over natural resources.

Although the two meanings of the principle of sovereignty — the legal and the economic meaning — have the same goal, that is the independence of the State, they are different, and their consequences might even be contradictory. While the legal sovereignty needs strict equality, in the rules applied to the States, economic sovereignty, which takes into account the socio-economic structures of the States, can allow legal inequalities in order to re-establish a materially unequal situation: that means that international law no longer feels compelled to treat equally unequal situations, but takes into account the existing inequalities in order to compensate for them by reverse inequalities: the whole system of generalized preferences of the Lomé Convention is based on that reasoning. Also, the Declaration on the establishment of an NIEO, insists on this aspect, providing for a 'preferential treatment without reciprocity for the developing countries in all fields of economic co-operation, whenever it is possible.'

In other words, the concept of sovereignty has been enriched. The

NIEO is not based on a new principle of international law, but on a more sophisticated expression of the old and uncontested principle of the sovereignty of States.

3 Legal Status of the Charter of Economic Rights and Duties of States

*Subrata Roy Chowdhury**

The restructuring of economic relations on a global scale by the establishment of a New International Economic Order (NIEO) presents many inter-related problems: political, economic and legal. The emerging norms of a dynamic concept like NIEO would perhaps require, at least to some extent, an unorthodox jurisprudential approach. This is indeed a challenge to legal creativity which the International Law Association (ILA) has now taken up after it adopted the Manila resolution in 1978.

We are now at the threshold of the preparations for a third development decade. It would be appropriate to remind ourselves of some pertinent observations made by Jan Pronk, the then Netherlands Minister for Development Cooperation, about the malady of the present international economic order. He said:[1]

The international system, as devised after World War II, served the Western world well. The tripling of total world output since 1945 cannot be considered a small achievement . . . Never have there been, both in relative and absolute terms, more people below minimum standards of living than today. The gap between the average income in developed and in developing countries has widened. According to World Bank calculations, the average income of developed countries will, in the period 1970–1980 increase by 900 dollars to a total of 4,000 dollars. In the same period the average income in the poorest developing countries will increase from 105 dollars to 108 dollars — a total increase of 3 dollars during the period of 10 years, or an increase in purchasing power per year equivalent to the price of a bottle of

*Supreme Court of India; International Law Association.

Coke. This means poverty and inequality. It means nearly 70 per cent of the children in the Third World are suffering from malnutrition, leading to incurable damage. It means unemployment, bilharzia and slums. But it also means the production of nonsense goods, heart attacks, pollution and overkill capacity. That is the present international economic order.

He has strongly supported radical changes in the existing order and the establishment of a new international economic order on ethical, political and economic considerations. Since the political will for economic accommodation has not been noticed on any significant scale, the process of development has not yet started. Accordingly Jan Pronk suggested a double-track approach, using both voluntary and less voluntary methods, with a view to reaching decisions favouring the Third World: first, the liberal way, based on the voluntary recognition that yielding of some power is also in the long-term interest of the powerful; secondly, a less liberal way, through the development of an appropriate countervailing power. He regretted that the first method of voluntary redistribution of power has not been tried until now, while the second method of building countervailing power by the developing countries, has thus far yielded hardly any concrete results except with regard to the action of OPEC countries.[2]

The formulation of norms and principles of international development law postulates genuine international co-operation in an intensely interdependent world community. This is the mandate of the UN Charter. The fundamental purpose of the recent exercise at the United Nations level in this direction is to promote the establishment of an NIEO based on equity, sovereign equality, independence, interdependence, common interest and co-operation among all States irrespective of their economic and social systems. The three basic instruments in this field are the three important resolutions of the General Assembly; (i) Declaration on the Establishment of a New International Economic Order — Resolution 3201 (S–VI) of 1 May 1974 (ii) Programme of Action on the Establishment of a New International Economic Order — Resolution 3202 (X–VI) of 1 May 1974 and (iii) Charter of Economic Rights and Duties of States — Resolution 3281 (XIX) of 12 December 1974.[3] While the first two resolutions were adopted without vote but with reservations from some developed countries, the third resolution was adopted by a vote of 120 in favour to 6 against with 10 abstentions.

With a view to effective implementation of the rights and duties of States broadly enumerated in the aforesaid instruments, the possibility of different types of control-mechanism systems are currently being debated in various forums of the United Nations. The Intergovernmental Working Group of the United Nations Commission on Transnational Corporations (CTNC) is preparing a code of conduct for TNCs which is expected to cover a wide variety of corporate activity including competition and restrictive business practices. The United Nations Commission on Trade and Development (UNCTAD) has set up two working groups: (i) an Ad Hoc Working Group of Experts on restrictive business practices which has drawn up a list indicating types of behaviour which may affect the trade and development of developing countries; (ii) the UNCTAD Intergovernmental Group on the transfer of technology is engaged in drafting a code which will include an important chapter on restrictive licensing practices. Both the developed and the developing nations have presented drafts of the code. The legal implications of an NIEO are also expected to be studied by a working group of UNCITRAL and specific proposals for introducing changes in the existing rules are now under consideration in other forums like GATT and WIPO.

The Charter of Economic Rights and Duties of States (hereinafter referred to as the Charter) has introduced certain norms or rules which some of the developed nations consider as fundamental departures from the traditional rules of international law. Accordingly they contend that the Charter is a non-binding instrument with no legal force.

It is a basic principle that the intention of the parties is the determining factor in ascertaining whether or not an international agreement creates legal rights and obligations. Broad generalization and imprecise formulation of aims and objects are often considered too indefinite to support the intention of creating legal obligations. But such considerations are not necessarily conclusive. For instance, the legal implications of the UN Charter and many other constitutional instruments, formulated in broad general terms, have never been questioned. Similarly, many international agreements for friendship and co-operation in the field of culture and trade, science and technology, are equally considered as binding. Even though a particular international agreement may be technically considered as non-binding, it does not necessarily follow that legal responsibility was intended to be excluded. Such a proposition, it has been stated, is not an analytical proposition (i.e. it does not simply follow from the definition of a non-binding agreement), but it is a conclusion based on state practice.[4]

The practice of the State Department in the USA indicates two relevant criteria. First, documents 'intended to have political and moral weight, but not intended to be legally binding, are not international agreements.'

Secondly, the agreement must have 'certain precision setting forth the legally binding undertakings.' 'For example, a promise to "help develop a more viable world economic system" lacks the specificity essential to constitute a legally binding international agreement. At the same time, undertakings as general as those of Articles 55 and 56 of the UN Charter have been held to create internationally binding agreements (though not self-executing ones).'[5] With regard to the first criterion it has been commented that the Congress might have adopted a less exacting interpretation with regard to agreements intended to have 'political or more weight', even if legally non-binding, in the light of the significance accorded to such agreements in international relations.[6] The second criterion no doubt represents a standard rule of international law as it does in municipal law. But the illustration given by the State Department appears a little confusing. Strictly construed, the 'specificity' test is satisfied by neither; yet a promise to fulfil the undertakings in Articles 55 and 56 of the UN Charter is considered a binding obligation but a promise 'to help develop a more viable world economic system' is considered nonbinding. It is clear that the purpose of the second promise is to give business efficacy to the legal obligations in Articles 55 and 56 of the Charter and should therefore be considered equally as binding. Again, as stated before, even a technically non-binding instrument can give rise to legal obligations, depending upon the nature and purpose of the instrument, despite the fact that it is couched in general terms.

On the other hand, the developing countries consider the Charter a legally binding instrument imposing rights and obligations on the States. The basic source of this legal obligation is to be found in Article 56 of the UN Charter. As stated in the first preliminary report of the Sub-Committee on the Study of Regional Problems in the Implementation of Human Rights of the ILA:[7]

> It seems clear, however, that any strategy for the implementation of human rights in regions made up of countries in which mass poverty exists must necessarily concern itself with transforming the material conditions and the environments in which the majority of people in such societies find themselves. Whether this process is characterised as 'economic development' or 'the realisation of economic and social rights', it must involve a substantial measure of international cooperation. The obligation of the international community in this regard is recognised in Article 56 of the UN Charter and is reflected in Article 2 of the Economic Covenant. It is in this context that such measures as are contemplated by e.g. GA Resolution 2626 (XXV) setting out

the international development strategy for the second UN Development Decade, the resolutions adopted at the Sixth and Seventh special sessions of the General Assembly relating to the establishment of the new international economic order, the Charter of Economic Rights and Duties of States, the UNCTAD Declarations, and other resolutions adopted on international economic relations acquire relevance in relation to the question of implementation of human rights.

The political and juridical organs of the United Nations have interpreted the provisions of Articles 55 and 56 as a whole to constitute legal obligations.[8] The trend of State practice is also in the same direction.

The Declaration on Principles of International Law Concerning Friendly Relations and Cooperation among States in Accordance with the Charter of United Nations adopted by the General Assembly in an important resolution 2625 (XXV) of 24 October 1970 supports the contention of the developing countries. The 1970 Declaration stipulates that the principles of the UN Charter which are embodied in the Declaration constitute basic principles of international law. One such principle is the duty of States to co-operate by taking joint and separate action in the economic, social and cultural field as well as in the field of science and technology and for the promotion of economic growth throughout the world, specially that of the developing countries. This duty is to be fulfilled in good faith and in co-operation with the United Nations and its agencies.[9] The view has been expressed that the Charter along with the Declaration and Programme of Action are clearly intended to be normative in character and will almost certainly rapidly attain the same status and significance for international law as, for example, the 1970 Declaration. The Charter is regarded by a large majority of the members of the United Nations as a development of legal norms for the development of international relations on a just and equitable basis. As Robin White has observed:[10]

It is the assertion of political power by the developing nations that makes the Declaration, Programme of Action and Charter so important. Quite clearly the documents are not perfect and have met severe criticisms from the highly industrialised nations, but they do present a comprehensive series of norm-creating statements on a new international law of co-operation in the sphere of making rights and duties. It is right that the Third World should assert itself in this area, and the developed nations were not only unable to challenge the philosophical underpinnings of the documents but many actively supported them . . . Nevertheless they will provide primary evidence and guidance for all nations of international legal norms governing international economic relations. It is not an overstatement to say that a new era in the international law of economic co-operation has arrived.

The legal character of the Charter will depend upon the view one takes of the effect of the resolutions of the General Assembly. One view is that such resolutions do not in any way have the force of law.[11] Another view is that although the Charter is not a legally binding document, it can be construed by those States rejecting traditional international law as a new standard of international law or as a device to pressure future international lawmaking.[12]

A third view emphasises the need for a new approach to the theory of obligation in international law. It has been suggested that, as a result of the active participation of the Afro-Asian States in international affairs and the growth of a global consensus, the need for a sociological re-orientation of the basis of international obligations in international law is called for. The purpose of this new approach is to make the emerging concept of consensus rather than the traditional concept of consent as the basis of obligation of the international community. Accordingly a quasi-legislative competence is attributed to the General Assembly resolutions of a constituent pattern. If international society is to function effectively, it requires a limited legislative authority, at a minimum, to translate an overriding consensus among the States into rules of order and norms of obligation despite opposition of one or more sovereign states.[13]

It is possible to argue that the provisions of the Charter have become a part of customary international law inasmuch as they are regarded as binding by a large number of States. In support of this contention reliance can be placed upon the decision of International Court of Justice in *North Sea Continental Shelf* cases: a norm-creating provision in an international agreement, while only conventional or contractual in its origin, may pass into the general *corpus* of international law so as to become binding even for countries that did not become parties to the convention. Indeed it constitutes one of the recognized methods by which new rules of customary international law may be formed.[14]

On the other hand, it may be argued on behalf of the developed States that the Court had observed in the *Continental Shelf* cases that one of the elements usually regarded as necessary for a conventional rule to become a general rule of international law, even without the passage of any considerable period of time, is that a very widespread and representative participation in the convention might suffice of itself, provided it includes the participation of the States whose interests are specially affected. It may further be argued, relying upon the *Fisheries* case,[15] that the reservations and negative votes in relation to the three instruments by some of the developed States make them persistent objectors, like Norway with regard to the ten-mile rule in that case, and accordingly they are not bound by the same.

At this stage it will be useful to examine some of the major areas of agreement and of controversy with regard to current debate on the implementation of the provision of the Charter. The areas of agreement include: first, there should be an NIEO and that the developed countries are willing to help build it.[16] Secondly, there should be a code or codes of conduct covering various aspects of international trade and commerce, such as, the conduct of TNCs, restrictive business practices and transfer of technology.

The areas of controversy broadly are: first, the terms and scope of specific rules to be formulated and incorporated in the code, but even here, it is generally agreed that the relevant code should incorporate provisions for preventing corrupt business practices. For instance, US Senate Resolution 265 of 12 November 1975 provides that the executive should negotiate for an international agreement with sanctions to eliminate the distortions of trade resulting from unfair competition, bribery and other corrupt practices.[17] Secondly, the major controversy relates to the nature and effect of the code — whether the rules to be formulated in the code should be merely voluntary guidelines or whether they should be considered as legally binding obligations subject to the same kind of sanction for non-compliance.

According to some of the developed countries, the codes should establish general equitable principles but should not be legally binding.[18] It was urged by the developed countries before the UNCTAD committee on restrictive trade practices that the code should be voluntary because of divergences in approaches to restrictive business practice among the members of United Nations and their varying stages of development. Again, before the UNCTAD committee on transfer of technology, the developed countries submitted an outline of a code of conduct consisting of guidelines for international transfer of technology.[19] Attention is drawn to the fact that even the guidelines for multinational enterprises framed by the Organization for Economic Co-operation and Development (OECD) have been expressly made 'voluntary and not legally enforceable.'[20] Another reason suggested in support of the voluntary nature of the guidelines is that insofar as the United States is concerned, there are various constitutional, legal and practical difficulties in implementing an international code by introducing corresponding domestic legislation relating to the activites abroad of TNCs of USA.[21]

On the other hand, various arguments have been advanced by the developing countries in support of their contention that the code or codes of conduct should be made legally binding and enforceable. First, it is contended that TNCs have become too powerful and dominating to be effectively controlled by a single host government. The behaviour of TNCs cannot be properly regulated by merely prescribing certain non-binding voluntary guidelines. It has become very difficult for the host government to obtain information about business practices of TNCs with headquarters abroad. Secondly, it is rather strange that some of the developed countries should continue to refuse to accept a code on restrictive business practice as binding when they strongly support the enforcement of anti-trust laws in their own jurisdictions. Thirdly, even though the OECD guidelines are technically described as voluntary there is an element of compulsion in it. All OECD governments have recommended to their respective TNCs the observance of some specific provisions, such as, the obligations to co-operate with the authorities of the countries investigating restrictive business practices. Any failure to co-operate may prejudicially affect the business interests of the TNCs concerned. Finally, it is pointed out that even in the developed countries there already exists the precedent of a legally binding code with a powerful enforcement machinery for non-compliance with the treaty provisions against restrictive business practices e.g. in the forums of the European Economic Community (EEC). Therefore, in principle, there should be no objection to extending the element of compulsion in an international code on a worldwide basis.

If an agreement can be reached as to a particular rule or rules to be incorporated into the code, even though described as non-legal, it will significantly change the voluntary character of the code. In the context of an important 'non-binding' agreement it has been observed by Oscar Schachter: 'Or when governments have agreed, as in the Helsinki Act, on economic co-operation or human rights the understanding and expectation is that national practices will be modified, if necessary, to conform to those understandings. The political commitment implies, and should give rise to, an internal legislative or administration response. There are often specific and determinate acts.'[22] The same analogy ought to apply to an international agreement relating to international economic co-operation.

There are at least two different ways in which the provisions of a code or codes can be made enforceable. First, an institutional device or supra-national authority may be created by the code or codes to regulate the conduct of TNCs, such as, the mechanisms introduced by the Treaty of Rome and Carteagena Agreement of the Andean Pact countries. Many of the developing countries, conscious of their newly acquired sovereignty and of their fragile social, economic and political infrastructures, are not in favour of such an international enforcement body. On the other hand, they would prefer the alternative method by which the conduct of TNCs can be regulated by introducing suitable national legislation in the home country pursuant to and in terms of conduct embodied in the code or codes. It is generally recognized in international law that the State has responsibility for the conduct of its nationals abroad.

Even if the provisions of the code do not become part of the law of the home country, a TNC operating in a particular host country will be bound by the provisions of an international code if the same becomes part of the domestic law of the host country. Again, there always remains the possibility that the developing countries will be able to persuade the General Assembly to adopt the code or codes of conduct by an overwhelming majority. The legal position will then depend upon the view one takes of the legal consequences of an overriding consensus reflected in the resolutions of the General Assembly.

It is necessary to refer to a few of the major controversial questions arising out of the provisions of the Charter. The first serious controversy relates to the principles laid down in Article 2 of the Charter which confers on every State the right to regulate foreign investment, the activities of TNCs within its national jurisdiction and the right to nationalize alien property on payment of adequate compensation. When Article 2 of the Charter is read with para. 4(e) and (f) of the Declaration as well as the General Assembly resolutions 1802 (XVII) of 14 December 1962 and 3171 (XXVIII) of 17 December 1973 relating to permanent sovereignty over natural resources, it is clear that three main principles have been enunciated. First, the theory of adequate compensation with some guidelines has replaced the traditional theory of 'prompt, adequate and effective' compensation. Secondly, in the computation of the quantum of compensation, the notion of unjust enrichment has been recognized. Thirdly, in the event of any dispute as to compensation, the tribunal under the domestic law of the nationalizing state has been recognized as the final authority unless there is mutual agreement to the contrary.

With regard to the reservation by the United States relating to the provisions in the Declaration, US Ambassador Scali commented:[23] 'the present Declaration does not couple the assertion of the right to nationalise with the duty to pay compensation in accordance with international law. For this reason we do not find this formulation acceptable. The governing international law cannot be and is not prejudiced by the passage of this resolution.'

The amendment of Article 2 proposed by USA and thirteen other countries would have (a) allowed appeals on investment disputes to international tribunals after the exhaustion of domestic remedies in the host country; (b) stipulated that the standard for compensation should be just compensation in the light of all relevant circumstances, but the proposal was defeated by a large majority.

Article 2 of the Charter has been described as 'a classic restatement' of the Calvo doctrine of Latin America which has always been and still is a fundamental principle of the jurisprudence of the Hemisphere.[24] Article 2 is therefore not a recent innovation but a global extension of the Calvo doctrine, particularly for the benefit of the entire developing world. The idea of an independent international authority for the resolution of investment disputes was never accepted by Latin America nor is it likely to be accepted by the rest of the developing world. For instance, Latin America rejected ICSID (Convention on the Settlement of Investment Disputes between States and Nationals of Other States proposed as a part of the World Bank system in 1965).

Robin White has observed:[25]

Although the United States regards the Charter as non-legal in character and non-binding, it is difficult to argue that, with a consensus of at least 104 states in favour of the new standard, there remains a requirement of just compensation as a precondition to the legality of any expropriation. The new standard, moreover, seems to remove expropriations from the international arena by making the provisions of national law of the expropriating state the governing legislation. Under such a standard there will be few disputes capable of examination on the international level. Of course it may still be in the interests of the expropriating state to pay compensation in some cases, but the Charter seems clearly to be a victory for those states which have maintained that the requirement of compensation operates as a denial of the right to expropriate when it may be that holdings of foreign capital are too small and economies too weak to sustain the level of payments needed fully to compensate the foreign investor. It remains an open and controversial question whether a discriminatory expropriation could be challenged; the UN documents envisage the exercise of the right in the promotion of the economy of the expropriating state. Given the wide nature of the right, such a challenge is probably rendered illusory because of difficulties of proof of motive except in the most blatant and extreme cases. There appears to be an in-built presumption in favour of the legality of the taking, which it is now even more difficult to rebut.

Even the US Supreme Court, in the *Sabbatino* case, relied upon the notion of consensus in the course of assessing the reality of an international legal obligation. It was held by the Court that traditional rules of international law imposing a duty upon an expropriating government to pay an alien investor 'prompt, adequate and effective compensation' were no longer supported by a consensus of sovereign states and, as a result, the validity of such rules was in sufficient doubt as to make them inapplicable to the dispute.[26]

It cannot be disputed that theoretically it is possible for a nationalizing State to lay down arbitrary standards for compensation of foreign property or to exercise the compensation provisions of Article 2 in an abusive manner. However, besides the fact that there are many practical constraints in abusing such powers, the nationalizing state is legally bound to act in good faith in dealing with the properties of an alien.

The solution to the sensitive problem of investment disputes cannot be found either by an arbitrary exercise of power by the developing States or in the retaliatory policies of the developed countries as reflected in the Hickenlooper and Gonzales Amendments in USA. Any rigid or uncompromising attitude on either side would be harmful to both. The feeling of interdependence will create an atmosphere for mutual accommodation; in such an atmosphere, friendly negotiations and quiet diplomacy can produce results which rigid adherence to the rival theories cannot do. A sense of pragmatism is becoming apparent in recent years as one finds in such instances as the solution of the Marcona dispute in Peru in 1976 and of the dispute arising out of Venzuelan oil nationalization of 1974. Addressing the Permanent Council of the OAS, President Carter observed on 14 April 1977: 'We support your efforts (to encourage private investment) and recognize that a new flexibility and adaptability are required today for foreign investment to be most useful in combining technology, capital management and market experience to meet your development needs. We will do our part in this field to avoid differences and misunderstandings between your government and ours.'[27]

Another area of controversy relates to price indexation and intergovernmental raw material arrangements. It is contemplated that there should be an equitable relationship between the prices of raw materials, primary commodities, manufactured and semi-manufactured goods exported by developing countries and the prices of raw materials, primary commodities, manufactures, capital goods and equipment imported by them. Thus a link should be established between the prices of exports of developing countries and the prices of their imports from developed countries: Declaration, paragraph 4 (j) and Programme Part I, paragraph 1 (d). Despite protests from the developed countries the provision for price indexation was incorporated in Article 28 of the Charter.

The intergovernmental raw material arrangements are to be achieved, *inter alia*, through associations of commodity producers. This right is recognized, *inter alia*, in Article 5 of the Charter read with paragraph 7 of the General Assembly resolution 3171 (XXVIII) of 17 December 1973, paragraph 4 (t) of the Declaration and Part VII, paragraph 1 (a) the Programme. The Programme welcomed the 'increasingly effective mobilisation by the whole group of oil-exporting countries of their natural resources for the benefit of their economic development'.

The opposition of the developed countries can be seen from the following statement of Ambassador Scali of the United States: 'Neither can the United States accept the idea of producer associations as a viable means of promoting development, or of fixing a relationship between import and export prices. Artificial attempts to manage markets which ignore economic realities and the legitimate interests of consumers as well as producers, run the risk of political confrontation on the one hand and economic failure on the other.'[28]

This is reminiscent of the retaliatory policy statement on expropriation of President Nixon on 19 January 1972[29] and the Hickenlooper-Gonzalez-Nixon doctrine. Perhaps a more balanced view was taken by Jan Pronk, when he said:

> The same holds true for the question of whether intergovernmental raw material arrangements should replace, or, rather, provide a framework for the present so-called free world market for commodities. Horror stories are told regarding the effects of interfering in the market, and the concept of an integrated commodity programme is considered a dirty word. But what is the actual situation? Apart from the fact that developed countries dominate most raw material markets and therefore are in a position to obtain the greatest advantages as regards price and processing, these markets show an inherent instability. Intergovernmental arrangements could diminish the degree of instability and at the same time keep the prices of raw materials on a level

that meets the interests of both consumers and producers. These arrangements would be in the long-term interests of the developed countries as well, not the least because the demand for some raw materials, particularly minerals, will be so large during the last two decades of this century that heavy pressure on prices will result. This pressure should be absorbed by stabilising market arrangements.[30]

Jan Pronk made another significant observation:

In the short term, and economically speaking, a new international order could very well be disadvantageous for developed countries. Higher prices of raw materials industrial redeployment will in the short term not be applauded by the public in the rich countries. But we should also tell them the other side of the story. One of the lessons of the recession of the last few years is the increased degree of inter-dependence in the world. It is not only the developing countries that need crucial imports from developed countries, but developed countries increasingly need the developing countries as sources of raw materials, energy and manufactures, and also as export markets, in view of distinct signs of saturation and diminished growth possibilities in the developed world.[31]

While fully appreciating the serious concern of the developed nations who are huge importers of raw materials from developing countries, the view has been expressed that 'it is difficult to see the ground upon which it can be argued that there is no right to associate. The economic repercussions are great but that alone cannot justify denial of the right.'[32]

The duties of the developed States to help the developing nations with a view to bridging the gulf between the rich and the poor are to be found in various provisions of the Charter. For instance, Article 13 refers to the obligation to transfer of technology; Articles 18, 19 and 26 provide for extending the system of generalized non-reciprocal and non-discriminatory tariff preferences to the developing countries and for their more favourable treatment to meet the trade and development needs of the developing countries. International trade should be conducted without prejudice to the aforesaid preferences in favour of developing countries.

Since there can be no equality among unequals, some minimum rules of preferential treatment of the poor by the rich nations is a mandate of the UN Charter read with the 1970 Declaration. Such preferential treatment does not suffer from the vice of unlawful discrimination which results from unequal treatment of equals. On the other hand, in the scheme of the Charter provisions for preferential treatment of the developing by the developed nations, one can find a rational and reasonable classification (viz. between the rich and poor nations) having a clear and proximate nexus with the objective of the Charter (viz. the establishment of a new international economic order based on equity, sovereign equality and interdependence).

These implementations of the Charter provisions are vitally important for the establishment of a new international economic order. These provisions reflect the emerging norms of meaningful international economic co-operation.[33] The developed countries are under a legal obligation under the law of the UN Charter to co-operate with the developing countries in the implementation of those norms in good faith. The mechanism of implementation has to be worked out by introducing specific rules.

NOTES AND REFERENCES

1   Jan Pronk, 'New International Order is in the Interest of the Developed Countries Too': address at the inaugural session of the SID, 15th World Conference, 1976: *International Development Review*, Vol. XVIII (1976), pp. 8–10.

2   Ibid., p. 9.

3   For the texts of the three resolutions see respectively: (1974) *International Legal Materials*, Vol. 13, 715–19; 720–36; (1975) *International Legal Materials*, Vol. 14, 251–61.

4   Oscar Schachter, 'The Twilight Existence of Nonbinding International Agreements' *American Journal of International Law*, Vol. 71 (1977), pp. 296, 300.

5   Ibid., p. 302 for extracts from the Memorandum by the State Department Legal Adviser dated 12 March 1976 on 'Case Act Procedures and Department of State Criteria for Deciding What Constitutes an International Agreement'.

6   Ibid., p. 302.

7   ILA Committee Reports, 1978 Manila Conference, p. 86.

8   Ian Brownlie, *Principles of Public International Law*, 2nd ed., 1973, Oxford, p. 553.

9   For text of the 1970 Declaration, see *International Legal Materials*, Vol. 9 (1970), pp. 1292, 1295–6.

10 Robin C.A. White, 'A New International Economic Order' *International and Comparative Law Quarterly*, Vol 24 (1975), pp. 542, 552; also see p. 543.

11 G. Haight, 'The New International Economic Order and the Charter of Economic Rights and Duties of States', *International Lawyer*, Vol. 9 (1975), pp. 591, 597.

12 C.N. Brower and J.B. Tepe Jr., 'The Charter of Economic Rights and Duties of States; A Reflection or Rejection of International Law?', *International Lawyer*, Vol. 9, pp. 295, 302.

13 Richard A. Falk, 'On the Quasi-Legislative Competence of the General Assembly' *American Journal of International Law*, Vol 60 (1966), pp. 782, 783. Also see H. Meijers and E.W. Vendag, eds., *Essays on International Law and Relations in Honour of A.J.P. Tammes* (1977), Sijthoff, pp. 72–73 for the views of the present writer on the legal effect of the General Assembly resolutions.

14 (1969) ICJ, *Reports*, 3. Also see *American Journal of International Law*, Vol. 63 (1969), p. 591, 620.

15 (1951) ICJ, *Reports*, 116.

16 Statement of US Secretary of State Cyrus Vance quoted in *American Journal of International Law*, Vol. 72 (1978), p. 247, fn. 5.

17 Ibid., p. 249, fn. 10.

18 Ibid., p. 249.

19 Ibid., p. 254–5.

20 *International Legal Materials*, Vol. 15 (1976), pp. 967, 970.

21 J. Davidow and L. Chiles, 'The United States and the Issue of the Binding or Voluntary Nature of International Codes of Conduct Regarding Restrictive Business Practice', *American Journal of International Law* Vol. 72 (1978), pp. 259–61.

22 Schachter, 'The Twilight Existence', pp. 296, 303.

23 *International Legal Materials*, Vol. 12 (1974), pp. 744, 746.

24 W.D. Rogers, 'Of Missionaries, Fanatics and Lawyers: Some Thoughts on Investment Disputes in the Americas', *American Journal of International Law*, Vol. 72 (1978).

25 Robin White, 'A New International Economic Order', p. 547.

26 *American Journal of International Law*, Vol. 60 (1966), p. 782, 785; 376 US 298.

27 Rogers, 'Of Missionaries', p. 14.

28 *International Legal Materials*, Vol. 13 (1974), p. 747.

29 Rogers, 'Of Missionaries', p. 15.

30 Jan Pronk, New International Order, p. 12.

31 Ibid., p.11.

32 Robin White, 'A New International Economic Order', p. 549.

33 The position taken in the paper is that principles embodied in the Charter of Economic Rights and Duties of States have the character of legal norms, albeit some of them may be characterized as 'emerging norms'. Juristic views expressed in recent literature, some of which are cited below, recognize that it is misleading and inaccurate to characterize these principles as 'non-binding' simply on the basis that resolutions of the UN General Assembly are not 'binding'; reference may be made to the following extracts from articles published in the *Virginia Law Quarterly*, Vol. 16 (1976): 'Obviously these formulations of the concept of economic coercion, resting as they do on resolutions of the UN General Assembly, lack the normative quality of a treaty provision. They are, however, indicative of the gradual acceptance of a concept whose influence cannot be ignored.' (Derek W. Bowett, 'International Law and Economic Coercion', p. 245.

'In the first place, what is the legal effect of the steady stream of near unanimous resolutions? Here conventional wisdom has it that such resolutions "cannot have legal pretensions . . . General Assembly resolutions do not in any way have the force of law . . ." (Haight) This attitude seems unnecessarily dogmatic. While technically such resolutions are not regarded as binding obligations under international law, their authoritativeness, in that they reflect the expectations of the international community, cannot be dismissed out of hand, a point well made by Bowett (supra) and acknowledged, albeit with some reluctance by Professor White.' (Richard B. Lillich, 'Economic Coercion and the New International Economic Order: A Second Look at some First Impressions', p. 232 at p. 257.)

'The removal of the word "obligations" together with other amendments to these passages, clarifies the intention of the States proposing the resolution that one should not subjectively regard it as having the force of a treaty codifying and declaring legal values. Instead the Charter represents only a collection of *policy prescriptions* supported by the overwhelming majority of UN members. How else can one explain the retention of the word "willing" in the preamble? If an instrument creates or re-states legal norms, a state's willingness to fulfil the provisions is legally irrelevant. This term indicates the exhortatory nature of the document.' (Gillian White, 'A New International Economic Order?', p. 323 at p. 330.)

'It was always the understanding of the Developing World that the Charter not only should include those rules and principles already generally recognized by customary international law, but also should have as its primary objective the development of new rules responsive to the present and future needs of the international community. To have been satisfied with the mere codification of existing customary international law, without the creation and development of new principles, would have been tantamount to accomplishing nothing. *A new international economic order required a new international legal order as a foundation* (italics added).

'. . . In view of the strong opposition manifested by the developed countries, however, and the dubious value of a treaty to which only one group is willing to become a party, the developing nations acceded to the proposal that the Charter should be a declaration. Their hope was that a solemn proclamation by the General Assembly, although not legally binding, would incorporate legal norms which would gradually acquire a certain force in the regulation of economic interaction. The Charter would differ from the Programme of Action and Declaration adopted by the Sixth special session of the General Assembly, in that it could not limit itself to expressing aspirations and recommendations; it would alter rules of the future by embodying rights and duties binding them in relation to the developed countries.' (Andres Rozental, 'The Charter of Economic Rights and Duties of States and the New International Economic Order', p. 309 at pp. 314, 316.)

4 The Legal Character of General Assembly Resolutions: Some Considerations of Principle

*Maurice Mendelson**

As Dr Bollecker-Stern has pointed out, the New International Economic Order bases itself in part on traditional sources of international law. However, a very large part of the effort to establish such an order has been channelled into the passing of United Nations General Assembly resolutions on this subject. The precise legal effect to be given to a particular resolution will depend, among other things, on its terms, accompanying statements, the number and (quite possibly) the importance in the relevant field of the dissenters and abstainers, and so on. Space obviously does not permit such a detailed investigation here; but in a session devoted to 'principles' it may not be inappropriate to examine in general terms the extent to which General Assembly resolutions may be said to have binding effect.

It is proposed to consider, first, the grounds upon which such resolutions might be said to be without binding effect, and then to look at some possible answers to these objections.

I   THE NEGATIVE VIEWS

Presumption of non-binding effect of General Assembly resolutions

We must start with the presumption that General Assembly resolutions have no binding effect. At the San Francisco Conference which drew up the UN Charter, Committee 2 of Commission II rejected by twenty-six

(*Note*. This paper attempts to embody the substance of two largely impromptu contributions made at the seminar. Nothing has been added to the substance of what was said, and consequently this paper is not to be regarded as a research paper, or as the definitive views of the author on the subject.)

*St John's College, Oxford.

votes to one a proposal by the delegation of the Philippines that the General Assembly should be vested with the legislative authority to enact rules of international law which would become effective and binding upon Members of the Organization after those rules had been approved by a majority vote of the Security Council.[1] The history of international conferences also bears out the proposition that resolutions of such conferences are generally devoid of binding effect on the States to whom they are addressed.

This presumption against binding effect is, however, a rebuttable presumption, and there are clearly cases where resolutions of the General Assembly can be binding. For example, what have been called 'house-keeping resolutions' are clearly binding — decisions to admit members, to apportion the budget and so on (at any rate, if the organ concerned is not acting beyond the scope of its legal powers). Secondly, an 'authentic interpretation' of the Charter is binding — that is to say, a decision taken to interpret the UN Charter for the purposes of an organ of the UN is binding so long as that decision is within the competence of the organ concerned. Thirdly, the General Assembly can be given the power to dispose of territory and there have been cases where, on one view, that is exactly what has been done. This sort of decision can have a dispositive effect. Somewhat analogous are those cases, like the termination of the Mandate over Namibia, where the effect of the decision is to create a legal status which is binding on all States and not just on those who vote in favour of the resolution.[2] On the borderline between law and politics it is also fair to point out, as others have done, that the General Assembly has a certain legitimizing role. That is to say even if, for example, the admission of a State to the United Nations does not constitute collective recognition proper, in the sense of being opposable against States who vote against admission on the grounds of lack of statehood and so on, in political terms, and in the long run, such a resolution may very well have the effect of consecrating the separate legal personality of the entity concerned.

Beyond this point, we get into rather softer ground. It has, for example, been suggested that General Assembly resolutions, particularly unanimously adopted ones, can create something like an estoppel binding all those who have voted in favour. Part of the difficulty here lies in the fact that there is no general agreement as to the precise rules relating to estoppel in international law. But if, put broadly, an estoppel can be regarded as a rule preventing States from denying assertions which they have made and which are relied on by other States (to their detriment?), the question immediately arises whether one can have an estoppel when the representation is about intentions or about the state of the law, as opposed to a fact or facts. It also raises the question whether there has been a reliance on the representation if the only reliance that can be said to have been made is the reliance by other States on the binding effect of the resolution; such an argument would beg the question.

Even unanimous resolutions are open to this objection. Furthermore, given the important political differences which exist between States, it is an observable fact that unanimity is rarely attained, and that, when it is, it is frequently at the expense of anything which a lawyer can do anything with. One of the most commonly cited illustrations of this is the provision in the Resolution on Permanent Sovereignty over Natural Resources[3] for the payment upon nationalization of 'appropriate' compensation. 'Appropriate' connotes widely differing methods of calculation of compensation for different states. To rely on such resolutions on the grounds that they represent the international 'consensus' does not take the argument any further. Furthermore, when the General Assembly decides a matter by the voting technique (or perhaps, more accurately, non-voting technique) known as 'consensus', this is usually a very good indication of the fact that there is a very strong disagreement and that cracks are being papered over.

General Assembly Resolutions and Traditional Sources of International Law

Because General Assembly resolutions are not in general binding as such, efforts have been made to assimilate them to recognized sources of international law. The attempt has often been made to find a home for these resolutions among the sources of international law listed in Article 38 (1) of the Statute of the International Court of Justice, namely, treaties, custom, general principles of law recognized by civilized nations and, as subsidiary means for the determination of the rules, judicial decisions and the teachings of highly-qualified publicists. If that list is taken (as it is by many commentators) as representing an authoritative and exclusive list of present-day sources of international law, it is understandable why supporters of the binding force of General Assembly resolutions should attempt to subsume those resolutions under one of other headings in that list. The incentive is all the stronger if, like Dr. Thirlway,[4] one takes the view that the list is a closed one, in the sense that, within the present framework of international law and international relations, the only way in which a new source can be added to the list is through the existing sources. This would mean, for example, that General Assembly resolutions could become binding as such if, for example, a customary rule grew up, or a treaty were concluded, to that effect. But if we go through the exercise of trying to subsume General Assembly resolutions under one of these headings (as traditionally interpreted) the result is likely to be negative.

(i) Treaties

These are essentially expressions of will on the part of states, and no special form is needed for the conclusion of a treaty in international law. So at first sight it looks as if one might be able to regard a General Assembly resolution as a treaty concluded by simultaneous or consecutive voting. The following objections may, however, be raised.

(a) International agreements are only binding if they are intended to be binding. Given the general presumption against the obligatory force of General Assembly resolutions, one would require positive evidence of an intention to create legally binding relations before a General Assembly vote could be assimilated to a treaty. But on the contrary, it is an observable fact that states frequently are prepared to vote for General Assembly resolutions only because they expect that no legal obligation will result from casting a positive vote.[5]

(b) Another difficulty is that even to negotiate the text of a treaty a representative normally requires to possess and exhibit full powers to perform that act; as I understand it, delegates to the General Assembly are not usually equipped with such powers. Still less are they empowered to make their States parties to such agreements — a step which often entails the observance of elaborate constitutional procedures.

(c) Furthermore, as is well known, treaties in general bind only the states who are parties to them; consequently, if General Assembly resolutions are to be assimilated to treaties, they can at the very best bind only those who vote in favour of them.[6]

(ii) General Principles of Law Recognized by Civilized Nations

Most commentators understand this item on the International Court's list as meaning general principles of national law which are capable of transplantation to the international sphere. Examples are the notion of the trust, the rule that a victim of a fundamental breach of contract can regard himself as released from the obligations under that contract, principles of procedural fairness, and so on. There seems to be little here which would provide a suitable niche for General Assembly resolutions.

(iii) Judicial Decisions and the Teachings of Publicists

These are listed in the Statute of the Court as subsidiary means for the determination of law. That General Assembly resolutions are capable of constituting evidence of what international law stipulates is not a particularly controversial proposition; but it is not one which supports the conclusion that such resolutions have binding force in and of themselves.

(iv) Custom

I have saved one of the most important sources of international law till last, because it is the one under which the most important — and the most controversial — attempts to subsume General Assembly resolutions have been made. Observance of a consistent pattern of conduct can, in certain circumstances, result in the emergence of a rule of law permitting or obliging (as the case may be) States to act in a way consistent with that practice. Such a rule is called a rule of customary law. There are some difficult theoretical problems about the elements and operation of customary law which, to this day, have not been entirely resolved; but for present purposes it will probably be sufficient to define custom as a consistent practice on the part of States, accompanied by a belief (*opinio juris*) that they are obliged to act in a way consistent with that practice. Clearly the passing of a General Assembly resolution, like many other events, can provide the impetus for a customary practice (accompanied by the requisite *opinio juris*) to grow up; that is not, however, the same as saying that the resolution has the force of law *proprio vigore*.[7] Similarly, to say that General Assembly resolutions are evidence of the rules of customary international law is not the same as saying that they themselves constitute the law. A few writers go beyond these limits and suggest that General Assembly resolutions make customary law. They seek to overcome the obvious difficulties in such a proposition by attempting either to minimize the importance of the psychological element (*opinio juris*) or of the material element (practice).

(a) *'Instant Customary Law'.* Some writers assert that customary law requires only one single constitutive element, and that is *opinio juris*; usage is a normal element, but merely provides evidence of the existence and content of the underlying rule and of the requisite *opinio juris*.[8]

A new *opinio juris* could be created instantly, and provided that the intention is expressed articulately and without ambiguity, a General Assembly resolution may in principle be used as a means for identifying the existence and contents of a new *opinio juris*. Though such a resolution would itself still be without binding force it could provide strong evidence of the existence and content of the rule in question, and those who vote for it may even be estopped from denying what it asserts.

It may be thought that the qualifications which have already had to be introduced will in practice deprive General Assembly resolutions of any significant role as sources of customary law. But there are further objections. In the first place, *opinio juris* is a rather unstable foundation upon which to build. For example, as many commentators have pointed out, to require a belief in the obligatory character of the practice makes it somewhat difficult to explain how a new customary rule of international law can come into existence, since the initiator of a new practice cannot realistically be described as having any belief in its obligatory character — on the contrary, such a new practice may well be inconsistent with existing rules of international law.[9] Furthermore, a basic premise of this school of thought is open to doubt because it justifies such heavy reliance on *opinio juris* on the basis of a voluntarist theory of international law — a theory that States are bound if they want to be bound, if they express their wish to be bound. Such a theory is open to serious objections; for example, it cannot satisfactorily explain how it is that new States are bound by customary law. Moreover, there is a certain amount of judicial authority for the proposition that mere paper claims by States, not backed up by acts putting those claims into practice, is an insufficient basis for the establishment of rules of customary international law.[10] Such an objection would apply with even greater force to a declaration which did not even purport to be a claim. On a more general level, the distinguishing feature of customary international law is surely usage; to speak of a custom without a usage is a contradiction in terms.

(*b*) The other approach is to regard the act of voting for a General Assembly resolution as a form of usage (thus satisfying the requirement of a material element), while denying the need for *opinio juris*. The difficulty about this theory is that, however unsatisfactory the notion of *opinio juris* may be in some respects, it is a notion that we cannot do entirely without. For instance, there are many practices which States habitually observe as a matter of international courtesy or comity, and without their regarding themselves or others as legally bound to continue to observe those usages. To jettison *opinio juris* entirely would deprive us of an important means of distinguishing law from non-law. So drastic a step would probably be unjustified in principle: if every act a State performed created a legal obligation it would act at its peril, which would be somewhat inconsistent with the notion of State sovereignty and would inhibit States from making concessions to other States through fear of creating binding legal obligations for the future. Above all, an approach which dispensed entirely with the need for *opinio juris* would be inconsistent with what can be observed of the way States behave; for example, if States who voted in favour of the General Assembly resolution 1962 (XVIII) on 'Legal Principles Governing the Activities of States in the Exploration of Outer Space' regarded this as binding, why have they felt the need to proceed to the conclusion of a treaty on the subject?

To sum up, it does not seem possible to equate General Assembly resolutions with customary law; and the attempt to accommodate them by re-defining the concept of customary law by suppressing either the psychological or the material element creates more difficulties than it solves.

Other Approaches

Faced with these obstacles in the way of subsuming General Assembly resolutions under the accepted headings of sources of international law, some commentators are content to allot a less ambitious role to General Assembly resolutions. For example, in the *Voting Procedure* case, Judges Lauterpacht and Klaestad seemed to suggest (albeit in very guarded language), that there might be some sort of legal obligation at any rate to consider in good faith repeated resolutions of the General Assembly;[11] but the obligation here is an obligation to *consider* the resolution rather than an obligation simply to observe it. The attempt has also been made to describe General Assembly resolutions as 'quasi-legislation'.[12] A distinguished English jurist, Sir Carleton Allen, once said that the word 'quasi' is often a signal of a certain evasiveness, an attempt to avoid a difficulty; and if we are going to talk about 'quasi legislation', we ought at any rate to be aware that we are not talking about legislation. But if all that this thesis means is that General Assembly resolutions can create political expectations which can in certain circumstances be turned into legal obligations, there does not seem to be any particular objection to that assertion. It is just that this seems to be little different from the unexceptionable claim that resolutions may provide the impetus for the creation of new rules of international law by means of custom or treaty.

II A MORE POSITIVE APPROACH

After this necessarily somewhat cursory recital of well-known, and largely negative, arguments, it is now time to consider a number of other possible bases upon which a greater legal significance might possibly be attached to General Assembly resolutions.[13]

(i) Subsumption under Article 38(1) of the Statute of the International Court

(a) Custom

Although, as previously indicated, there are serious difficulties in the way of regarding General Assembly resolutions as capable of creating rules of customary law, it is important to recall that the formation of law by custom is a *dynamic*, not a static process. A house can be gradually altered by the addition of new features (extensions, windows, balconies, etc.). A house also needs to be constantly kept in repair by the addition of new materials; otherwise it gradually disintegrates. Similarly, customary rules are constantly in a state of mutation: if not maintained and observed they gradually disappear; and by the gradual accretion of usage their character can be fundamentally altered. To put this metaphor in another way, although state practice and *opinio juris* may constitute the basic bricks and mortar of the edifice of a customary rule, such a rule can both be reinforced and undermined by other substances, such as General Assembly resolutions. If customary law is seen as a dynamic process, these resolutions can play an important part in it.

(b) General Principles of International Law

As previously indicated, the majority of commentators regard Article 38 (1) (c) of the Statute of the Court as referring to the general principles of national law. It is, however, well known that at any rate some of those who drafted the Statute in its original form intended by this phrase the general principles of *international* law. Now, some of these general principles of international law are axiomatic rules. That is to say, without them there would be no international law; the principle of the sovereign quality of states is a good illustration of this. Others are not, perhaps, axiomatic, but they happen to be the principles obtaining at a particular time. For example, the freedom of the high seas is not an axiomatic rule;

it was challenged at one stage before it became established. There is a very interesting though complex interaction between legal principles and legal rules and it has, for example, been suggested that in certain circumstances legal principles can over-ride legal rules.[14] I would very tentatively like to suggest that in certain very limited circumstances a General Assembly resolution may constitute, or bring about the birth of, a principle of international law. For example, it might perhaps be argued that the General Assembly resolutions on the freedom of outer space established a principle of international law rather analogous to the principle of the freedom of the high seas. The fact that it was thought necessary subsequently to conclude a treaty on this subject would not detract from this argument. In the first place, treaties have the advantage of laying down more specific and precise norms than principles can do; secondly, since principles do not have pre-ordained weight, it is certainly desirable to establish clearly binding legal rules on the subject. But notwithstanding the somewhat elusive and nebulous character of principles, they undoubtedly do play an important part in all legal systems, and the potential of General Assembly resolutions, in appropriate circumstances, for creating or helping to create such principles, is a subject which could well repay further investigation.[15]

(c) Equitable Principles

While the power of an international tribunal to decide a case purely on the basis of what it thinks would be fair and reasonable in all the circumstances is — as Article 38 (2) of the Statute of the Court attests — a power quite distinct from the power to dispense the law, it is a fact that the International Court of Justice and other international tribunals have made fairly frequent use of general equitable principles,[16] though it would be misleading to say that they have *carte blanche* to do so. To some extent, these principles may be drawn from those to be found in municipal law or from certain fundamental principles of international law, such as the principle of good faith. However, it may be that in certain circumstances General Assembly resolutions, particularly repeated ones, could give rise to notions of what is just and equitable which were widely shared but could not necessarily be neatly subsumed either under the rubric 'general equitable principles of national law' or 'general principles of international law'. The statements of Judges Lauterpacht and Klaestad could conceivably be regarded as harbingers of such an approach.[17]

(ii) Non-exclusiveness of Article 38(1) of the Statute

Although most of the commentators regard the sources listed in Article 38 (1) of the Statute as exhaustive, this is not necessarily the case.

(a) Unilateral Declarations

Although, with great respect, one would not necessarily agree with the decision, the judgment of the majority of the International Court of Justice in the *Nuclear Tests* cases[18] certainly strengthened the arguments of those who contend that unilateral declarations of States can, in some circumstances, have the force of law. If this be so, then successive or simultaneous unilateral declarations by States voting for a General Assembly resolution could, in principle, have a like effect. To those who would object that it is necessary for the unilateral declaration concerned to be at the very least intended to create legal relations, it might perhaps be riposted that there was little evidence of such an intention on the part of the French Government in the *Nuclear Tests* cases. The subject is difficult and rather undeveloped, but the possibility of treating General Assembly resolutions — or at any rate some of them — in this way might merit further investigation.

(b) Article 38(1) Not a Closed List

Even fairly conservative commentators like Thirlway[19] admit that new sources of international law could be created through existing sources; for example, a custom could grow up that unanimous General Assembly resolutions were binding, and that rule of law would itself be binding. It may be possible to go even further than that and suggest that the list is not closed and that if some of the assumptions of the international community were to change, new ways of law-making could emerge. Looking at it pragmatically, if the international community developed new assumptions about the ways in which binding obligations could come about, there would seem to be no reason why a particular process should not be elevated to the status of a source of law. Such an approach may also be justified on a more theoretical level. So far, no-one has successfully identified a unifying basic norm which explains what treaties, custom and the other sources of international law have in common. This failure helps to explain why the list is regarded as a closed one. I would very tentatively suggest that there may be a unifying basic norm to the effect that States have to fulfil the legitimate expectations of other States.

Now, that raises all sorts of questions about what constitutes a 'legitimate expectation', and a good deal of further exploration and refinement is needed. But if there is a basic rule of international law that States have to fulfil the legitimate expectations of other States created by custom or treaty or in various other ways, then there seems to be no reason in principle why certain types of General Assembly resolutions should not, in appropriate circumstances, give rise to legitimate expectations. I am not necessarily arguing that such a development has already occurred; it is sufficient for the purposes of the present discussion to indicate the possibility of its occurrence.

(iii) A different orientation

Finally, I would like to suggest that to approach the problem of the sources of international law primarily from the point of view of what the International Court of Justice will do, and what sources it will apply, is somewhat misconceived. Most of us international lawyers are trained as municipal lawyers, and municipal lawyers tend very much to think in terms of what a court will do. Now, as we know, it is a fact — perhaps a very unfortunate fact, but a fact all the same — that the role of the ICJ (and courts generally) in the international community is sporadic and peripheral in the extreme. That being so, it would seem to follow that what a court will do is of much more limited significance than is the case in a municipal context. It may still be of some importance because lawyers, when they talk to each other, have a kind of *lingua franca*, a sort of set of stable expectations which *to some extent* are based on predictions of what courts will do. But I think that the situation is rather more fluid and would like to indicate some of the ways in which it is more fluid.

(a) First of all, legal advisers of foreign offices are very busy men who very often do not have the time to conduct a detailed investigation into what is the State practice etc. in the relevant field. So what they tend to do is resort to unratified treaties, for example the Vienna Convention on the Law of Treaties. There are some indications that in these circumstances legal advisers will also resort to General Assembly resolutions, even though technically they may not be binding.

(b) Secondly, the categories of discourse in international relations are rather blurred. Although we can, I would strongly assert, distinguish between rules of law, morality, comity, political obligation, etiquette and so on in some respects, undoubtedly they blur into each other at the edges; and in these cases governments tend sometimes to invoke General Assembly resolutions even if they do not think that they are strictly binding on them. For example, although a good deal of the legal debate on the status of Gibraltar turns on the interpretation of the Treaty of Utrecht, General Assembly resolutions on self-determination and decolonization have been referred to by both the United Kingdom and Spain, even when neither party considers itself bound by such resolutions.

(c) Thirdly, legal advisers of foreign offices have to be diplomats as well as lawyers, and they have to have some sense of what other legal advisers, who are also partly diplomats, are going to regard as acceptable. Just as a municipal lawyer needs a nose for what a court will find acceptable in a debatable case (because the law is often somewhat unclear), so legal advisers of foreign offices need a sense of what is acceptable to other States. Here, General Assembly resolutions can be a very good guide, because they articulate what is acceptable to other States. This is particularly the case where the resolution is unanimous or where it is one to which both parties to the dispute have subscribed. Of course, all the relevant circumstances have to be taken into account, and this may reduce the utility of such resolutions in particular circumstances; nevertheless, I would suggest that they do in this way play a significant role in the international legal process.

(d) Finally, it must be borne in mind that one of the most important ways in which the rules of international law are made effective is by being transmuted into municipal legal or bureaucratic rules. Now, if a General Assembly resolution is fortunate enough to find its way into national legal or bureaucratic systems (which has on occasion occurred), its effectiveness in the real world may be even greater than that of a legal rule properly so called which has not been so transsubstantiated. This is not to say that all legal rules undergo this transformation, still less that everything that undergoes this transformation is a legal rule. But since we lawyers are apt to forget that when we pass laws people do not necessarily twitch, it is important to recall that it is results in the real world that count. If General Assembly resolutions, such as those on the New International Economic Order, are fortunate enough to become incorporated into an ever-widening circle of national legal or bureaucratic systems, that consequence may be equally or more important in the real world than the elevation of the resolutions to the status of international law properly so called.

Whether that consummation will come about is beyond the scope of this paper, and the powers of its author, to predict.

NOTES AND REFERENCES

1   *UNCIO* Documents (1945), 70.
2   See International Court of Justice, Advisory Opinion on *Legal Consequences for States of the Continued Presence of South Africa in Namibia (South West Africa) Notwithstanding Security Council Resolution 276 (1970)*, ICJ Rep. 1971, p. 16.
3   UN General Assembly resolution 1803 (XVII).
4   H.W.A. Thirlway, *Customary Law and Codification*, Sijthoff, Leyden, 1972.
5   The fact that States sometimes attach reservations to their votes in favour of a resolution is (*pace* those who have made the suggestion) an insufficient reason for inferring that the States concerned consider that they would, without such reservations, be legally bound by the terms of the resolution. Lawyers often act *ex abundanti cautelae* and diplomats try (or should try) to avoid misunderstandings.
6   The provisions of treaties may reflect or give rise to practices which are or become binding on non-parties: however this is as *customary* law, which is dealt with below.
7   See O.Y. Asamoah, *The Legal Significance of the Declarations of the General Assembly of the United Nations*, Nijhoff, The Hague, 1966.
8   See esp. Bin Cheng, *Indian Journal of International Law*, Vol. 5 (1965), p. 23.
9   The present author hopes to make a contribution to this subject in the near future.
10 See, for example, Judge Read in the *Anglo-Norwegian Fisheries* case, ICJ Reports, 1951, p. 116, at 191.
11 Advisory Opinion on *Voting Procedure on Questions relating to Reports and Petitions concerning the Territory of South-West Africa*, ICJ Reports, 1955, p. 67 at 88, 118–20.
12 See, for example, R.A. Falk, *American Journal of International Law*, Vol. 60 (1966), p. 782.
13 It should, of course, be borne in mind that these approaches do not necessarily entail the conclusion that General Assembly resolutions (either generally or in particular) are *ipso facto* 'binding' as a matter of present-day law.
14 See, for example, Dworkin, *Taking Rights Seriously*, Duckworth, London (1977).
15 That such a resolution could create a rule of *ius cogens* — 'a peremptory norm from which no derogation is permitted' (cf. Vienna Convention on the Law of Treaties, 1969, Art. 53) seems unlikely, if only because such norms are few and far between at the present stage of development of international law.
16 See, for example, *North Sea Continental Shelf* cases, ICJ Reports, 1969, p. 3.
17 See above, p. 57.
18 ICJ *Reports* 1974, pp. 253 and 457.
19 Thirlway, *Customary Law and Codification*.

5 Justice and the New International Economic Order

*Salman Khurshid**

Much as a municipal lawyer may complain about the vagueness of international law it cannot be denied that it is a system. It is *sui generis* but it certainly does not lack method. The method might often be devious but it is seldom dubious. This paper recognizes the fact that there is method in international law and at the same time completely rejects the conventional view of this method. The rejection might at times appear so complete that it might give rise to the common suspicion that the real attempt is to smuggle 'ought' into a discussion about 'is'. Consequently, it needs to be stated categorically that the accepted foundations of international law are not being challenged. But the interpretation that has been used now for a long time is certainly under challenge.

The question ultimately is of obligation. Dr Mendelson's paper[1] very lucidly reminds us of the acts of the international community that create obligations and those that do not. Consent seems to be the accepted basis of such obligations. Of course, there is consent and consent.[2] But broadly speaking we all understand what we mean by consent. There is hardly any pleasure or profit in arguing about the different methods in which true consent can be obtained and to what extent implied consent falls within the concept of consent. There is, however, need to look at a related but distinct question — when does ostensible consent fail to reflect the true mental state of the putative consentor? Municipal legal systems recognize doctrines such as *unconscionability*. This is quite different from the doctrines of duress. In the latter there is the use of the vocabulary of consent without the psychological ingredients that are essential. Normally these are easy situations to identify. Duress, however, is not a

*Trinity College, Oxford.

static concept, for the human situation throws up new situations and novel engines of coercion. The cases get progressively harder. But even if we take care of them there remains the other problem that has been labelled *unconscionability* for the present. There is no conceptual or logical escape for the putative consentor in such a case. There is undoubtedly consent on his part. But intuitively it is not a very satisfactory situation. If one has to deny the existence of obligation in such a case one needs to go to the roots of consent itself to isolate the important factor that links consent with obligation.

There is no denying that the present endeavour at pointing directions for the New International Economic Order challenges a great deal that the positivists cherish and revere as the indispensible requirement for an intelligent conversation regarding law of any kind, international or municipal. However for more reasons than one, the challenge shall be from within their framework rather than without. The basic tenet of positivist lawyers is the existence of 'fact'. 'Fact' itself should be made the source of challenge. But it will have to be a different 'fact'. International lawyers have to become instrumental in changing the 'fact' of international law since the 'fact' of the past years has been found to be manifestly biased in favour of certain national units at the expense of others. For lawyers such an attempt has to be based in principle rather than politics. We have to search for a principle or sets of principles that will accommodate the requirement of consent because our endeavour is to work from within the existing framework. To an extent it might be said that we are really working towards international law reform rather than a revolution. But at the same time we cannot be content with cosmetic surgery since the nature of international economics is becoming much more complex every day.

To return then to the concept of consent. It has relevance in moral terms because of the legitimate moral expectations it creates. For the present purpose there is no need to consider various forms of consent, i.e., representation, acquiescence, or — the strongest of them all — promise, with reliance on the promise by the promisee, etc. It is pertinent to cite here from the living leader of the positivist camp in England, H.L.A. Hart: 'if there are any *moral* rights at all, it follows that there is at least one natural right, the equal right of all men to be free'.[3] There can be fine adaptations and variations of this basic proposition but even its present form adequately supports the thesis being propounded here. Only when one starts from the basic equal liberty position can one meaningfully create certain binding obligations by voluntarily giving up a portion of this liberty. There might at that stage appear a surface inequality but in fact the initial equality subsists. Without this equality there is no true consent and therefore no binding norm no matter how long established a particular practice might be. Of course there would be expectations if there is a standing practice. But these would surely be illegitimate. There cannot be an argument that the continuation of a wrong for some duration somehow makes it right. That is not what we really mean by consent.

What then are to be the principles of justice that will adequately provide for a normative international legal order? We cannot, consistent with the argument made till this stage, choose any principles that might appear atttractive to any particular section of the international community no matter how exploited and deprived it might claim to be in the present international economic order. There is a very strong requirement of rationality in the choice of binding principles. At this stage it would be inadvisable to venture any definitive versions but after suggesting the methodology one might just briefly consider one or two examples that are likely to be thrown up.

This is no place for a further digression on the matter of rational choice theories. Suffice it to say that there are many models familiar to lawyers and philosophers alike. One can see no reason why international lawyers should not make use of them in their arguments instead of relying upon desperately out of date, fossilized notions associated with international law. A model that has a strong claim is the one suggested by John Rawls in his book *A Theory of Justice*.[4] The problem with a principle that emerges from such a model is that in practice, if not in theory, there is tension between equality and liberty.[5] Even in our times the controversy that looms large in any political discussion is the one between human rights' enthusiasts and radical egalitarians. But on the international plane that is neither here nor there. There is no practical necessity in international law for a trade-off between equality and liberty. We can safely move towards a principle of total equality.

Undoubtedly 'equality' is a difficult term to come to grips with but more often than not objections to an interpretation of it are made for ideological and tactical reasons rather than due to a genuine disagreement about its content and substance. In any case, the most important contribution of John Rawls is not that his model takes us to an egalitarian principle but that it is intrinsically an egalitarian model. When people in *absolutely* equal positions come to negotiate a system of governance (which includes a method for distributing the available resources) they invariably arrive at the principles of fairness suggested by Rawls. The second principle, though subject to the priority of the first principle (which is not quite relevant to the international institutions) is very significant — 'Inequalities to be permissible only if to the maximum benefit of the least advantaged person.'

Intuitively that is an attractive proposition. Intuition can be used at this stage to confirm the moral validity of the principles we arrive at using the suggested methodology. On its own, intuition would be terribly inadequate. In a similar manner one may proceed to give further substance to the system of fair international norms. One might usefully call this system International Equity. We have now come a full circle to the existing frame-work of international law. The concept of equity is not unknown to the international lawyer, no matter how sceptical he might be about its practical potential. It found a prominent place in the *Anglo-Norwegian Fisheries* case, though its formulation there might leave a lot to be desired. Again, the Declaration on the Establishment of a New International Economic Order makes several references to 'equity'. It appears together with sovereign equality, independence, common interest and co-operation among all States etc., but there is no elaboration of this broad concept. In a way that is sensible and useful. Unless we can associate equity with a moral sanction and validity in the manner suggested in this paper, it will remain a weak negotiating technique instead of becoming the core of the international system.

Similar in potential is the concept of the 'common heritage of mankind' in the context of the emerging law of the sea. But even that is merely a starting point for negotiations. The real thrust must come from a pervasive model. It need hardly be said that attractive as this model might appear to the Group of 77 when dealing with the developed world (North), in dealings amongst themselves the countries of the South might find it to be a different matter altogether. The principle of total equality would place a tremendous responsibility on the Group of 77 or at least those in the group who have the advantage of a good coastline. They cannot expect to have their cake and eat it too. One cannot consistently expect a fair share of the seabed profits without submitting to the moral claim of land-locked States to the benefits of the Exclusive Economic Zone. On the same tack there is an argument for Affirmative Action or Reverse Discrimination between the North and the South. But so is there between one country of the South and another.

Some eminent jurists are sceptical about applying institutions and principles of municipal law to the international sphere. If the objection is theoretical it is certainly quite misplaced. When one is talking about developing a new morality as opposed to enforcing it, there is no *a priori* obstacle to defining its content. If a country like the United States, in the application of its constitutional law, can accept the idea of reverse discrimination as being a delayed *quid pro quo* for what has unfairly been denied in the past, it cannot honestly and logically deny the relevance of the concept 'redressing past injustices' in international law. Universality is after all an inherent characteristic of moral propositions. In talking about a new order for the world community, a macro-cosmic projection of the national model, Reverse Discrimination is very much in point. Moral pressure has to be put on countries that claim to be in a morally superior position. At the same time it must not be forgotten that they are not being asked to do acts of charity. They are not being asked to concede a bonus to the claimant nations and that is where the relevance of the earlier discussion on the binding nature of international norms becomes very great. They are binding because they are fair and only when they are fair. Consent is merely prima facie evidence that they are fair or at least considered fair by the parties concerned.

The type of pressure that is permissible can also be discovered with the help of the principles we choose. Certainly a form of international civil disobedience or non-cooperation would be well within the bounds set by our model.[7]

NOTES AND REFERENCES

1   See pages 51 to 62.
2   See H. Pitkin, 'Obligation and Consent I and II' in *American Political Science Review*, Vol. LIX (1965) and Vol. LX, No. 1 (1966).
3   'Are There Any Natural Rights?' in A. Quinton, ed., *Political Philosophy*, Oxford University Press, Oxford, 1967.
4   J. Rawls, *A Theory of Justice*, Oxford University Press, Oxford, 1972, esp. Chaps. 2 and 3.
5   But see R. Dworkin, *Taking Rights Seriously*, Duckworth, London, Chap. 6 and 'Liberalism' in Stuart Hampshire, *Public and Private Morality*, Cambridge, 1979.
6   See R.M. Hare, *Freedom and Reason*, Oxford, 1963, esp. Chaps. 1–4, 7.
7   J. Rawls, *A Theory of Justice*, Chap. 6; P. Singu, *Democracy and Disobedience*, Oxford, 1974.

6 Equity and the New International Economic Order: A Note

Tawfique Nawaz *

In spite of its acceptance as a source of law, a wide variety of meanings has been ascribed to equity. The jurisprudence of the international courts has rejected the view that it is to be understood in either (1) the Anglo-American sense or (2) that it is a separate entity from the law. The Anglo-American concept of equity was rejected in the *Norwegian Shipowners Claims* case, where the Tribunal of the Permanent Court of Arbitration opined: 'The majority of international lawyers seem to agree that these words (law and equity) are to be understood to mean general principles of justice as distinguished from any particular system of jurisprudence or the municipal law of any state'.[1]

That it is not a separate entity distinguishable from the law was emphasized by Judge Hudson in the *Diversion of the Waters of the River Meuse* case, where he stated:

A sharp division between law and equity, such as prevails in the administration of justice in some states should find no place in international jurisprudence . . . whether the reference in an arbitration treaty is to the application of 'law or equity' or to justiciability dependent on the possibility of applying 'law or equity' it would seem to envisage equity as part of the law.[2]

In a more substantive sense equity has been deemed to mean equality[3] but such a description is question-begging and leaves a host of questions unanswered. How is 'equity' to be measured in different situations? What factors must an international tribunal consider in order to determine

*Centre for Research on the New International Economic Order, Oxford.

equality? And in what situations would a departure from formal equality be justified? The problem may be illustrated by considering for example the construction of a dam across an international river by two riparian States. If the contribution made by one state is greater than the other ought the waters to be shared equally? Should the state making a greater contribution be allowed a greater share of the waters, even though the other riparian state may be economically more dependent on the waters of the river than the former? Should a long-term arrangement be made whereby equitable shares are determined by a formula which takes a variety of factors into account? Each of the above propositions for departures from equality may be supported by reference to equity, yet the identification of the relevant circumstances justifying such departures raises complex issues. To treat equity as equality would in many cases ignore a certain set of circumstances which may justify departures from equality. In the instance where a division of waters on the principle that shares ought to be commensurate with contributions made towards the construction of the dam, a series of factors such as the level of economic development, the principle of permanent sovereignty over natural resources, avoidance of waste in utilization may be relevant for purposes of effecting an equitable apportionment.

Under Article V of the Helsinki Rules on the Uses of the Waters of International Rivers there is an attempt to list the factors that comprise equity and reasonableness in the sharing of the waters. Thus, factors such as the geography, hydrology, the climate, past utilization, economic and social needs, the population dependent on the waters of the basin, comparative costs of alternative means, the availability of other resources, the avoidance of unnecessary waste in the utilization of the waters, the practicability of compensation to one or more of the co-basin States and the degrees to which the needs of a basin State may be satisfied, are enumerated.[4] But even these are not deemed to be exhaustive enough and recourse to generality is recommended. Thus, under Article V para. 3, it is stated: 'The weight to be given to each factor is to be determined by its importance in comparison with other relevant factors. In determining what is a reasonable and equitable share, all relevant factors are to be considered together and a conclusion reached on the basis of the whole'.[5] Further, Article VI enunciates: 'A use or category of uses is not entitled to any inherent preference over any other use or category of uses'.[6] The juridical task in these cases is to spell out criteria by reference to which deviations from formal equality may be justified.

Thus, for example, in the *Anglo-Norwegian Fisheries* case, equity was understood to operate as an exception to the general rule. A similar view was also adopted by Fitzmaurice when he said that a single recalcitrant State could dissociate itself from a general rule on the basis that the practice of that state was an exception.[7] But the operation of equity as an exception, it has been suggested, is fraught with danger. Thus, Akehurst observes that by creating an exceptional precedent states would be enabled to invoke the precedent in subsequent cases, whenever obedience to the rules of law would be irksome.[8]

Closely related to the above criticism is one which underlines that a degree of arbitrariness is inherent in an equitable determination by a court or arbiter. What factors ought a tribunal to take into account in determining whether or not its decision is equitable? Thus, some could argue that determination could vary with time and circumstances, or in cases involving apportionment of the continental shelf among adjacent states (as in the *North Sea Continental Shelf* case) a tribunal may consider not only the length of the coastline of states but the standard of living of the population and the degree of their dependence upon the continental shelf for resources, and take into account geological and geographical aspects of the situation.[9]

But the inclusion of economic and geographic interest hardly diminishes the complexity of the issues involved in a judicial determination. The question of the 'frontiers' of geographic and economic interests remains as do the problems relating to the relevance of the criteria to be applied. The use of equity has been seen not strictly as a source of law, but as an element of the process of judicial determination, thus: 'Strictly it cannot be a source of law, and yet it may be an important factor in the process of decision. Equity may play a dramatic role in supplementing the law or appear unobtrusively as part of judicial reasoning.'[10]

In some cases an international tribunal is faced with situations involving distribution or apportionment in areas in which there are no substantive rules by reference to which apportionment may be made. In these cases, it characterizes the problem as one calling for an 'equitable solution' and delineates a method by which such a solution may be found. It has thus been observed 'the court cannot itself adjudicate on the issue . . . it therefore directs that the appropriate method to be adopted in such a case is negotiation in good faith aimed at arriving at an agreement. The court could also logically urge that failing agreement the appropriate method for settlement could be ex aequo et bono.'[11] Often the courts in such cases do not decide the exact quantum of resources that will accrue to a state as in the *North Sea Continental Shelf* cases, where the International Court of Justice did not delimit the shelf but gave a direction as to the principles upon which delimitation ought to take place through negotiations.

The above analysis reveals that equity is invoked in different international contexts; (a) in a substantive sense, to support a claim to alter existing legal relationships or the application of existing rules; (b) in a procedural sense in the matters relating to distribution or apportionment.

EQUITY AND RESTRUCTURING OF THE INTERNATIONAL ECONOMIC ORDER

Equity is extensively invoked in support of proposals for changes in the existing international economic order. An examination of the specific references to equity in the different basic documents, envisaging proposals for the establishment of the new international economic order, reveals that equity is invoked not only to deal with cases involving distribution or apportionment, but also as a basis for claims to (a) alteration of existing legal relations (b) alteration of existing rules (c) establishment of new regulatory frameworks to restrict freedom of action of states or entities such as TNCs in areas where previously unrestricted freedom of action was enjoyed by them. Such alterations or innovations are sought to be justified on the basis that the existing legal framework is 'inequitable' or 'unjust' in that it operates unevenly — it favours the developed states, and is detrimental to the interests of the developing countries. It is in this perspective that the specific proposals on NIEO contained in the documents may be appraised.

(A) The Declaration on the Establishment of a New International Economic Order[12]

The Declaration makes a number of references to 'equity'. First, it appears as a criterion on the basis of which the New International Economic Order requires to be established. It appears together with sovereign equality, interdependence, common interest and co-operation among all States etc., but there is no elaboration of this broad concept.

In paragraph 1 the Declaration states the 'benefits of technology are not shared equitably by all members of the international community.' Technology is thus conceived as a 'community resource' akin to the concept of the common heritage of mankind, and equity is seen as the appropriate principle of apportionment to be applied.

Paragraph 4 of the Declaration states that the New International

Economic Order should be founded on full respect for certain principles. Among these it incorporates 'equity' in sub-paragraph 4(b) as follows: 'The broadest cooperation of all the state members of the international community based on equity whereby the prevailing disparities in the world may be banished and prosperity secured for all.' It would appear that in the paragraph itself 'equity' appears in the widest sense possible. It neither states the meaning of the term itself nor does it attempt to say to what specific areas of co-operation it will be applied, except in the 'broadest' manner. There is a reference to the elimination of all prevailing disparities and the attainment of prosperity as an objective of the Declaration.

(B) Programme of Action on the Establishment of a New International Economic Order[13]

The Declaration enunciates as one of its principles: 'the broadest co-operation of all the state members of the international community based on equity whereby the prevailing disparities in the world may be banished and prosperity secured for all.' The Programme of Action spells out specific areas where re-structuring of relations on the basis of equity is called for. These include:

    (i)   the fundamental problems of raw materials and primary commodities as related to trade and development;

    (ii)   the international monetary system and financing of development in developing countries;

    (iii)   industrialization;

    (iv)   the transfer of technology;

    (v)   the regulation and control over the activities of transnational corporations;

    (vi)   the matters covered by the Charter of Economic Rights and Duties;

    (vii)   promotion of co-operation among developing countries;

    (viii)   assistance in the exercise of permanent sovereignty over natural resources;

    (ix)   strengthening the role of the United Nations system in the field of international economic co-operation;

    (x)   matters related to the Special Programme of the United Nations.

(C) The Charter of Economic Rights and Duties of States[14]

In the Preamble to the Charter the General Assembly declared: 'it is a fundamental purpose of this Charter to promote the establishment of the New International Economic Order, based on *equity*, sovereign equality, common interest and co-operation among States irrespective of their economic and social systems.'

Further the Charter enumerates certain rights and duties whereby this may be done. It states:

(a) that States have a right to remunerative and *equitable* prices taking into account, in particular, the interests of developing countries (Article 6);

(b) that all States have a duty to adjust export prices to their imports in a manner which is remunerative for producers and *equitable* for producers and consumers (Article 28);

(c) that all States have a right to participate in the international decision-making process for the solution of world economic, financial and monetary problems through the appropriate international organizations and to share *equitably* in the benefits resulting therefrom (Article 10);

(d) that every State has a duty to co-operate in promoting trade liberalization in an *equitable* way, taking into account the specific problems of the developing countries (Article 14);

(e) that international trade should be conducted without prejudice to generalized non-discriminatory and non-reciprocal preferences in favour of developing countries, on the basis of mutual advantage, *equitable* benefits and the exchange of the most favoured nation treatment (Article 26);

(f) that every State has the right to enjoy the benefits fully and *equitably* of world invisible trade (Article 27);

(g) that the benefits derived from the deep seabed ought to be *equitably* shared by all States taking into account the particular needs of developing countries (Article 29).

In each of these cases there is an invocation of equity.

Implicit in the Charter, therefore, is a complex notion of equity whereby it is invoked to support claims to special treatment on the basis of a recognition of the special needs of States such as those emanating from the Special Programme in the Programme of Action for the Establishment of the NIEO; it also invokes equity as the appropriate principle for the apportionment of resources of the deep seabed.

(D) Equity in other Resolutions and Declarations

Cognizance has also been taken of principles enunciated in the above resolutions of the General Assembly, *inter alia*, in (i) the Declaration on Development and International Economic Co-operation[15] and (ii) in the Lima Declaration and Plan of Action on Industrial Development and Co-operation[16] through a reaffirmation and a further spelling out of those principles. Thus the Declaration on Development and International Economic Co-operation includes a list of subjects to which the General Assembly resolutions on the NIEO and the Charter of Economic Rights and Duties apply and refers to the payment of 'remunerative and *equitable* prices for commodities of export interest to developing countries.'[17] Similarly, the Lima Declaration refers to the resolutions on the NIEO and declares that 'countries, particularly developed countries, should undertake an objective and critical examination of their policies and make appropriate changes in such policies so as to facilitate the expansion and diversification of imports from developing countries and thereby make possible international economic relations on a rational, just and equitable basis'.[18]

(E) The Informal Composite Negotiating Test of the Third UN Law of the Sea Conference[19]

In the INCNT there are at least six areas to which equity applies. The first of these is the familiar one relating to the delimitation of physical boundaries. Articles 74 and 83 lay down the principles whereby the Exclusive Economic Zone and the Continental Shelf may be apportioned between adjacent or opposite States. Where *benefits* accrue such as in the Continental Shelf beyond the 200 nautical mile zone (Article 82, paragraph 1) or in the EEZ (in the not unusual case where more than one State has the beneficial rights — Article 59) or in the deep seabed equitable principles may be employed for apportionment. Indeed Article 151, paragraph 9 states: 'The Authority shall establish a system for equitable sharing of benefits derived from the area, taking into consideration the interests and needs of developing countries and peoples, particularly the land-locked and geographically disadvantaged among them, the countries which have not attained full independence or other self-governing status.'

As in the case of the apportionment of resources from the deep seabed, equity provides the basis for equitable sharing of financial and other economic benefits derived from activity in the deep seabed (Article 158,

XII). It further calls for the principle of 'equitable geographical distribution' to be applied to recruitment of 'nationals of developing states, whether coastal, land-locked or geographically disadvantaged for the purposes of training as members of the managerial, research and technical staff constituted for its undertaking' (Article 275 (a)).

With regard to the constitution of the Authority and its organs, (the Assembly and the Council together with the subsidiary organs), equity emerges as a concept with structural connotations. Articles 154–68 describe the manner in which it applies. Particularly important are Articles 158(2) (v) and 160(2) (iv) wherein the powers and functions of the Assembly and the Council are outlined. Under both these principles of equitable geographical distribution and special needs are taken into account, in defining the composition of their subsidiary organs.

Equity is the basis of the right, claimed by special categories of States such as land-locked States, and certain developing coastal States, ('geographically-disadvantaged') to participate in the exploitation of resources which they would not otherwise have been entitled to do. Thus under Article 69(1) 'land-locked states have the right to participate in the exploitation of the living resources of the exclusive economic zones on an equitable basis taking into account the relevant economic and geographical circumstances of all states concerned.' Article 70(1) provides a similar right to certain 'geographically disadvantaged' developing coastal states in a sub-region or region.

Under Article 74 provision is made for delimitation of EEZ boundaries by the application of 'equitable principles', thus: 'The delimitation of the exclusive economic zone between adjacent or opposite States shall be effected by agreement in accordance with equitable principles employing where appropriate, the median line and taking into account all the relevant citcumstances.'

(F) Draft Outline of an International Code of Conduct on Transfer of Technology[20]

In the Draft Code it is stated that among its objectives it shall: 'Establish general *equitable rules* for the international transfer of technology taking into consideration particularly the needs of the developing countries and the legitimate interests of technology suppliers and technology recipients.' Pursuant to the above objective, the Code includes the following principles:

(i) Improving access to technology at fair and reasonable prices and costs, both direct and indirect, and regulating business practices, particularly those arising from transfer pricing and transfer accounting;

(ii)   Eliminating restrictive practices arising out of or affecting technology transfer;

(iii)   Promoting unpackaging of transactions involving transfer of technology, evaluation of costs, organization forms and institutional channels for the transfer;

(iv)   Establishing an appropriate set of guarantees to suppliers and recipients of technology, taking fully into account the weaker position of recipient enterprises of developing countries;

(v)   Facilitating an orderly implementation of national laws and policies on transfer of technology through the establishment of minimum international standards;

(vi)   Promoting the development of indigenous technologies particularly in developing countries.

Thus the Draft incorporates equity as a basis for the restructuring of legal relations in the field of technology transfer.

Support for a wide variety of claims is thus sought to be derived from equity — equity as a basis for claims to change existing rules, existing legal relations, existing structures. It is invoked to support claims for new regulatory frameworks and to change the constitutions of international organizations and decision-making procedures. At root is the basic premise that all these changes would 'correct' or 'redress' existing injustices or disparities which characterize the existing order.

The working out of specific proposals for change based on equity presents no less, indeed greater, difficulty than the working out of equitable solutions to problems of distribution and apportionment. Whether it is through adjudication, arbitration, or negotiation that equity is to be achieved, the task of establishing criteria by reference to which what is relevant can be discerned, presents a challenge. Perhaps, lawyers can make a contribution towards the establishment of the New International Economic Order by elucidating the different elements which are relevant to determining what is equitable in different situations and in helping to formulate criteria for this purpose.

NOTES AND REFERENCES

1   1.R.I.A.A. (1922), p. 309 at p. 331.
2   (1937), Permanent Court of International Justice, Series A/B, No. 70 at p. 73.

3 Ibid.; see also *North Sea Continental Shelf* cases (1969), ICJ, *Reports*, 3, para. 91.
4 Helsinki Rules on the Uses of Waters of International Rivers, Article V (j).
5 Ibid., Article V, para. 3.
6 Ibid., Article VI.
7 *Barcelona Traction* case, Judge Fitzmaurice (1970), ICJ, *Reports*, p. 84–6.
8 M. Akehurst, 'Equity and General Principles of Law', *International and Comparative Law Quarterly*, Vol. 25 (1976), p. 789–826 at p. 809.
9 *North Sea Continental Shelf* cases (1969), ICJ, *Reports*, 3, para. 91.
10 Ian Brownlie, *Principles of Public International Law*, Oxford, 1973.
11 K. Hossain, see Chap. 15.
12 UN General Assembly resolution 3201 (S–VI).
13 UN General Assembly resolution 3202 (S–VI).
14 UN General Assembly resolution 3281 (S–XXIX).
15 UN General Assembly resolution 3362 (S–VII).
16 Adopted at its Second General Conference, 6 December 1973.
17 See note 15.
18 See note 16.
19 Informal Composite Negotiating Text, A/CONF. 62/WP. 10.
20 Presented by the Group of 77 experts.

Part II

TRANSNATIONAL CORPORATIONS AND TRANSFER OF TECHNOLOGY

7 United Nations Efforts at International Regulation of Transnational Corporations

*Samuel K.B. Asante**

This decade has been characterized by a sustained and intense international interest in the nature, role, operations and strategies of transnational corporations. The discussion of transnational corporations in various international forums has revolved around two main themes. On the one hand, it has been stressed that transnational corporations have the requisite economic power and resources to act as effective instruments of development, particularly in developing countries, and that they have, in fact, played a meaningful and constructive role in this regard. On the other hand, the pervasive role attributed to transnational corporations in the world and the disclosure of certain instances of corporate misconduct have generated a grave concern about the impact of transnational corporations on economic development and political and social affairs, both at the national and international level. The various international and regional efforts towards the promulgation of a multilateral system for the regulation of transnational corporations stem from this concern about the negative aspects of the operations of transnational corporations, as well as the recognition that national regulation and control is clearly inadequate to deal effectively with the global strategies of transnational corporations.

The Group of Eminent Persons appointed by the Secretary-General to study the impact of multinational corporations on development, recommended the establishment of a Commission which would, *inter alia*: 'Evolve a set of recommendations which, taken together, would represent a code of conduct for governments and multinational corporations to be considered and adopted by the Economic and Social Council, and

---

*UN Centre on Transnational Corporations.

review in the light of experience the effective application and continuing applicability of such recommendations.' Similarly, the concern about the activities of transnational corporations found concrete expression in the deliberations on the establishment of a New International Economic Order. In drawing up the Programme of Action on the establishment of a New International Economic Order, the General Assembly emphasized that 'all efforts should be made to formulate, adopt and implement an international code of conduct for transnational corporations' in order:

'(a) To prevent interference in the internal affairs of the countries where they operate and their collaboration with racist regimes and colonial administrations;

(b) To regulate their activities in host countries, to eliminate restrictive business practices and to conform to the national development plans and objectives of developing countries; and in this context facilitate, as necessary, the review and revision of previously concluded arrangements;

(c) To bring about assistance, transfer of technology and management skills to developing countries on equitable and favourable terms;

(d) To regulate the repatriation of the profits accruing from their operations, taking into account the legitimate interests of all parties concerned;

(e) To promote reinvestment of their profits in developing countries.'

The United Nations Commission on Transnational Corporations was established by the Economic and Social Council in consequence of the above developments and specifically charged with the responsibility for the formulation of a code of conduct for transnational corporations. The Programme of Work of this Commission expressly mandates it 'to secure international arrangements that promote the positive contributions of transnational corporations to national development goals and world economic growth while controlling and eliminating their negative effects'.

As intimated above, the attempt to devise an international code of conduct for transnational corporations has not been confined to the United Nations. Several regional organizations have embarked on such an exercise. The Andean Group, established under the Cartagena Agreement, adopted an Andean Foreign Investment Code, 'Decision 24', in December 1970, which established common regulations on foreign investment in the Andean Group. Decision 24 provides for (i) appropriate restraints of entry of new direct foreign investment; (ii) closure of certain areas, economies to direct foreign investment; (iii) regulation of repatriation of capital and profits; and (iv) restrictions on transfers of technology. The Organization of American States has also done preliminary work towards the formulation of a code of conduct for transnational corporations.

Similarly, the OECD adopted a comprehensive code of conduct on 21 June 1976, embodying guidelines for multinational enterprises. The guidelines are recommendations jointly addressed by the member countries of OECD to multinational enterprises operating within their territories and 'lay down standards for the activities of these enterprises' in such areas as questionable corporate payments, involvement in local political activities, competition, taxation, employment and industrial relations, science and technology and disclosure of information. The EEC has also promulgated decisions against restrictive trade practices by transnational corporations operating within its member countries.

The movement for *international* control of transnational corporations has been endorsed by important non-governmental organizations, such as the International Chamber of Commerce, the International Conference of Free Trade Unions, the World Federation of Trade Unions and the World Confederation of Labour which have produced documents spelling out their views and proposals in regard to the activities of transnational corporations.

Within the United Nations system, several organizations and agencies are engaged upon the formulation of international regulations on specific aspects of the activities of transnational corporations. Thus, UNCTAD is preparing a Code of Conduct to regulate the transfer of technology and also multi-laterally agreed principles and rules on restrictive business practices. The ILO has developed a code on labour, whilst the Social and Economic Council has established an Ad Hoc Intergovernmental Group to draft an international agreement to prevent and eliminate corrupt practices in international commercial transactions. However, the formulation of the most comprehensive code of conduct relating to the activities of transnational corporations has been entrusted to the Commission on Transnational Corporations.

THE UNITED NATIONS CODE OF CONDUCT FOR TRANSNATIONAL CORPORATIONS

In accordance with the above-mentioned mandates, the Intergovernmental Working Group established by the United Nations Commission on Transnational Corporations to draft a code of conduct relating to transnational corporations, commenced its task in January 1977 — a task which has been accorded the highest priority by the Commission. The Working

Group has now reached a stage where its discussions centre around a working paper prepared by the United Nations Centre on Transnational Corporations, embodying, for purposes of discussion only, broad, tentative formulations of the position which the Group might adopt on the substantive provisions of the Code. Some of the major issues which have emerged during the deliberations of the Group are as follows.

1   Conduct to be affected by the Code

A crucial issue that emerged during the early stages of the Working Group's deliberations was whether the code of conduct should be addressed exclusively to transnational corporations or whether it should encompass the treatment of transnational corporations by governments. The developing countries at first insisted that the only issue before the Working Group was the regulation of the conduct of transnational corporations and that the conduct of governments was outside the purview of the code. This position was strongly resisted by the developed countries who ultimately succeeeded in bringing the treatment of transnational corporations by governments within the purview of the code. Thus, as presently structured, the code has two parts; part A, which deals with the regulation of transnational corporations and part B which prescribes standards to be observed by governments in relation to transnational corporations.

2   The legal nature and form of the Code

Preliminary discussions on the nature and form of the code have alluded to several alternatives, including the following

(i)   a binding code, that is, a code which prescribes specific rules and is legally binding on all parties concerned – state parties, transnational corporations and other persons;

(ii)   a voluntary code, that is, a code which contains broad, equitable principles or guidelines to be observed by all parties concerned but which is not legally binding on such parties. A voluntary code would, in effect, prescribe general corporate standards but not legally enforceable rules;

(iii)   a code which is binding in part and voluntary in part, that is, a mixture of alternatives (i) and (ii) above; and

(iv)   an international agreement or convention which is binding on state parties with respect to inter-state relations, but contains a voluntary code of conduct for transnational corporations and other entities.

On the whole, the developing countries and socialist countries have intimated a preference for a binding or mandatory code of conduct, whilst the developed countries from the market economies have argued for the adoption of a voluntary code of conduct. However, the Working Group has deferred in-depth consideration of these issues as well as the modalities for the implementation of the code pending a clearer appreciation of the substantive provisions which the code might contain.

3 Substantive provisions of the Code

The first stage of the Working Group's deliberations consisted in the delineation of the subjects to be included in the Code. As intimated above, this broad outline has now been elaborated into tentative formulations prepared by the Centre on Transnational Corporations for purposes of discussion, of the substantive provisions of the code which are organized under two main sections, the first part dealing with 'Major principles and/or issues related to the activities of transnational corporations', and the second part, 'Principles and/or issues relating to the treatment of transnational corporations'.

The first section encompasses two main categories of prescriptions, (a) general and political and (b) economic, financial and social. Among the prescriptions of a general and political significance are the following:

(i) Transnational corporations should respect the national sovereignty of the countries in which they operate and the exercise by each state of its right to full permanent sovereignty over the wealth and resources within its territory. A further requirement of these standards would require transnational corporations to observe the laws and regulations and administrative practices in the countries in which they operate and respect the right of each such State to regulate and supervise the activities of transnational corporations. These prescriptions are reminiscent of the various United Nations resolutions on permanent sovereignty and, to some extent, the New International Economic Order.

(ii) Transnational corporations are further required to respect the economic goals and developmental objectives of their host countries. Transnational corporations should, in particular, support the development efforts of developing host countries and effectively participate in these efforts at the national level and, where appropriate, at the regional level within the framework of regional integration programme. At the instance of the developed countries from the market economy countries, the general obligation of transnational corporations to take all necessary steps to ensure that their activities are consistent with the established objectives and priorities of their host countries, was qualified by the phrase 'with due regard to sound commercial practices'. Representatives of developing countries have maintained that this qualification would virtually nullify this obligation of transnational corporations.

(iii) Transnational corporations are also urged to adopt a more flexible approach to the principle of sanctity of contracts by recognizing the need to renegotiate or review contractual arrangements in certain cases — such as a fundamental change in the circumstances surrounding the conclusion of the contract or where such circumstances were marked by a clear inequality of the parties or duress. The developed countries from the market economies have strenuously maintained the position that renegotiation or review of contracts should be the exception to the well-settled principle of *pacta sunt servanda*.

(iv) Transnational corporations are required to respect the social and cultural objectives and values of the countries in which they operate. In this regard, transnational corporations should co-operate with governments with a view to ensuring that their practices, products or services do not cause major distortions in the basic cultural patterns or have other socio-cultural effects considered undesirable by the countries in which they operate, beyond those which necessarily follow industrialization and the introduction and generation of new technologies.

(v) An important prescription requires transnational corporations to respect human rights and fundamental freedoms. More specifically, transnational corporations in their employment practices should avoid discrimination on the basis of race, colour, sex, religion, political or other opinions or social origin.

(vi) The code prohibits political interference of various types. Transnational corporations should not interfere in the internal political affairs of countries in which they operate, particularly by resorting to subversive activities, attempting to overthrow governments or to alter by pressure or coercion, the political and social systems in these countries. Transnational corporations should act as good corporate citizens and abstain from activities of a political nature clearly inconsistent with the domestic legislation or established practice in such countries.

(vii) Transnational corporations are further to abstain from improper interference in inter-governmental relations. More explicitly, transnational corporations, in pursuing their corporate interests, should not request their home governments to act on their behalf in any manner that exceeds normal diplomatic representation or other regular intergovernmental communication and, in particular any manner that amounts to the exercise of political and economic pressure on other governments. In this regard, transnational corporations should, in accordance with international practice, exhaust legal means available in host countries for resolving disputes before seeking diplomatic support from their home governments.

The code's prescriptions on the economic, financial and social aspects of the activities of transnational corporations deal specifically with such subjects as ownership and control, balance of payments, taxation, transfer pricing, consumer protection, environmental protection and disclosure of information, all areas which have perennially generated conflicts in the relations between governments and transnational corporations. Examples of the formulations under this heading are as follows:

(i) Transnational corporations should structure their corporate arrangements in such a manner as would permit an effective division of the decision-making process among their various entities in different countries so as to enhance their contribution to the economic and social development of the countries of operation and enable them to act as good corporate citizens. Transnational corporations are further called upon to be amenable to joint venture and participation arrangements and to avoid any action which would impede the effective exercise or sharing of local control in their undertakings under such joint ventures or other arrangements. In this regard, transnational corporations are specifically required to provide local personnel with the requisite managerial training and to ensure that qualified nationals of the host countries hold positions of management and direction and participate effectively in the decision-making process of the local subsidiaries.

(ii) With regard to balance of payments, a broad prescription is stipulated enjoining transnational corporations to co-operate with governments regarding the achievement of established balance of payments objectives. More specifically, transnational corporations are required, with due regard to the established balance of payments objectives of the countries in which they operate and consistent with sound commercial practices, to contribute over an appropriate period of time to the expansion of exports, particularly by avoiding the imposition of undue restrictions on exports by their affiliates, and by utilizing domestic raw materials and other domestic resources. Another refinement of this prescription requires transnational corporations to refrain from excessive or untimely remittance of profits, royalties and fees, in a manner that aggravates balance of payment problems in the country in which they operate, taking into account the development goals and particularly the balance of payments objectives of that country as well as sound commercial practices and the legitimate interests of all parties concerned, including those of the home countries. Transnational corporations should also avoid excessive or untimely outflows of funds and intracorporate capital transactions which aggravate the balance of payments problems of the countries in which they operate.

(iii) Transfer pricing is the subject of rather emphatic regulations. In their intracorporate transactions, transnational corporations should desist from the application of pricing principles which, in violation of the laws, regulations and practices of the countries concerned, evade taxation or substantially reduce the tax base on which they are assessed or have adverse effects on competition, employment, technological development, credit policies and balance of payments objectives of such countries. To reinforce this prescription, transnational corporations are required to use pricing policies based on 'arms-length' principles or other analogous principles applied in transfer pricing and all relevant information upon request by government authorities.

(iv) The prescription with regard to consumer protection requires transnational corporations, in accordance with national laws, regulations and administrative practices of the countries concerned, to perform their operations in a manner that is not injurious to the health and safety of consumers while at the same time maintaining a consistent quality of goods. In particular, transnational corporations should disclose to the public in the countries in which they operate all appropriate information on the contents and possible dangerous or other adverse effects of the products they produce or market in the countries concerned by means of proper labelling, informative and meaningful advertising and other appropriate methods. Subject to the requirements of confidentiality, transnational corporations should also disclose to the appropriate governmental authorities information relating to the experimental aspects and uses of products which they propose to produce or market in the country concerned.

The Working Group has deferred consideration of subjects such as restrictive business practices, employment and labour, transfer of technology, corrupt practices in international business transactions and taxation, pending the conclusion of the work of various agencies of the United Nations which are charged with the formulation of regulations in these specific areas.

Corporate obligation to disclose information constitutes an important part of the draft of code of conduct. The prescriptions in the area go substantially further than the requirements of the municipal laws of many countries. There is a general standard that transnational corporations should, with due regard to their nature and relative size, regularly provide to the public in the countries in which they operate, clear and comprehensive information on their activities, consistent with, and in addition to, the requirements of its national laws, regulations and administrative practices. But the draft code goes on to provide more specifically as follows:

(i) The information should cover activities of the corporation as a whole as well as by geographical area, country of operation and by major line of business as appropriate and include financial as well as non-financial items, such as: structure of the transnational corporation, financial statements (including sources and uses of funds), employment, investment, and statements on transfer pricing policies and on the accounting principles used in compiling and consolidating the information, taking into account the cost of producing the information and the need for confidentiality to avoid adverse effects on competition. In providing a suitable breakdown of information, account should also be taken of the significance of the transnational corporation operations in a particular country or group of countries and the links with operations in other countries. (ii) Transnational corporations should disclose upon request to the governments of the countries in which they operate information required for legislative and administrative purposes relevant to their affiliates in the countries concerned and specifically needed to assess the performance of such affiliates. Such information may include items held in other countries and related to the transnational corporation as a whole and its operations in other countries, subject to relevant national legislation of all countries concerned.

The second part of the code dealing with the principles or issues relating to the treatment of transnational corporations by governments first prescribes norms for intergovernmental co-operation in matters relating to the activities of transnational corporations and also in the implementation of the code. Thus, governments are required to co-operate on a bilateral as well as a multilateral basis with a view to encouraging the positive contributions that transnational corporations can make to economic and social progress and to resolving, as feasible, difficulties to which the operations of transnational corporations may give rise.

Governments should also co-operate with one another in order to promote the effective implementation of the code.

The principles which address the treatment of transnational corporations are organized under three broad headings, namely (a) general treatment of transnational corporations by home and host countries (b) nationalization and compensation and (c) jurisdiction.

Among the prescriptions under subtitle (a) are the following:

(i) Transnational corporations should be treated by their host countries in a fair and equitable manner consistent with the interests of all concerned and in accordance with national laws, regulations and administrative practices, as well as international norms and contractual obligations which have freely been assumed.

Non-discriminatory treatment is to be assured by the prescription that, subject to the requirements of public order and national security, transnational corporations should be accorded treatment under national laws, regulations and administrative practices no less and no more favourable than that accorded to domestic enterprises, in situations where the operations of transnational corporations are comparable to those of domestic enterprises.

(ii) Transnational corporations should be treated by their home countries in a way that recognizes the rights of host countries to regulate the activities of transnational corporations operating within them.

(iii) The concerns of transnational corporations about the uncertain and unpredictable nature of host country laws and regulations are to be allayed by the prescription that national policies, laws, regulations and administrative practices significantly affecting the activities of transnational corporations should be clearly defined.

Changes deemed necessary in the light of evolving circumstances should be made in an orderly way with proper regard to the rights of transnational corporations established at the time. The notion of predictability, however, raises exceedingly difficult problems of interpretation which might make it inappropriate for a code of conduct, particularly in view of the differences in the level, stage and pace of development in the various countries, and differing perceptions and needs of those in the various countries. The problem arises of either construing the term so flexibly as to deprive it of all significance or so narrowly as to make it too rigid and standard.

(iv) Improper use of transnational corporations by countries as instruments for the attainment of foreign policy objectives is to be prohibited. Another prescription addressed to home countries enjoins them to ensure that action taken toward other countries in support of the interests of transnational corporations remain within the bounds established by international norms concerning normal diplomatic representation and the submission of international legal claims. Such action should not amount to the exercise of economic or political pressure.

The formulations of the appropriate standards regarding nationalization and compensation are probably the most tentative and controversial. A compromise proposal, yet to be fully discussed, reads as follows:

In the exercise of their sovereignty, states have the right, acting in the public interest, to nationalize property in their territory. Transnational corporations should expect, as part of fair treatment by the host countries, that just compensation will be paid in the event of nationalization or other taking of their property, under due process of law and without discrimination between enterprises in comparable situations. These principles do not affect the right of private individuals and entities to present their claims to appropriate authorities. These principles do recognize a mutuality of interest between host countries and transnational corporations on the basis of which disputes between them may be avoided or, should they arise, be amicably settled.

With regard to the issue of jurisdiction over the activities of transnational corporations by governments of the countries in which they operate, the discussion revolves around the following formulations:

(i) In view of the jurisdiction that States have over their territories, transnational corporations are subject to the jurisdiction of the countries in which they operate.
(ii) In the exercise of its jurisdiction over transnational corporations and their entities, each State should refrain from such acts as many infringe on the jurisdiction of another State, due regard being had to the interests and policies of that other State and any relevant international agreement.
(iii) Investment disputes between a State and a transnational corporation are subject to the jurisdiction of the courts and other authorities of that country. Where the Government and the transnational corporation have freely agreed to submit their disputes to arbitration or other method of settlement of disputes, the Government should observe in good faith its obligation under such agreement, with due regard to cases where the State's vital national interests are involved.
(iv) The validity of contractual arrangements between private parties in

one country concerning application of the law of another country or submission of disputes to the courts of another country or to commercial arbitration is to be determined by national law.

(v) In order to avoid and, as necessary, settle conflicts of jurisdiction between States arising in connexion with the operation of transnational corporations, States, on a bilateral or multilateral basis, should adopt mutually acceptable principles and procedures.

4 Implementation and Sanctions

As intimated above, the Inter Governmental Working Group has not addressed itself to the intricate issues concerning the legal nature and form of the code and the modalities for its implementation. It is evident, however, that the system of sanctions which would eventually be established would substantially depend on the legal nature and form of the code. The following summarizes the main implications of the various alternatives as to the nature of the code.

Binding Code

If the code of conduct assumes the form of a multilateral treaty or convention, then it would impose legally binding obligations on State-parties to such treaty or convention. The provisions of the code which affect the conduct of transnational corporations would then be enforced either by individual legislation and the enforcement machinery of each State, or by some intergovernmental or supra-national machinery established for the express purpose of enforcing the code. Such an intergovernmental authority would be competent to make determinations as to violations by transnational corporations and impose appropriate sanctions, in the manner of the EEC Commission in the enforcement of its anti-trust provisions. Technically, a treaty or convention embodying a mandatory code provides the basis for an unequivocal regime of legal sanctions to be effected by a national, regional or an international mechanism.

Voluntary Code

Implementation becomes a much more complex, though probably no less effective phenomenon when the code is voluntary. If such a code is adopted by way of a resolution of the General Assembly of the United Nations, fully supported by an overwhelming majority of State-members, then, although it may not be mandatory in the strict sense, it may ultimately be effective for a number of reasons. Firstly, inasmuch as such a resolution represents the collective view of a preponderant majority of nation-States as to the appropriate standards of corporate conduct or State conduct, it would have a strong moral standing as an international standard which cannot be violated with impunity. Secondly, it is arguable that such a resolution represents an emphatic restatement of the subscribers' conception of the current status of customary international law or State practice in this area and is therefore entitled to respect as such. Finally, United Nations resolutions fully endorsed by the international community could ultimately be a source of law, whatever the immediate technical legal effect of such resolutions may be.

The effectiveness of a voluntary code need not depend on the interposition of a United Nations resolution. A code recommended by the international community for adoption on a voluntary basis could have a meaningful impact in a number of ways. First, the adoption of such a code in itself would create a climate of public opinion which would induce expectations of compliance as evidence of good corporate conduct or fair acceptable state practice. A corporation which violates such a code would attract public censure and probably disqualify itself from the diplomatic support of its home country in the face of reprisals by its host country.

Secondly, host States could adopt such voluntary codes by incorporating them as part of their municipal laws or by setting them up as standards of acceptable corporate behaviour. In either case, what was originally a voluntary code could become enforceable as municipal law or State policy. Violation of the code could then be a basis of normal legal sanctions or economic sanctions such as the denial of economic privileges or the imposition of restrictions. In this regard, it is conceivable that a host State may set off such a violation against a claim by the corporation for compensation or other reliefs.

Thirdly, the promulgation of voluntary codes may influence professional bodies such as accountants in determining what is acceptable corporate behaviour, particularly in the area of disclosure of financial matters. If the prescriptions embodied in voluntary codes are endorsed by professional bodies as evidence of custom or responsible corporate behaviour in a particular business activity, then breach of the relevant part of the code could be material in the determination of such issues as negligence or good business practice before national courts or international adjudicatory authorities.

A learned author has summed up the likely impact of codes of conduct as follows:

Codes of conduct are likely to become prevalent in the coming years as a multilateral response to the activities of multinational corporations throughout the world. Codes embodied in international treaties will, of course, have the effect of law. Even voluntary codes will be of concern to multinational corporations, however, not only because of the adverse publicity engendered by public disclosure of violations of such codes, but because of the standard of behaviour that such codes will set which may be enforced by courts of host countries notwithstanding that these codes are not incorporated into the municipal law of such countries.[1]

REFERENCE

1. Stephen K. Chance, 'Codes of conduct for multinational corporations', *The Business Lawyer*, Vol. 33, No. 3, April 1978, 1799 at 1820.

8 'National Treatment' and the Formulation of a Code of Conduct for Transnational Corporations

*Elsa Kelly**

1 THE SETTING OF THE PROBLEM

One of the issues which falls within the scope of the North–South negotiations for the establishment of a New International Economic Order is the regulation and control of the activities of transnational corporations. Several UN resolutions reflect serious misgivings related to those activities, particularly — though not exclusively — on the part of the developing countries. This debate is far from being new. Foreign investment, one of the ways in which highly industrialized market economy countries expanded their economic interests beyond their national boundaries, has carried with it, since its inception as a normal event in world business, the seeds of conflict among investors and their governments, on the one hand, and the receiving countries on the other. Whether in the form of a call for restraint in the use of force by States for the recovery of debts early in this century, or of a dispute over the issue of compensation to be paid as a result of the expropriation by a State of alien-owned property, foreign investment in its different modalities has been the object of scrutiny by politicians, economists and lawyers alike. It is not surprising that concerns arising from the issue of foreign investment have given place to various conflicting and contradictory views, since what is at stake is not always entirely explicit. The task would be simple if the issues involved were merely economic. However, the question of foreign investment is far more complex, given the fact that the problems which have arisen relate also to social, political and cultural concerns at the domestic level as well as to issues derived from the

*Centre for Research on the New International Economic Order, Oxford.

different and differing interests of states at the international level. These problems have become more evident as a result of the activities of transnational corporations, the most elaborate form of foreign investment, and the widespread increase of their operations in the aftermath of the Second World War. Their special characteristics *vis-à-vis* other forms of foreign investment have increased and deepened the sources of conflict among states, particularly between developing and developed countries. These conflicts are mere manifestations of a more general and complex phenomenon that may be more properly characterized as an emerging *de facto* system of transnationalization or globalization of economic relations, the transnational corporation being one of its institutional mechanisms. This process, which has tended to undermine the power of individual nation-States, particularly that of developing countries, is moving towards the establishment of a new international division of labour, the emerging features of which seem to be highly unfavourable to that group of countries.

It is from this perspective that the ongoing debate on transnational corporations should be envisaged in order to evaluate properly the results of the negotiations that are being carried out within the United Nations system with a view to establishing some kind of legal control over their activities.

In order to undertake a meaningful assessment of these negotiations, the analytical framework should include the broader issues involved in the process of transnationalization of economic relations from which a new pattern of asymmetric structural economic relationships, both at the national and international levels, is emerging. To look at the mere institution of the transnational corporation as such, devoid of the power-structure in which it operates, would be a candid conceptualization which may obscure the basic facts relevant for any agreement between the developed and developing countries.

It would also be misleading to concentrate solely on the sources of conflict between transnational corporations and the home State *vis-à-vis* the host State as if they were the real cause originating the call for international regulation. Such conflicts have certainly triggered off this call but should be considered rather as the effect of the broader phenomenon, that of the transnationalization of economic relations, the international control of which is the real issue.

Therefore, the basic assumption in this paper is that the questions concerning transnational corporations – either in the context of the North–South dialogue or of the political debate within individual nation-States – should be addressed to the problem of transnationalization of economic relations, as well as that of its institutional instrument, the aggregate body of transnational corporations, which is tending to transform the international economic system in a way which accentuates the disadvantages of developing countries.

Another assumption is that legal regulation is the means through which political and other objectives are achieved within a society; legal formulations — especially at the international level — cannot replace a lack of political will in concretizing those objectives. At the same time, the adoption of a set of rules implies that certain standards of behaviour are considered more adequate than others, whether any individual state or minority group of States agree with them or not. The establishment of standards should be part of the general strategy of the developing countries towards the achievement of an orderly change of the international economic system. These standards or rules should, at best, create conditions which will favour their position, at worst, should not legitimize objectives which are at odds with their specific interests, especially in areas defining structural relationships within the system.

The initial position of the Group of 77 with respect to the formulation of a code of conduct relating to transnational corporations, according to which such a code should be concerned only with the behaviour of these corporations, was in line with this strategy, given the fact that the major success of the developing countries had been attained with the adoption of three important General Assembly resolutions, embodying the Declaration on the Establishment of a New International Economic Order (3201 (S-VI)) and the Programme of Action thereof (3202 (S-VI)), and, in particular, the Charter of Economic Rights and Duties of States (3281 (XXIX)) which defined the rights and duties of States in this area. It is clear that the objective behind Article 2 of the Charter was to strengthen the legal position of host States (*vis-à-vis* the transnational corporations and their home States) concerning the treatment of transnational corporations. This achievement did not mean that major changes in that relationship to the benefit of the developing countries, would in fact occur but, rather, that if an individual host State or a group of them had the political will to attempt such a change, their attempt, within the limits set forth by the Charter, would conform to an international standard adopted by a wide majority of members of the international community. Even if it were conceded — which it is not — that the precise nature of that standard, i.e. whether it is a rule of law or not, may be arguable, there is no question that acts of states which are in agreement with Article 2 of the Charter cannot be held as unlawful.

It is difficult to foresee if further negotiations on this topic of treatment of transnational corporations by States in the United Nations will lead to the adoption of standards or rules that will be more favourable or improve the position of the developing countries. In fact the formulations by the Chairman of the Intergovernmental Working Group on a Code of Conduct on transnational corporations suggests that the acceptance by the Group of 77 of the proposal to discuss and incorporate a section dealing with the treatment of transnational corporations by States may not bring about an improved version of the Charter considered from the point of view of the interests of developing countries. One of the issues that deserves careful consideration is the one concerning 'national treatment' as a minimum standard to be applied to transnational corporations within each State. This issue bears upon two main themes which in fact represent the two levels on which the discussion of the impact of the process of transnationalization of economic relations is centred: (a) the erosion of the powers of nation-States as decision-making centres within their territories, especially those of developing countries; and (b) the establishment of a new international division of labour creating a kind of interdependence between developing and developed countries that will expose the former to greater vulnerability.

The question of 'national treatment' also bears upon the extent to which certain principles, rights or freedoms laid down both in the Declaration and the Charter shall be recognized, such as those implied in the concept of self-reliance, as well as on the possibility of extending the application of certain principles defined in connection with specific issues (such as, for example, international trade) to the one concerning the treatment of transnational corporations.

In any event, the inclusion of this aspect of the question within the scope of the code of conduct can be viewed as a negotiating concession towards the developed countries. Nevertheless, it is important to bear in mind that any substantive concession towards the position of the developed countries in this area will jeopardize the objectives achieved with the adoption of the Charter. On the other hand the UN Commission on Transnational Corporations has already determined the relevance of the aforementioned resolutions to the issues involved in its programme of work, adopted at its second meeting, in which the question of the formulation of a code of conduct was given the highest priority. One of the stated objectives of the Commission in submitting its programme to the Economic and Social Council was to 'strengthen the negotiating capacity of host-countries, in particular the developing countries, in their dealings with transnational corporations'. Therefore this paper will be concerned with the question of 'national treatment' in the context of the work carried out within the United Nations for the formulation of a Code of Conduct. To this effect the following aspects related to this question shall be analysed in the light of (a) the applicable principles derived from General Assembly resolutions 3201 (S–VI) and 3202 (S–VI) and the Charter, (b) the interests of the developed and developing countries as reflected in position papers and other international agreements, (c) the formulations arrived at by the Intergovernmental Working Group set up by the Commission on Transnational Corporations, and will attempt to derive some conclusions with respect to the future position of the developing countries compatible with their interest in the establishment of a new international economic order.[1]

2   PRINCIPLES APPLICABLE TO THE ISSUE OF THE TREATMENT OF TRANSNATIONAL CORPORATIONS

The Declaration for the Establishment of a New International Economic Order is based on the concept that two overriding values apply to the political and economic relations between States: equality and equity. Both values are linked inasmuch as equity, in the pursuit of equality, requires the establishment of a preferential regime in favour of the developing countries in order to 'correct inequalities and redress existing injustices' and 'make it possible to eliminate the widening gap between the developed and developing countries'.

To achieve this balance within a new international system the Declaration determines the principles which embody those values in a concrete manner. Those principles tend towards the strengthening of the power of States generally and particularly that of developing countries (individual and collective self-reliance) and towards the recognition of a preferential status in favour of developing countries as the basis for the development of the rules of the new order. Within this framework the treatment of transnational corporations and the regulation and control of their activities are given special consideration.

The following principles of the Declaration are relevant in relation to the issue under consideration:

(a) Full and effective sovereignty of every state over its natural resources and economic activities, which includes the right to nationalization, expropriation or transfer of ownership to its nationals;

(b) Regulation and supervision of the activities of transnational corporations to safeguard the interest of the national economies where they operate, on the basis of the full sovereignty of those countries;

(c) The strengthening, through individual and collective actions, of mutual economic trade, financial and technical co-operation among the developing countries, mainly on a preferential basis not extendable to the developed countries.

The Charter of Economic Rights and Duties provides a legal formulation of the above mentioned principles. Article 2 is particularly relevant to the question of the treatment by States of transnational corporations:

1. Every State has and shall freely exercise full permanent sovereignty, including possession, use and disposal, over all its wealth, natural resources and economic activities.

2. Each State has the right:

(a) To regulate and exercise authority over foreign investment within its national jurisdiction in accordance with its laws and regulations and in conformity with its national objectives and priorities. No State shall be compelled to grant preferential treatment to foreign investment.

(b) To regulate and supervise the activities of transnational corporations within its national jurisdiction and take measures to ensure that such activities comply with its laws, rules and regulations and conform with its economic and social policies. Transnational corporations shall not intervene in the internal affairs of a host State. Every State should, with full regard for its sovereign rights, co-operate with other States in the exercise of the right set forth in this sub-paragraph.

(c) To nationalize, expropriate and transfer ownership of foreign property, in which case adequate compensation should be paid by the State adopting such measures, taking into account its relevant laws and regulations and all circumstances that the State considers pertinent. In any case where the question of compensation gives rise to a controversy, it shall be settled under the domestic law of the nationalizing State and by its tribunals, unless it is freely and mutually agreed by all States concerned that other peaceful means be sought on the basis of the sovereign equality of States and in accordance with the principle of free choice of means.[2]

Other rules of the Charter are also relevant inasmuch as they relate to the right of States to determine freely their priorities and means in pursuit of development (which may have a bearing on the question of the role of foreign investment and of transnational corporations); to the co-operation among developing countries for the expansion of their mutual trade through the grant of trade preferences to other developing countries without the obligation to extend them to developed countries (which may include preferences granted to the products produced by enterprises or corporations wholly or partially owned or controlled by developing countries or their nationals); and to the principle of collective self-reliance in order to enhance the effective mobilization of the resources of developing countries (Articles 7, 21 and 23 of the Charter).

It is possible to draw the conclusion that the rationale behind the relevant provisions of the Declaration and the Charter is to ensure that States will exercise freely their sovereign right to determine their economic policies, including the right to freely determine the regime applicable to transnational corporations, however liberal or restrictive, within their jurisdiction and to definitively legitimize (since certain concepts of the 'old' order could be interpreted as colliding with those of the new system) those agreements or other international undertakings between developing countries establishing a preferential treatment not extendable to developed countries.

This, of course, was seen as a serious setback in the task of providing a legal framework compatible with the process of unrestricted trans-nationalization of economic relations which several developed countries had attempted to develop throughout more than two decades.

There is, however, one provision in Article 2.2 of the Charter that may leave room for some doubt as to its implications: 'No State shall be compelled to grant preferential treatment to foreign investment'. The meaning of the word 'compelled' in this context is not clear. However, assuming that it may be interpreted as meaning that no State is under the obligation to grant preferential treatment to foreign investment, the question arises as to whether States have, by implication, a duty to grant a no less favourable treatment than the one accorded to its nationals.

This paragraph should, rather, be considered in the light of the past experience of developing countries. The argument put forward by certain host States (for example, the United States to the Mexican government) in connection with the criteria to be applied for determining the amount to be paid as compensation for the expropriation of foreign-owned property, was that a 'minimum standard was required by international law' whether the expropriating State applies it to its own nationals or not. Thus, in this context, the concept of 'national treatment' introduced by some host countries was put forward with a view to limiting the international responsibility of the host-State with respect to the question of compensation, and of asserting the principle that questions arising from compensation in the case of expropriation are governed by the law and should be subject to the jurisdiction of the expropriating State.[3]

Therefore, if any implication relevant to the question of 'national treatment' could be derived from this provision in Article 2.2, it can only relate to the issue of compensation. On the other hand any other interpretation leading towards the recognition of this clause as an international standard would not be consistent with the practice of States as reflected in their national legislation and in other international agreements, particularly in the 'Declaration by the governments of OECD members on international investment and multinational enterprises' as will be seen in the following section.[4] Furthermore, it would appear to be inconsistent with the purpose of the other paragraphs of this Article and that of other Articles of the Charter.

3 INTERESTS OF THE DEVELOPED COUNTRIES AS REFLECTED IN POSITION PAPERS AND INTERNATIONAL AGREEMENTS

The defensive stand adopted by some developing countries during this decade with respect to foreign investment, especially in relation to the transnational corporation, as a result of the experience of their impact on the national economies — reflected in the position adopted by the Group of 77 in the various United Nations meetings in which this issue was considered and debated — has brought about a reconsideration by the industrialized countries of their strategy towards the fostering of the process of transnationalization of economic relations. This strategy involves the need of establishing a standard concerning their treatment by host States which in fact would operate as a double standard, one applicable to the economic relations between developed States and the other to the relationship between developed and developing countries. Contrary to what has been laid down in the Charter of Economic Rights and Duties where discrimination, if established, should favour the developing countries, the kind of discrimination envisaged by the developed countries would tend to favour them. In order to achieve this they would attempt to obtain, through bilateral agreements with developing countries, national treatment for their enterprises not subject to reciprocity, and to ensure a more favourable treatment with respect to certain aspects related to the protection of the investment. In this respect, the American Branch of the International Law Association has undertaken, as a response to the interest expressed by the US Government in pursuing the negotiation of new treaties that would afford greater protection to American-owned interests, particularly in the developing countries, the task of drafting a model bilateral convention on protection of private investment. As a basis for the drafting of this model, consideration has been given to the experience of several Western European countries which, in the opinion of the Committee concerned, 'have been more successful than the United States in establishing a comprehensive network of bilateral treaties protecting investments of their nationals in developing countries'. According to the 'Working checklist of Basic Protections' to be given as 'government undertakings' included in certain bilateral treaties (presumably those entered into with developing countries) for the protection of foreign investment, the following are included:

(a) Refraining from application of unreasonable or discriminatory measures impairing legally acquired rights;
(b) National treatment to engage in commercial, industrial, financial and other activities for profit subject to certain reserved activities (no reciprocity is considered);
(c) Right to acquire and dispose of personal property;
(d) National treatment and most-favoured-nation treatment in levy of taxes, fees or other charges based on reciprocity.

With respect to the last 'protection' one may well ask when would that reciprocity apply if reciprocity is not a condition for granting national treatment with respect to commercial and other activities engaged for profit. In any case, even if reciprocity for the granting of 'national treatment' would be envisaged with respect to those activities, the fact remains that that clause would benefit almost exclusively the enterprises from the industrialized countries given that the developing countries have not reached the stage of economic development that would enable their enterprises to make use of that reciprocity.

At the multilateral level the developed countries have endeavoured to offset, if not reverse, the standards established through the adoption by the UN General Assembly of the Declaration for the Establishment of an NIEO and of the Charter of Economic Rights and Duties of States.

The first step in this direction was taken by the OECD countries who adopted in 1976 a 'Declaration on International Investment and

Multinational Enterprises'[5] which determined (besides the 'Guidelines for Multinational Enterprises' which are annexed to the Declaration) their policy towards a number of issues related to the treatment of foreign investment. The question of granting 'national treatment' is considered in the following manner:

> The governments of the OECD Member Countries declare . . . National Treatment II.
>
> 1. That member countries should, consistent with their needs to maintain public order, to protect their essential security interests and to fulfil commitments relating to international peace and security, accord to enterprises operating in their territories and owned or controlled directly or indirectly by nationals of another member country (hereinafter referred to as 'Foreign-Controlled Enterprises') treatment under their laws, regulations and administrative practices, consistent with international law and no less favourable than that accorded in like situations to domestic enterprises (hereinafter referred to as 'National Treatment');
>
> 2. That Member countries will consider applying 'National Treatment' in respect of countries other than Member countries;
>
> 3. That Member countries will endeavour to ensure that their territorial sub-divisions apply 'National Treatment';
>
> 4. That this Declaration does not deal with the right of Member countries to regulate the entry of foreign investment or the conditions of establishment of foreign enterprises . . .
>
> Review II. That they will review the above matters within three years with a view to improving the effectiveness of international economic co-operation among Member countries on issues relating to international investment and multinational enterprises.

Notwithstanding the aim to set a standard, the provisions set forth in the Declaration require voluntary compliance and, therefore, do not have a binding effect on the countries which signed it. Furthermore, the decision adopted by the Council on National Treatment establishes a procedure for notifying the Council of measures adopted by the Member countries which depart from 'National Treatment', though it also entrusts the Committee on International Investment and Multinational Enterprises with the reviewing of 'the application of National Treatment (including exceptions thereto) with a view to extending such application', and the making of proposals, 'as and when necessary' in this connection.

The commitment of OECD countries to the application of 'national treatment' to their mutual relations does not appear to be very strong and seems indeed shallow with respect to its extension to other countries. It would be interesting to ascertain what new developments have occurred that might change this impression. Given the difficulties that appear to exist in the application of this clause between the OECD Member countries, the question arises as to what was the purpose of putting it forward as a standard.

This question of 'national treatment' was further pursued by the industrialized countries in the United Nations Commission on Transnational Corporations. In determining the areas of concern related to the relations between transnational corporations and governments,[6] a number of developed countries stated that one of such areas (in fact the first identified) is:

> The extent to which host country legislation and regulation may discriminate, either in favour of TNCs or against TNCs as compared to domestic enterprises, in the treatment of enterprises on the basis of whether or not such enterprises are under foreign control; the extent to which any such discriminatory treatment affects the activities of TNCs as well as the contribution of TNCs to the development objectives of host countries.

This document also contains an indication of the possible value these countries attached to the OECD Declaration and its consideration as a precedent for the determination of international standards:

> The extent to which existing codes of conduct and guidelines concerned with any aspect of the range of issues relating to the activities of TNCs may already exist, including the study of materials underlying such codes and guidelines, commentaries thereon and the implementation and/or effects of such codes and guidelines upon TNCs and Governments.

It is obvious, by comparing the relevant provision of the OECD Declaration with the relevant 'area of concern' that the real issue here is the one related to discrimination against transnational enterprises since the 'national treatment' clause is referred to as a minimum standard.

As has already been noted, upon the insistence of the developed countries the issue concerning the treatment of transnational corporations was re-opened in the context of the formulation of a Code of Conduct. The question of the inclusion of a provision on 'national treatment' is, therefore, before the Intergovernmental Working Group.

4   INTERESTS OF DEVELOPING COUNTRIES AS
     REFLECTED IN POLICY PAPERS AND OTHER
     INTERNATIONAL DOCUMENTS AND AGREEMENTS.

Much speculation has been made, after the Paris Conference on International Economic Co-operation (CIEC), on the degree of differences in the position of the developing countries and on the thin layer of solidarity among them. Notwithstanding the fact that indeed some very important differences do exist with respect to certain areas, the issues concerning the need to safeguard and increase the bargaining power of developing countries in real terms, and the need for fostering individual and collective self-reliance (as a means to ensure that a re-definition of structural economic relationship *vis-à-vis* the developed countries will benefit them) have been a recurring theme among developing countries, which allows one to infer that these words form only the bases of their solidarity in the North–South dialogue. In this respect, as has been reflected in the UN Declaration on the establishment of an NIEO and in the Charter of Economic Rights and Duties of States, self-reliance includes both the right of granting a preferential treatment to national economic interests, as defined by the State, at the national level as well as the right to grant preferential treatment, among others, to developing countries without being obliged to extend such treatment to other countries. The whole thrust of self-reliance rests upon the acceptance and protection of these rights by the international community. In fact, these rights have been and are exercised by the developed countries as has been seen already in the previous section. Notwithstanding this practice, the experience of developing countries has been that the developed nations have exerted their influence and, when necessary, their power to demand from them national treatment as a minimum and, most times, more favourable treatment at the national level, thus deepening the gap of an unequal relationship. This was reflected — amongst others — in several areas related to foreign investment. Therefore, the issue of self-reliance at the national level involves as a pre-condition the requirement that no State shall be compelled either to grant 'more favourable treatment' or 'national treatment'.

The position and interests of the developing countries relative to these matters is reflected in the note submitted by the Group of 77 to the UN Commission on Transnational Corporations entitled 'List of areas of concern regarding the operations and activities of transnational corporations', where (amongst others) the following concerns were put forward:

(a) Preferential treatment demanded by transnational corporations in relation to national enterprises;

(b) Obstruction by transnational corporations of the efforts of the host country to assume its rightful responsibility and exercise effective control over the development and management of its resources, in contravention of the accepted principle of permanent sovereignty over their natural resources;

(c) Acquisition and control by transnational corporations of national corporations of national, locally capitalized enterprises through controlled provision of technology among other means;

(d) Super-imposition of imported technology without any adaptation to local conditions, creating various types of distortions;

(e) Failure by transnational corporations to promote research and development in host countries;

(f) Obstruction or limitation by transnational corporations of access by host countries to world technology.

The position paper presented by a group of Latin American countries, which expands on the concerns expressed by the Group of 77 is in a way more explicit in defining the powers of the state related to the issue of foreign investment and transnational corporations which bears upon the demand for recognition by the developed countries of 'national treatment' as a minimum standard and goal to be achieved generally.

In the first place, reference is made to the principle (recognized in Article 2 of the Charter) that 'the transnational corporations shall be subject to the laws and regulations of the host country and, in case of litigation, they should be subject to the exclusive jurisidiction of the courts of the country in which they operate'. The explanatory note which follows determines the rationale behind this statement as:

the reflection of an old Latin American concern which has its origin in the claim of the transnational corporations to a status, or to be beneficiaries of a privileged treatment, in the country where they operate. To validate this claim would signify the provision of a preferential and discriminatory status in favour of foreign enterprises. It would also pre-suppose the establishment of different treatment for nationals and foreigners, which would be unacceptable. But in the last analysis, the exemption of transnational corporations from the international juridical order would bring, as a consequence, injury to the fundamental basis upon which the sovereignty of the state resides, which implies full competence over the entire area in which the power of the state is exercised.

The third paragraph of the explanatory note may be the source of some confusion and misunderstanding inasmuch as it may be taken as suggesting 'national treatment' as a standard applicable to all aspects related to the economic life of a country. What is emphasized in the explanatory note is the inadmissibility of the pre-supposition that a state is under obligation to place its own nationals in a situation where they are discriminated against, which would be the case if it were recognized that foreigners (individuals or enterprises) are not subject to the laws and to the jurisdiction of the courts of a State. Therefore, with respect to this principle and to the extent to which a derogatory position may affect unfavourably and *ab initio* the status of nationals *vis-à-vis* foreigners, both are considered equally subject to the laws and jurisdiction of the State. This does not mean that a limitation exists as to the right of granting, for economic purposes, preferential treatment to nationals (or to any other, for that matter) by law or through other measures (such as the signing of an agreement of treaty). In fact, this right is implicit in the concept of 'full competence over the entire area in which the power of the state is exercised'.

There are of course a series of implied and related principles. In the first place, subjection to the law of a State means that certain minimum standards required by international law should be respected. This question of defining minimum standards is in itself a very complex, delicate and controversial issue which includes the application of human rights standards, a full survey of which would be beyond the scope of this paper. Suffice it to say that insofar as economic and developmental policies are concerned, these standards do not apply equally in all respects to nationals and aliens (including enterprises). Equality of treatment is required, for example, with respect to access to courts and administrative tribunals or, in cases of expropriation or nationalization, with respect to the criteria for determining the amount of compensation. In other respects, the law of a State may grant preferential treatment to nationals in pursuit of certain political or economic objectives and may even extend them to some specific foreigners (as may be found in some regional arrangements) or under certain conditions. This is implied both in the papers submitted by the Group of 77 and by a group of Latin American countries which express their concern in the following areas:

(a) Full exercise by the home country of its permanent sovereignty over all its wealth, natural resources and economic activities;
(b) Creation of indigenous technology;
(c) Subjection of transnational corporations to policies, objectives and priorities for development;

(d) Conduct of the operations of transnational corporations in a way which results in a net transfer of resources (especially financial resources) to the host country;

(e) Transfer of useful technology;

(f) Promotion of exports.

The exercise by the State of its powers to regulate economic activity in a way conducive to the attainment of certain goals may imply — though not necessarily — the establishment of preferential treatment, the extension of which to all foreign companies would jeopardize the effect of an economic policy oriented towards their achievement. In certain cases the need to control economic mechanisms at the national level may involve the need to establish a different treatment for transnational corporations operating in very sensitive sectors of the economy. In others, the need to stimulate national industry or technology may lead a state to provide incentives applicable only to nationals. In others still, given the need to ensure that vital and scarce national resources are deployed adequately, the state may decide that foreign capital or enterprises shall not have access to long-term credit provided by national financial institutions, or shall not subsidize them while subsidizing national enterprises operating in the same sector.

An example of what kind of interests of developing countries may be involved in the issue of 'national treatment' is the Andean Foreign Investment Code (Decision 24 of the Commission of the Cartagena Agreement approved in 1970),[7] which established a common regime of treatment for foreign capital and of trademarks, patents, licences and royalties with a view to giving 'preference, in the economic development of the subregion, to authentically national capital and enterprises of the Member countries', in order among other objectives, to 'strengthen the negotiating capacity of the Member countries *vis-à-vis* other countries, enterprises which supply capital and technology, and international organizations which are concerned with these matters'. As made explicit in the introductory part which quotes the 'consensus of Vina del Mar' in this respect Decision 24 establishes a link between this kind of preferential treatment and the principle of individual and collective self-reliance, when stating that 'economic growth and social progress are the responsibilities of their peoples and that attainment of national and regional objectives depend fundamentally on the effort of each country'.

Decision 24 establishes a series of mechanisms and procedures to make possible 'a growing participation of national capital in existing or future foreign enterprises in Member countries', among others:

(1) The withholding of authorization of any direct foreign investment in activities which are adequately covered by existing enterprises, or for the purpose of acquiring shares, participations or rights owned by national investors;

(2) Previous authorization of foreign credits contracted by an enterprise;

(3) No endorsement or guaranteeing in any form by governments of the Member countries, either directly or through official or semi-official institutions, to external credit transactions carried out by foreign enterprises in which the State does not participate;

(4) Domestic credit of foreign enterprises is restricted to short-term credit only;

(5) Establishment of incentives for the promotion of sub-regional technology and protection thereof;

(6) The advantages deriving from the duty-free programme of the Cartagena Agreement is restricted to products produced by national or mixed enterprises of the Member countries;

(7) Foreign enterprises of the production of which 80 per cent or more goes into exports to the markets of third world countries, are exempted from the provisions regarding the obligation to place for sale for purchase by national investors of shares, participation or rights for the transformation of such enterprises into 'mixed enterprises' (as defined in the Decision), though in this case their products shall not enjoy the advantages deriving from the duty-free programme of the Cartagena Agreement;

(8) Foreign bankers operating in the territory of Member countries are not entitled to receive local deposits in current accounts, savings accounts or time deposits;

(9) Member countries shall not grant to foreign investment any treatment more favourable than that granted to national investors.

It is, therefore, clear the existing regimes adopted by some developing countries, of which the Andean Foreign Investment Code is only one example, in furtherance of the principle of individual or collective self-reliance, have established a preferential treatment which benefits their nationals or those foreign enterprises which adapt to the conditions and regulations established by such countries with a view to ensuring the achievement of those objectives, goals and priorities required for its development.

5   THE QUESTION OF NATIONAL TREATMENT IN THE
    CONTEXT OF THE FORMULATION OF A CODE OF
    CONDUCT BY THE UN COMMISSION ON
    TRANSNATIONAL CORPORATIONS

As has already been stated, the Intergovernmental Working Group (IWG) on a Code of Conduct decided upon the insistence of the developed countries to include, among the areas to be covered by the Code, the question of the treatment of transnational corporations by the countries in which they operate. At its seventh session[8] it will have before it a document[9] containing formulations by its Chairman of provisions to be included in a code of conduct on transnational corporations. A draft code of conduct or a report by the IWG on the progress towards its promulgation is expected to be presented at the next session of the Commission on Transnational Corporations.[10]

This document, which according to the Introductory Note should be regarded as an attempt to consolidate the discussions so far held by the IWG, includes as paragraph 47 the following provision:

> Consistent with national needs to maintain public order and to protect national security, transnational corporations should be accorded the same treatment under national laws, regulations and administrative practices of countries in which they operate as that accorded to domestic enterprises, in situations where the operations of transnational corporations are comparable to those of domestic enterprises.

This paragraph runs counter to the interests of the developing countries to the extent that it establishes the 'national treatment' clause as a minimum standard to be applied to transnational enterprises, thus divesting the developing countries of the rights that constitute pre-conditions for the exercise of self-reliance policies, with the further effect of diminishing the bargaining power of the developing countries (which, according to the objectives set forth by the Commission for its programme of work,[11] should be strengthened, particularly in their dealings with transnational corporations). This standard, even in the case of the code being voluntary, as the developed countries have proposed, would offset the provisions established in the Charter. One may well imagine the arguments put forward in favour of the inclusion of this clause.

In the first place, it may be argued that the 'national treatment' clause would apply and benefit equally developing and developed countries. In fact, this argument is based on the assumption that all countries have equal *effective* rights and the capacity and power to use and enforce them. It is wrong, of course, and the reasonings and conclusions derived are fallacious. One relevant question that should be asked is how many transnational corporations from developing countries would be in a position to request 'national treatment', in order to determine who will benefit from it if that clause is accepted as a standard. Another question relevant to the issue, is to ask, bearing in mind regimes of the nature of the Andean code, who it is who will lose as a consequence of the recognition of the clause as a principle. A third very pertinent question to ask is why a clause which has not been practised as a general or international standard by any significant group of countries, not even by the OECD countries, should now be enthroned as a principal applicable to the treatment by States of foreign enterprises.

Secondly, one may speculate that another argument in favour of the formulation in paragraph 47 might be that it represents a 'compromise solution' between the position of the developing and the developed countries. The formulation of the OECD Declaration refers to a treatment 'no less favourable than that accorded . . . to domestic enterprises' thus implying that a more favourable treatment would be an acceptable standard as well. This formulation of the clause would be in disagreement with the position adopted both by the Group of 77 and by the Latin American countries as expressed in their papers submitting the 'areas of concern'. Therefore, the 'compromise solution' would be to formulate the clause in a way that would avoid the implication of legitimizing discrimination against nationals.

Had it been put forward, this kind of argument, (quite common in international negotiations) would confuse the issues at stake, since what would be put to the question, if the clause were accepted, is the right of every State to adopt measures of self-reliance which derive from its full sovereignty over all its wealth, natural resources and economic activities, as recognized in the Charter, and not the legitimacy of the requirement or demand made to a State, to discriminate against its nationals. In other words, what is disputed is the definition of a structural relationship between developed and developing countries, implying the recognition or the denial of the right of the latter to exercise as far as they are concerned some kind of control on the process of globalization of economic relations.

Among the options open to the developing countries with respect to the issue of the 'national treatment' clause in the context of the present negotiations relating to the formulation of a Code of Conduct, the following may be considered;

(a) Refusal to include any such clause in the Code of Conduct;
(b) Restricted acceptance of the clause limiting its application to the aspects of access of foreign enterprises to the tribunals of the country in which they operate and of compensation in cases of expropriation or nationalization;
(c) Acceptance of the clause but limiting it with the insertion of a sentence enabling developing countries to depart from it in exercise of their right of unilateral or collective self-reliance as recognized by the Declaration of Principles of the NIEO and the Charter of Economic Rights and Duties of States.

This provision would not preclude developing countries from freely accepting on a case-by-case basis the granting of 'preferential' or 'National Treatment' to whatever country or foreign enterprise they decide it should be accorded to; what it would prevent is the establishment of a general standard which would be used to promote the generalized recognition by developing countries of 'National Treatment' as a legitimate demand.

NOTES AND REFERENCES

1 The Intergovernmental Working Group held its seventh meeting in March 1979 and the Commission on Transnational Corporations met in May 1979.
2 The Programme of Action did not include the question of the treatment of transnational corporations among the areas to be covered by the Code of Conduct. The Code was to be addressed exclusively to the behaviour of transnational corporations.
3 Other host-states simply refused to recognize the existence of an obligation to compensate, as in the case of the Soviet Union.
4 Report of the Centre on Transnational Corporations: *Transnational Corporations: Issues involved in the formulation of a Code of Conduct*, pp. 31–32.
5 According to the foreword of the Secretary General of the OECD, 'the consensus thus reached (which does not include Turkey who did not participate in the Declaration and abstained from the decisions) represents a joint philosophy and common approach on the part of a group of countries accounting for most international investment. This should have an influence even beyond the OECD area'.
6 Annex II of the Report on the Second Session of the Commission on Transnational Corporations.
7 Decision 24 was modified later, in 1971 by Decision 37 and 37A.
8 To be held in the month of March 1979.
9 Document E/C. 10/AC. 2/8.
10 To be held in May 1979.
11 See Report of the second meeting.

9   Transfer of Technology and Developing Countries

*Oscar Shachter**

Transfer of technology is one of the currently popular United Nations topics. It is by no means a new subject. United Nations organs and the Secretariat took it up thirty years ago and it has never ceased to appear on the agenda or work programmes of some UN bodies. At present at least a dozen UN organs concern themselves with the subject. Several international conferences have also dealt with it and others surely will. It is not entirely clear that such multifarious activities have significantly helped needy countries. It is somewhat clearer that they have created employment opportunities for numerous experts, even for lawyers.

From the very beginning, the remedies could be divided into broad segments. One concerned 'structural weaknesses' in the developing countries and in the international system. The main concerns under this heading were the weak bargaining positions of the developing countries, the lack of adequate domestic institutions to select and make good use of technology, the shortages of trained personnel, the inadequate facilities for selecting appropriate technology — in short, all the conditions that accompany 'underdevelopment'. The second broad segment was concerned with laws and contracts with particular emphasis on restrictive business practices. Remedies were considered to lie in legal regulations — both international and national and in more equitable contractual arrangements. Obviously, this second area is of primary interest to lawyers.

The proposed code of conduct deals only generally with the structural weaknesses. It includes, for example, provision on technical assistance, training and other forms of international co-operation which would strengthen the capabilities of recipient developing countries. But most

*Columbia University.

of the Code is naturally directed to legal regulation. It seeks to prescribe obligations and prohibitions. It does this especially in respect of restrictive business practices. Some two dozen different varieties of such restrictive practices are described and prohibited outright or under certain conditions. All of such restrictions are disadvantageous in themselves to the recipients and ideally should be eliminated. However, many of the restrictions are inherently bound up with the commercial character of the technology transfer and the proprietary interest in technology. An obvious example is the common provision that precludes the recipient from exporting the product and thereby reducing the market for the supplier. But if that provision is prohibited by law, will the supplier refuse to sell the technology as he is free to do? The issue therefore is not whether the restriction can be eliminated by treaty or law but whether the technology will be made available at all. The treaty may have an effective prohibition but how far can legal rules be used to impose a duty on the private sector to provide technology against its own perceived interest? That duty is, to some extent, envisaged under the draft Law of the Sea Convention but there it is an element in a complicated package of quid pro quos.

It should be noted that some restrictive practices seem abusive and unfair even in the light of commercial interests. An example is the grant-back clause under which a recipient who makes an improvement in the technology is obliged to give ('grant back') that improvement to the supplier alone. Tying arrangements are also often seen as unfair in that they limit the ability of the recipient to go into the market for items he needs because the supplier has, as a condition of the sale, imposed an obligation to buy such items from the supplier exclusively. Developing countries naturally have objected to this and have demanded 'unpackaging'. It is not certain they will always benefit from unpackaging; in some cases, economic and technical benefits may come with the package that exceed the benefit of shopping for bargains in the market. There are situations where the initial problem for a developing country is the inability to combine all the essential factors — finance, equipment, knowledge, skill, etc. — in an effective working unit. In such cases, the ability of a multinational firm to provide the entire package may be more helpful than the right to shop around for the various items so as to get the best bargains. This is mentioned here for the general point that a rule or prohibition intended to enhance the position of the developing country may operate against its interest.

On the issues of exceptions and derogations, first, there is the question whether specified practices should be flatly prohibited or whether the prohibition should apply only where the practice in the particular case is unreasonable. The latter — the so-called 'rule of reason' — has been favoured by the developed countries and generally opposed by the developing countries. The latter obviously fear that a test of reasonableness would weaken the prohibition. The absence of adjudicative procedures contributes to that weakness. However, the developing countries seek their own form of escape clause, which would provide that when a recipient developing country decides that a transfer of technology is in its public interest, it shall be valid notwithstanding the rules against restrictive practices. Thus instead of a 'rule of reason', there would be a very broad exception available to the developing countries only. The effect would be that the strict binding code favoured by the Group of 77 would be much less 'binding' on the developing countries; indeed, they could 'opt out' of the rules whenever they so decided.

It is easy to see why that exception is desired. In many cases, a recipient may find it to its advantage to agree to a 'package' or to a restrictive clause because other elements of the deal would be favourable. Or it may be that there would be no transfer at all without a restrictive clause. But one may ask whether the right to make such unilateral exceptions would not result in the breakdown of the entire system. Might it not result in the developing countries 'under-cutting' each other by accepting restrictions otherwise prohibited? Developed countries might also be adversely affected by the uncertainty inherent in special deals that depart from what are supposed to be binding rules of a code. There is an additional consequence. If the developing countries are accorded a unilateral right to opt out of the rules, would not the developed countries demand similar rights or other concessions before they accept the code? They now press for excluding intra-corporate transactions (an important category of restrictive practices). The socialist countries, in turn, wish a broad exception for State-owned enterprises. The effect of one broad exception is to breed others. We may end up with a code of rules that is more illusory than real because of such exceptions. Whether that is desirable or not depends mainly on whether one considers that sweeping legal prohibitions and obligations are a useful way to promote transfer of technology. I must confess to some scepticism about that proposition. It seems to me that structural reforms such as those I referred to earlier are much more useful and that the attempt to impose legal restrictions may impede the flow of technology. However, there are good reasons to seek to build a common consensus and a set of legal rules that would bring about the elimination of certain abusive and inequitable practices. For that reason, I favour continued efforts to achieve a code though I would not expect a code to make a major difference to the actual flow of technology.

Two other questions of legal significance may be discussed briefly. One relates to applicable law and the settlement of disputes about technology agreements. The developed countries insist that parties should be free to choose the law and forum to settle their disputes. The socialist countries are basically in agreement with the principle of the autonomy of the parties in regard to applicable law. They also favour arbitration, as agreed. In contrast the developing countries insist that the law of the receiving country must apply and its jurisdiction shall be exclusive. They also reject any reference to international law standards as favoured by the developed market states. This problem is difficult to resolve. It may be a good subject for further analysis by a group of legal experts even if the underlying difference transcends legal issues.

The other question relates to the issue of international machinery to apply the code and further compliance. It is virtually certain that a code will involve in some way an international body that would provide a forum for exchange of views between States on the application of the code. This is likely to become a forum for specific complaints. The developed countries wish to avoid that body (which they see as necessarily a political organ dominated by the majority of developing countries) acting 'like a tribunal' and reaching conclusions on the conduct of particular governments or parties to a transfer of technology agreement. Whether such a body may be established by agreement remains to be seen. Certainly the issue of 'balanced representation' will have to be faced. It will also be necessary to agree on the scope of authority in regard to individual complaints and findings of fact and legal conclusions. No easy answers are available.

Part III

LAW OF THE SEA AND THE NIEO

10 The International Seabed and the Third UN Law of the Sea Conference: Some NIEO Issues

*T. Koh**

As a lawyer, miseducated at Harvard, and thus preoccupied with searching for specificity in concepts, I have always had some difficulty with the concept of the NIEO. My problem is, therefore, compounded when I am invited to speak about the interface between the NIEO on the one hand and the current negotiations in the Law of the Sea Conference on the other. I will try to do my best by identifying four areas in which there is an interface or intersection between very specific objectives of the NIEO and the Law of the Sea (LOS) Conference.

Let me begin with the first objective of the NIEO. One of the declared objectives of the NIEO and, indeed, the one on which the Group of 77 at the moment places the greatest interest is the establishment of an integrated programme of commodities supported by a common fund. The economic objective of this is to stabilize the prices of commodity exports by developing countries. If I am right in identifying this as one of the objectives of the NIEO then I hope I am also right in suggesting that there is an interface or intersection between this and one aspect of the negotiations in the Law of the Sea Conference. In the first Committee of the Conference and in Negotiating Group No. 1, which deals with matters concerning seabed exploitation, we have agreed that the international seabed authority which we propose to establish will be authorized to negotiate for and to participate in commodity arrangements and commodity agreements in respect of the four metals which are to be found in manganese nodules − nickel, copper, cobalt and manganese. I think this is a very significant aspect of the LOS Conference. The International Seabed Authority, by the consent of all participants, North and South, OECD as well as the Group of 77, agree that this authority

*Permanent Representative of Singapore to the United Nations.

will have the mandate to negotiate for, and to become party to, commodity arrangements and agreements.

Second, when commodity agreements or arrangements come into existence on these four commodities, the International Seabed Authority is authorized to become a party to such agreements and arrangements and production from the seabed will thereafter be regulated by the commodity arrangements and agreements. Now, the sticking point is this — until such commodity arrangements or agreements come into existence what is to be done? And here there are two points of view in the Conference. The industrialized countries say that for an interim period of twenty-five years, production from the seabed may be controlled. The developing countries, especially the developing countries that produce these four minerals, argue that the interim period should not be limited in time but shall exist for so long as the commodity arrangements and agreements do not exist. But anyway there is common ground between the two sides that something ought to be done in the interim period, however the interim period may be conceived. And what is to be done? Well, it is also the common position of North and South that in the interim period the production of these four metals from manganese nodules shall be controlled by a specific formula. And what is that formula? The formula, very briefly, is this: of the four metals, you pick nickel because it is felt that production of seabed nickel will have the most appreciable effect on the price of nickel as compared to the other three metals. You then look at the historical trends in the world consumption of nickel and you thereby work out the growth factor. In the interim period the production of nickel, and therefore of the other three metals as well, is to be limited to 60 per cent of the growth factor in the world demand for nickel. Land-based production, of course, is unlimited. If land-based production were more economic than seabed production it could cater for the entire growth segment. But seabed production is limited by a ceiling and the ceiling is 60 per cent of the growth segment of nickel. At the moment both the EEC countries and Japan are not happy with this production control formula and it is difficult to predict what will happen at the eighth Session of the Conference.

Let me turn next to another aspect of the NIEO: transfer of technology. The developing countries, members of the Group of 77, aspire to obtain transfer of technology, more rapidly than they have in the past, and on fairer terms, from the developed countries. If I am right in identifying this as one of the objectives of the NIEO then the question is — is there an intersection between this objective and the negotiations in the Law of the Sea Conference? The answer to this question is yes. I would like to describe very briefly where the intersecting points are. In the negotiations, the developing countries have demanded as one of the prices which the industralized countries must pay for the acceptance of the parallel system of exploitation, that a contractor who obtains a mining contract from the International Seabed Authority, shall have a legal obligation to transfer his technology to the Enterprise. There is provision in the document I have already referred to which says roughly, that after a mining contract has been awarded and if that fails, then it may be referred to compulsory arbitration. The criterion which will be used in the compulsory arbitration is that the technology shall be transferred or sold on fair and reasonable commercial terms. Now, what is the state of this text in the Conference? The Group of 77 can live with this although some of them would prefer to make it even stronger, to make it a precondition for the award of the contract, rather than leave it as an obligation which can be enforced after a contract has been awarded. The industrialized countries, as I understand them, cannot accept this mandatory transfer of technology and certainly the industries, the private sector, in these industrialized countries, all claim that they cannot accept this obligation. Whether this is true or not, whether this is just a bluff in order to obtain some concessions from the Group of 77 or whether they are asking for trade-offs in other areas I am not sure.

There is a clause in our present text which is sometimes referred to as the 'Brazilian Clause'. The so-called 'Brazilian Clause' is a provision that would also require the contractor to transfer technology to a developing country. The position of Brazil, being one of the more developed of the developing countries, is that it has aspirations that soon it too will be a seabed miner and not merely a beneficiary of the exploitation of seabed resources by industrialized countries. So Brazil is naturally very interested in a mandatory transfer of technology to developing countries. The position of Brazil is supported by other developing countries, especially the more developed amongst them.

Let me turn to my third point. Another objective of the NIEO is to obtain for the developing countries a more equitable share of the power of decision making in international financial institutions. Now, if I am right in identifying this as another objective to the NIEO, then I would like to draw attention to an intersecting point between this and one aspect of our negotiations in the Conference. The International Seabed Authority cannot, I think, be accurately described as an international financial institution of the same genre as the World Bank or the IMF. It clearly is not. In fact one can very logically argue that it is a unique institution with no precedent. It is an institution to be established to control and manage the exploitation of resources which are the common property of all of us and there is really no precedent for the International Seabed Authority. But some of the issues which have arisen in our negotiations on the composition of the Council of the International Seabed Authority, the distribution of voting power, and the procedures for taking decisions are very similar to the kind of issues that have been raised about giving the LDCs a more equitable share of the power of decision-making in international financial institutions. The ongoing discussions on the composition of the Council and on the voting procedure are extremely difficult, and they involve matters of principles which are felt very strongly on both sides of the negotiating table as well as realities of economic and political power which one has to take cognizance of. Let us take two examples. The developing countries insist that we now live in a day and age when the only applicable principle in decision-making is one State one vote and that the days of the veto power, the days of permanent Members, the days of weighted voting are gone. On the other side, our industrialized colleagues remind us that decisions taken by the UN General Assembly have no binding effect on anyone and indeed, in most cases, have no impact on the economic behaviour of States of their private entities but decisions taken by the Council of the International Seabed Authority will have a very real impact on the economic behaviour of States and private entities. They, therefore, argue that those States which have a greater economic stake in seabed mining ought to have commensurate power in the Council. And somehow one must balance the aspirations of the Third World which is embodied in the 'One State One Vote' principle and the aspirations and fears of the industrialized countries that their very real economic interests will be overridden in the Council. One has somehow to vindicate the principle but safeguard the interests of the industrialized countries. One has somehow to think of a meeting point between the Group of 77, that has argued that the composition of the Council shall be governed by simple, geographical distribution and the industrialized countries, which claim that it is more logical if its composition were to reflect the different categories of special interest – the category of land-based producing countries, and on the other side, the category of countries which will make major investments in seabed mining.

Let me turn to my fourth and last point. I am afraid that I am going to make myself very unpopular on this fourth point with some of my colleagues in the LOS Conference. But nevertheless I will make it. If I am right in thinking that an overriding objective of the NIEO is to narrow the existing gap between the rich and the poor nations I think it is pertinent to close my remarks by asking: will the new Law of the Sea Treaty promote this objective? I said I would make myself unpopular but I wish to argue that far from promoting this objective the new Law of the Sea Treaty is likely to widen the gap between the rich North and the poor South. You will ask me why I say this. I say this because with the establishment of the 200 mile exclusive economic zone, with the inexorable, and in my view, the unstoppable tendency by coastal States to claim not only the Continental Shelf but the whole of the Continental Margin, my calculations, and these calculations can be confirmed by any geographer, is that most of the ocean's wealth, especially in the form of offshore oil and gas resources, will be reaped by the world's rich and powerful nations, especially the United States, the Soviet Union, the United Kingdom, Japan, Norway, Canada, Australia and New Zealand. Only a very small handful of developing countries will make major gains of living and non-living resources from the new Treaty. The great majority of the developing countries, especially the land-locked countries, the least developed countries, will gain little or nothing. So I think those of us who belong to the Group of 77 must sometimes be troubled in our own conscience as to why we have designed a new Law of the Sea Treaty which, instead of building a more progressive and equitable world order for the oceans, appears to have the very paradoxical effect of bringing new and greater wealth to the rich nations of the North and a very in-equitable, and in my view, undesirable consequence for the many miserably poor countries of Asia and Africa.

11 The Future Legal Regime of Seabed Resources and the NIEO: Some Issues

*Felipe H. Paollilo**

There are certain noteworthy developments in the Conference on the Law of the Sea that are relevant to some of the basic aspects of the new international economic order. The evolution of the position of the Group of 77 on the question of the exploitation of the resources of the seabed reflects some of the attitudes and concerns that have inspired the Declaration on the establishment of the NIEO.

If a more equitable distribution of the world's wealth and power among nations is the fundamental goal of the new international economic order, then the oceans and the seabed will, with their vast riches and their changing legal status, provide particularly appropriate areas for the implementation of such a goal.

There are at least three main reasons that make the current negotiations on the Law of the Sea an event of particular relevance for the establishment of the NIEO. In the first place, due to the increasing importance of the seas and their resources in the economic life of the nations, it seems impossible to conceive of any future international economic system without including in it the economy of the oceans. Secondly, to be effective, the principles and purposes of the NIEO have to be applied to all economic activities, on land as well as in the sea. And thirdly, because the traditional legal order of the seas is either collapsing or is not adequate to solve the problems posed by the new needs of the international community, the new uses of the oceans, and the development of the marine technology. The oceans provide the ideal environment to test the set of legal and political concepts underlying the NIEO, such as sovereign equality, interdependence, common interest and co-operation. It is no

*Third UN Law of the Sea Conference

wonder that the Conference has been called in this context a 'laboratory' where new ideas, institutions and goals are being proposed and analysed.

So far the most daring concept being tested in this laboratory is that of declaring the seabed beyond the national jurisdiction and its resources as the common heritage of mankind. This concept embodies in itself some of the basic principles on which the NIEO is founded. The common heritage of mankind involves the substitution of the traditional ideas of territorial sovereignty, national interest and free exploitation with the ideas of community, non-appropriation, international management and equitable sharing of benefits.

The principle of common heritage of mankind has been embodied in a Declaration of the General Assembly which secured an overwhelming majority of the votes of the members of the international community. The impact of the Declaration on political realities may be measured by the fact that all the countries in the Conference, without exception, are negotiating on the assumption that the provisions of the future convention dealing with the seabed will be based on that principle. Even the most conservative positions, that is the position held by some of the industrialized countries during the first sessions of the Conference, were based on the acceptance of this principle and its implications.

Of course, there have been and there still are differences about how to implement this basic principle. These differences seemed to be irreconcilable during the early stages of the negotiations. Then the developed countries maintained that to make the idea of the common heritage of mankind a reality, it was necessary to rely on a system of exploitation based on free access to the deep seabed (the Area) and payment of royalties from private enterprises and consortia to an international organization. The developing countries gave greater weight to the idea of international co-operation and management, and proposed a system of exploitation in which an international body, the Authority, would play a virtually monopolistic role.

This initial opposition was considerably reduced through long and difficult negotiations seeking agreement on the middle ground. Agreement seems to have been reached by the acceptance of the so-called 'parallel' system in which the Authority, through the international Enterprise, as well as States and other entities would participate simultaneously in the exploitation of the resources of the area according to a somewhat complex system of rights and duties, checks and balances. The development of the negotiations on this particular issue may be seen as a clear example of the realization that the interests neither of the developed nor of the developing countries can be secured in isolation — one of the basic premises of the Declaration for the establishment of the NIEO.

There are two features of the parallel system, which will almost certainly be included in the text of the Convention and which respond to the philosophy of the New International Economic Order. The first one is that the exploitation of the Area and its resources shall be carried out according to the provisions of the Convention and the policies and rules set out by the Authority, in such a manner as to meet some specific economic objectives set forth in the Convention for the common interest of all countries. Amongst these objectives are the following: the orderly development and rational management of the resources of the Area; the availability of minerals; just and stable prices for minerals; and the protection of developing countries producers of the same minerals to be produced from the Area. All these involve some form of international production planning or international regulation of minerals originating in the Area, including the limitation of production and the participation in commodity agreements in order to maintain the prices and income of developing countries engaged in land-based mining. Therefore, negotiations on these questions must be considered as an application of the general principles of the NIEO related to raw materials.

The second feature is that all the benefits, financial and others, derived from the exploitation of the Area, would be shared by all countries taking into particular consideration the interests and needs of developing countries. It is in this area that one of the most interesting developments has taken place in the current negotiations. The idea of exploiting the Area and its resources for the benefit of mankind has evolved during the negotiations in such a way that its meaning and consequences are today substantially wider than those that the authors of the Declaration could possibly have imagined eight years ago. In the first place, the concept of benefits has been expanded through the various texts of negotiation and it now includes not only the financial benefits derived from the marketing of minerals produced from the Area but also other non-financial benefits. In the discussions held in the Seabed Committee and in the Conference the following non-financial benefits have been mentioned: availability of additional mineral resources, increasing knowledge of the marine environment and seabed area, stability of raw material markets, development and acquisition of technology, etc.

This conceptual expansion has a direct impact on the structuring of the system of exploitation, namely, on the determination of 'who' will exploit the area and 'how' the area will be exploited. Indeed, while a system of international licensing with free access to the Area for national enterprises might have ensured optimum revenues to be distributed amongst all countries, it does not provide in the view of the developing countries an appropriate framework for the creation and sharing of other kinds of benefits such as the acquisition of technology or training of personnel.

This consideration leads us to the second conceptual evolution, even more important than that of the expansion of the concept of benefits, namely the priority given by developing countries to the idea of participation in the activities in the Area, over the idea of merely sharing in the benefits. Actually the developing countries are not happy with a mere distribution of revenues. The view taken by them is that there are benefits to be derived from participation as well and that without such participation in the activities in the Area they would be deprived of substantial benefits that might otherwise have accrued to them. This is the reason why during the last session of the Conference most of the effort and time has been devoted to negotiating this new approach in the negotiating group which deals with the question of the system of exploitation. These efforts have successfully attempted − at least in theory − to change the role initially assigned to them from one of passive recipients of financial benefits to that of active participants in the operations in the area. Article 158 of the Informal Composite Negotiating Text now reflects the principle of the effective participation of developing countries in the activities in the Area. This principle had not been embodied in the first versions of the text.

A mere incorporation in the body of the Convention of this general and abstract principle could however, be no more than another addition to the realm of political rhetoric and myths with no legal or practical consequences. The lack of technological and financial means that affects developing countries would reduce the principle of effective participation to a sort of political fiction impossible to transform into reality, unless specific measures are adopted to enable those countries to play an active role in the operations in the Area.

This is why developing countries have insisted on the incorporation of special mechanisms as essential components of the system of exploitation so as to mitigate the disadvantaged position in which they are placed, with respect to the possibility of carrying out operations in the seabed.

These mechanisms are, *inter alia*, the following:

(a) The establishment of an inter-governmental body, the Enterprise, as an operational arm of the Authority. Through the participation in the management of the Enterprise and in the adoption of decisions concerning the Enterprise, developing countries can participate indirectly in the carrying out of activities in the Area. The degree of influence of developing countries in the decision-making process will depend on the structure, the composition and competence of each of the main organs of the Authority. Some aspects of this question are still pending, and constitute at present important obstacles in the way of agreement.

(b) In order to make the Enterprise operational, provisions have been included dealing with its financing, the training of personnel, and the transfer of data and technology. In this sphere (transfer of technology) the Conference appears to have made a greater degree of progress than other international fora. This may perhaps be an optimistic view but I think that there are good reasons to believe that with regard to transfer of technology the Conference is close to a satisfactory compromise. Not only does the draft convention contain the general principle referring to the transfer of technology to the Enterprise but also an elaborate set of provisions have emerged from the last round of negotiations, according to which the applicants for contracts and the contractors have to accept concrete undertakings in this field. This has been a significant development in the last round of negotiations.

(c) Another mechanism is the system of reserved areas also called the banking system, according to which any applicant for a contract must propose to the Authority an area sufficiently large, or two mining sites of approximately equal size and value. The Authority will select one of the sites to be exploited directly by the Enterprise or make it available to developing countries. This procedure ensures the Enterprise of the availability of areas with potential commercial value that have already been prospected by the applicant.

(d) Finally, there are some provisions establishing incentives for contractors that enter into associations with the Enterprise or with developing countries and their enterprises. The association with operators of industrialized countries seems to be the only real possibility for developing countries to effectively participate in ocean mining in the near future. Ocean mining requires large amounts of capital, complex and expensive technology and managerial skills that at present developing countries are not able to provide by themselves. For these reasons ocean mining constitutes a natural field for international joint ventures. Thus it does not seem to be too unrealistic to think of joint ventures with enterprises of developed countries in which developing countries contribute funds, manpower, or land facilities such as ports, deposits, plants for processing, transport, etc.

Some developing countries are important consumers of minerals to be extracted from the area and therefore the association with them may bring about attractive benefits, economic as well as political, for industrialized countries operating in the area.

All the features described are devices conceived to provide an equitable solution to a situation in which competing parties are unequal in knowledge and capabilities.

In conclusion, developing countries are still unable to envisage the exploitation of the Area by themselves due to their technological and financial shortcomings. But they have refused to play the role of spectators in the conquest of the seabed; for them only the active participation in that enterprise with all its implications in matters of acquisition of technology, scientific knowledge, managerial skills, industrial and commercial expertise, and financial management, will contribute to accelerate the process of development and to reduce inequalities.

12 NIEO, Law of the Sea and Common Heritage of Mankind: Some Comments

*Judge Shigeru Oda**

A confrontation concerning marine resources that faces us today is the varied interpretation of the concept of international common interest in the deep ocean floor. The concept of the international common interest in international society was traditionally evolved in the form of freedom. 'The high sea is for free access to all' was a typical philosophy in the past. For many centuries, fishing in the vast ocean was considered to be free, except in the limited offshore zone off a coast. In the case of mineral resources of the seabed of the vast ocean, international legal norms relating to their exploitation did not exist. Or, at least, there has been no rule of international law to prohibit the exploitation of the seabed beyond the continental shelf.

The Maltese proposal by Arvid Pardo was submitted to avoid the unregulated development of the deep ocean floor and any disturbance that might be caused by uncontrolled development. Thus the words 'common heritage of mankind' were introduced. What do these words mean? What is the substance of the concept of 'common heritage of mankind'?

At the initial stage of the UN Seabed Committee, Mr Pardo explained that this was a socialist concept. Afterwards a delegate from a socialist country told me: 'Obtaining profit without working is against socialism. It is just like an absentee-landlord theory'. The thesis that benefits from the common heritage of mankind should be shared equally whether you work or not is certainly one possible view, but on the other hand it can also be said that since it is a common heritage anyone can develop it and profit from it.

*International Court of Justice.

A significant feature of the 1970 United Nations Declaration of Principles Governing the Deep Ocean Floor is that the Declaration does not necessarily specify by whom and how the deep ocean floor could be developed nor by whom and how the benefits derived would be shared. The substance of the common heritage of mankind involved various interpretations. Thus, today, we have confusion in Committee I of the Law of the Sea Conference. Some autonomous principles work within the idea of freedom itself. If, however, this idea of freedom is to be denied and replaced by some new idea of justice then new principles must be worked out. The mere words 'common heritage of mankind' are meaningless. Simply to formulate some machinery is also useless. The issues discussed in Committee I are related to the areas which are considered to be those pertaining to the common heritage of mankind. The interests of the land-resource-possessing and non-possessing countries are so conflicting as to lead to bloody confrontations. What kind of idea in principle can we obtain if we are to put substance into the concept of 'common heritage of mankind'?

The same difficulty arises also in ocean fishing. Certainly in the case of ocean fishing the problems are different from the problems encountered in seabed development, as some nations may claim that they already possess certain fishing rights in the vast ocean, acquired on the basis of long-standing fishing operations. Yet these advanced nations are very limited in number. At the Fourth Law of the Sea Conference that might be convened some day in the future, I think that discussions will be held on the new concept of the common heritage of mankind applicable to ocean fishing similar to those discussions now taking place on the seabed mineral resources in Committee I.

Let me turn to the issues relating to the interests of the geographically disadvantaged States and land-locked States. Today, the land-locked countries, the most typical countries in the geographically disadvantaged group in terms of access to the ocean, are now going to be given some specific consideration particularly in the case of the developing nations. However, States can be geographically disadvantaged not only in terms of access to the ocean but also in some other terms, particularly in terms of the quantity and quality of land resources, features of land, etc. This problem applies not only to the developing nations of the Third World but also to the developed nations, geographically advantaged and disadvantaged States (in terms of the access to the ocean) and there are still some other types of geographically advantaged and/or disadvantaged States.

The different features as mentioned above are combined in one way or another in each country, and one of the most serious problems the world community will face will be the accommodation of these different types of interest into one universal legal order to meet the various needs and demands of everyone. An example of the difficulties facing NIEO is clearly shown in the troubled negotiations of the Third Law of the Sea Conference.

One further point relates to the question concerning the right of a State when it does not have the capacity to exploit its living resources to the maximum within its exclusive economic zone. It has been suggested that a State that does not have the capacity to exploit these resources must give the surplus to some land-locked or disadvantaged State.

How can one define that a coastal State is incapable of exploiting to the maximum the fishing resources within its exclusive economic zone? Any State is always capable of exploiting its resources up to the maximum with assistance from outside countries. Even the least developed country can exploit fishing resources within its own area by introducing some capital or by getting technological assistance from some outside countries, or even granting concessionary rights to another country, thus earning some foreign exchange from these undertakings. My point is that, if there is no rule which prohibits a coastal State from acquiring assistance, be it in the form of capital, technology or concessionary rights, to exploit resources within its own area, I cannot see any case in which a coastal State is incapable of exploiting its resources in its own exclusive economic zone.

13 Is it wrong for the Third World to Compromise? The Debate Over the Regulation of Seabed Activities

*Julio Faundez**

For nearly six years the Law of the Sea Conference has been trying to agree on a comprehensive document governing activities related to the sea. In the course of these lengthy negotiations, several thousand delegates have met in many parts of the world, in sessions of various types, in an attempt to identify and systematize the wide range of problems that fall under the 'law of the sea' label. The Conference has made an important contribution towards improving our awareness and understanding of many of these problems. Over the past few years, however, the Law of the Sea Conference appears to have reached a deadlock. This deadlock has stood in the way of a prompt and successful completion of the Conference's objectives. It has also provided the many critics of the Third World position with plenty of ammunition in support of their views that the political immaturity of many Third World governments is to blame for this excessively long Conference. The feelings of nostalgia for the good old days, when a few nations could impose discipline on the conduct of international affairs, emerges very clearly from this type of criticism and it probably reflects the mood of many people in the industrialized world.

One among the various areas accounting for the paralysis of the Conference concerns the regulation of seabed activities.[1] The importance of the seabed as a source of mineral resources has been firmly established. The existing technology already makes it possible to recover nickel, aluminium and copper from the manganese nodules found in the seabed. In the future, further advances in technology may add new names to the list of minerals, and probably other resources could also be recovered

*University of Warwick.

from the area.[2] The technological breakthrough which has made the exploitation of seabed resources a viable proposition has created a novel situation which calls for original solutions. For the first time humanity is attempting to establish an international machinery designed to organize the production and distribution of resources which are supposedly owned by humankind.

The sheer quantity of information and debate which the Sea Conference has already generated and the intricate technical details involved, make it impossible for an outsider to the Conference to understand the real implications of each point under discussion or to risk predicting the likely outcome of the negotiations. So far, however, the failure of the experts has allowed the focus of the discussion to change. Indeed, the possibility that the Conference may actually fail to produce an agreement has forced the debate away from the technical minutiae and back to the central political questions: what kind of political arrangement should be established in order to regulate seabed mining? Should seabed mining be controlled by an international authority? How much power should be vested in this international agency?[3]

The answers to these questions have, to a large extent, been determined by the broader division between industrialized and Third World countries. This dividing line has shaped the two main views which are confronting each other at the Law of the Sea Conference. The position of the socialist countries has tended to oscillate somewhere in between the two main positions. Thus, seabed negotiations are an important arena where the North–South dialogue is taking place.

At the start of the seabed negotiations the Third World countries called for the creation of an international agency with full and exclusive powers to control activities over the seabed. Some industrialized countries, on the other hand, put forward a very strong case against any type of regulation over manganese nodules. The negotiations have so far produced a compromise which is still the subject of further negotiations. This compromise envisages the establishment of an International Seabed Authority (ISA) which will administer a parallel system of exploitation of seabed resources. The ISA will have the power to license and regulate mining activities of state and private entities and, at the same time, it will be directly involved in mining.

The basic agreement on the parallel system has been regarded as an important step forward in the efforts to bring the Law of the Sea to a successful conclusion. Negotiations over the actual details on how to implement the proposed parallel system have been more difficult and have in fact become a major obstacle in the progress of the Conference.

The purpose of this paper is to attempt a preliminary evaluation of the proposed compromise in the light of the original negotiating position of the two opposing sides. I will be mainly concerned with two questions: to what extent does the proposed compromise accommodate the interests of the two opposing camps? How is it likely to work out in practice? The interpretations put forward in this paper are tentative. They merely purport to draw attention to some issues which still remain unresolved and unfortunately, judging by the publications specializing on Third World affairs, do not seem to generate much interest beyond that of a small circle of officials who have become the only experts on the topic.

THE POSITION OF THE THIRD WORLD COUNTRIES

The Law of the Sea Conference has been one forum where solidarity among Third World countries has been put to a severe test. Because the issues raised by the seabed negotiations are so varied and complex, the position adopted by participating countries has often been motivated by specific interests at stake rather than according to the North–South distinction. Thus, for example, the conflict of interests between land-locked and coastal states and between mineral producers and States expecting to become seabed miners has often severely shaken the co-hesiveness of the Third World position as expressed by the Group of 77. The description of the Third World position that follows is a reconstruction based upon the policy followed by the Group of 77 during the course of the negotiations. It may not adequately account for the many differences which have emerged among Third World countries on detailed technical points. In its general outline, however, the position of Third World countries is based upon a firm conviction that a comprehensive system for the regulation of seabed resources is absolutely essential and that, in order to ensure an equitable share of the resources recovered from the seabed, this regulatory system must be controlled by an international machinery fully equipped to engage directly in seabed mining.[4]

The starting point of the Third World countries is one of principle: seabed resources are the common heritage of mankind. This general principle, affirmed by a resolution of the United Nations General Assembly, supports the general conclusion that the exploitation of seabed resources should be regulated by an international machinery. According to this view, only an international regime would be consistent with the common heritage principle. As the costs involved in launching this type of mining operation are extremely high, the majority of countries will be financially and technologically excluded from it. This fact requires that the international machinery entrusted with seabed matters should become directly involved in seabed mining. The direct involvement of the international community in the mining process will ensure an equitable distribution of seabed resources.

The Third World position is, therefore, built around two major principles: the common heritage principle, which justifies the need for an international regulatory system; and the principle of equitable distribution of resources, justifying the direct involvement of the International Seabed Authority in the mining process.

THE POSITION OF THE INDUSTRIALIZED COUNTRIES

There has been a wide range of opinions concerning the regulation of seabed resources among industrialized countries. These differences are not always reflected in the positions they adopt in the Law of the Sea Conference, although some have been influential in persuading the hardliners, such as the United States, to accept a compromise formula. Unity among the industrialized countries is preserved by the fact that research on and development of seabed mining are carried out by companies based within their jurisdictions. The large sums which have already been laid out by these private mining concerns and the prospects of substantial resources and profits benefiting their national economies, act as an irresistable magnet in maintaining solidarity among industrialized countries. The United States, which has played a leading role in these negotiations, has provided, through the writings of its diplomats and some academics, the most coherent intellectual justification in support of the industrialized countries. This justification, which is a plea for allowing market forces to follow its natural course, perhaps does not fully represent the views of some governments, such as the British government before Mrs Thatcher, which are firmly rooted in the social-democratic tradition. Bearing in mind these reservations, I will outline the basic argument justifying the position of industrialized countries.

The position of the industrialized countries starts from assumptions which are diametrically opposed to those underlying the position of Third World countries.[5] To the common heritage principle, they oppose the principle of freedom of the seas. This principle, as contained in Article 2 of the High Seas Convention is interpreted as a set of complementary principles designed to ensure all nations the right to use the high seas, including seabed mining as one of the activities falling within this freedom.

The principle of the freedom of the seas is therefore interpreted as the unequivocal policy decision of the international community concerning the exploitation of seabed resources. According to this interpretation, the existing principles governing international relations already accommodate seabed mining, thus making superfluous any further regulation over this matter. In the context of this broad interpretation of the freedom of the seas principle, the fact that industrialized countries have accepted to negotiate over the future seabed regime is regarded by them as a major concession. Furthermore, their current acceptance, on principle, of the system of parallel exploitation is proclaimed as a sign of their good faith, flexibility and generosity.

In their argument, industrialized countries do not totally ignore the common heritage principle and the equity considerations which are raised by the position of the Third World countries. They simply re-interpret them in order to accommodate them to their argument. This process involves two stages. First, the force of the common heritage principle is devalued on legalistic grounds in order to conclude that the freedom of the seas principle is more universally accepted. The common heritage principle is thus relegated to a secondary principle, embodying a mere programmatic aspiration. Second, the redistributive aspiration of the Third World position is acknowledged, but the establishment of a complex regulatory scheme in order to achieve this objective is rejected as superfluous.

This discussion about principles is complemented by an argument derived from economic theory.[6] The main conclusion of this economic analysis is that the establishment of any type of system for the exploitation of manganese nodules would be economically inefficient and politically unnecessary. This argument, which takes the form of a plea to free manganese nodules from the fetters of property rights, follows roughly along the following lines. Although manganese nodules are not free goods in the sense that they can be recovered from the seabed without incurring heavy costs, the costs involved in running a regulatory system which would assign and enforce rights over nodules would be far greater than the harm resulting from the absence of regulation. The absence of regulation over seabed mining would not therefore create inefficiencies such as those associated with under-investment or over-investment. Seabed mining does not – according to this argument – require any form of regulation in order to reach an optimum level of efficiency. Therefore, any political intervention designed to alter the structure of rights – a licensing office or a fully-fledged international miner – would generate inefficiencies which would eventually harm the whole of the international community. Market forces, according to this view will resolve any harm resulting from seabed mining and will distribute the product on an equitable basis.

Thus an International Law principle and a specific kind of economic theory are combined to support the initial position of the United States and other industrialized countries.

AN EVALUATION OF THE TWO OPPOSING VIEWS

The message implicit in the position of the industrialized countries has a very appealing tone. Their slogan calling to 'free the nodules from the fetters of an international bureaucracy' is bound to have a sympathetic reception among the many old and new converts to the ideal of de-regulation. Yet, upon close inspection, their argument turns into a plea to treat seabed mining as a foreign investment venture in which one of the parties — the host State — has been eliminated. According to it, the six or seven multinational consortia involved in seabed mining should be free to recover the nodules and transport them back to their own national territories, unhampered by any type of *international* regulation. The free-nodules doctrine would thus legalize appropriation by those investors powerful enough to get at them first. It is important to note that the argument of the industrialized countries is not really about de-regulation. The international consortia which would be allowed free access to the nodules would simply be projecting onto the nodules — and the seabed — the regulatory and property systems of their own nation-states. Indeed, nation-state regulation in the form of police protection would be an essential component in facilitating the activity of these adventurous miners. Other forms of nation-state regulation would be implicit in the nature of the activity: laws protecting property over technology, laws regulating labour relations, and law imposing taxes on the proceeds. The regulatory function of some form of political entity cannot be wished away by mere analytical fiat or by means of the artificial distinction between the international and the domestic components of the specific mining activity.

The position of the Third World countries is, predictably enough, more concerned with the problems of distribution than with the subtleties of economic efficiency.[7] Their attitude stems from the deep-seated conviction that unless a powerful mechanism for the regulation of seabed mining is established promptly, multinational companies will move in, thus leaving the Third World countries on the fence, yet again. Apart from this increasing awareness about the behaviour of multinationals, some Third World diplomats have acquired a strong faith in the virtues of concerted political action. Consistent with this newly acquired faith, some of these officials are displaying an excessive, and often misplaced, optimism about the power of political imagination and the durability of Third World solidarity. It seems as if for some, the success of the North–South dialogue could be ensured by a mixture of good ideas, well-trained negotiators and a bottomless common fund of solidarity among the Group of 77. Consistent with this attitude the top priority of some Third World officials seems to be to establish the ISA as soon as possible, leaving other problems for a later stage.

It may be instructive, perhaps, to take a second look at the position of the industrialized countries. Although it may be rightly characterized as a justification designed to serve the interests of large mining consortia, it does nonetheless raise an important point, the implications of which may not have been adequately assessed by the advocates of the Third World position. The argument of the industrialized countries basically states that seabed mining can be carried out efficiently without any type of international regulation. The argument, as we have already shown, takes domestic regulation for granted. The important point which this interpretation raises, albeit indirectly, concerns the impossibility of reconciling State regulation with an ill-defined international regulatory system.

Unless the international seabed machinery clearly predominates over the regulatory jurisdiction vested in individual nation-states, the co-existence of two regulatory systems will inevitably create inefficiencies. Because, on the one hand, a weak international regulatory agency may simply duplicate work already done at the domestic level; on the other hand, this agency could be more receptive to the influence of conflicting political interests, thus leading to continuous deadlocks in its operation. In order to make the ISA involvement in mining viable, a massive delegation of power is an indispensable pre-condition. The powers delegated to this international agency should not differ much from those vested in existing regulatory agencies or nationalized enterprises at the domestic level. An important difference, however, is that at the domestic level there usually exists a great degree of unity of purpose — either spontaneous or imposed — about the goals which a particular form of state involvement ought to pursue. This political cohesiveness is much more difficult to find, or even conceive, at the international level, particularly if the agency is to consist of nearly all the states on earth.

Nothing of what has been said here about the nature of state intervention in economic matters is particularly new. Yet it may be relevant to ask whether the Third World countries have adequately grasped the political prerequisites needed for a successful operation of the political body they are attempting to establish. It is important to enquire whether Third World governments are actually prepared to delegate such enormous power to an entity which, individually, they will not control, and which in practice may not develop along the lines envisaged by its advocates.

THE COMPROMISE FORMULA

The parallel system of exploitation, which is at present on the agenda of the seabed negotiations, represents a compromise of the two opposing sides. It attempts to accommodate conflicting political and economic interests within a framework of an international organization that is expected to be involved in mining activities. The compromise formula is contained in the *Informal Composite Negotiation Text/Rev. I* (ICNT),[8] which is a preliminary draft of a treaty dealing with all the matters within the scope of the Law of the Sea Conference. The compromise formula provides for a separate mining agency — the Enterprise — endowed with a certain degree of autonomy to carry out the technical process of production. The two main organs of the proposed International Authority, the Assembly and the Council, are somewhat like their counterparts in the United Nations system. The general outline of the international organization emerging from the Conference reveals a very determined effort to reconcile, within a single institutional framework, the political requirements of universal participation with the demands of economic efficiency. A brief review of the main features of the compromise solution will enable us to discuss some of its political implications.

The Assembly, described as the supreme organ of the ISA, has the power to establish general policies, and to discuss any matter within the jurisdiction of the organization. All member-states are represented in the Assembly, each having one vote. Some important Assembly decisions, 'questions of substance', require the vote of two-thirds of the members participating in the relevant session. Apart from some important powers concerning budgetary and other administrative matters, the Assembly examines the periodic reports issued by the Council and the Enterprise. The Assembly also has the important power of adopting rules and procedures for the equitable sharing of financial and other economic benefits derived from activities in the seabed.

The Council is a smaller body, consisting of thirty-six members, membership being proportionate to the interest a group may have in seabed mining. States involved in seabed mining and states which consume or import more than 2 per cent of total world consumption or exports of the minerals obtained from the seabed, will each have four seats in the Council. Another four seats will be held by the major exporters of the minerals. Six members will be elected from among developing countries having 'special interests'. This category of special interest includes states with large populations, land-locked or geographically disadvantaged states, states which are major importers of seabed minerals and the least-developed states. The remaining eighteen members of the Council will be elected on the basis of an equitable balance among geographical regions.

The Council is the Executive organ of the ISA, entrusted with the task of adopting specific measures in accordance with the general policies approved by the Assembly and the provisions of the Convention. Decisions on questions of substance require a qualified majority of three-quarters of the members present and voting. The Council must perform the delicate function of approving plans for the conduct of activities on the seabed; it also has the responsibility for controlling activities of the Enterprise and exercising overall control over activities.

The Enterprise is the operating arm of the ISA. It is governed by a Board of fifteen qualified individuals and a Director-General elected by the Assembly. The Enterprise operates under the direct control of the Council, to which it must submit proposals of mining projects. The Enterprise is also required to follow the general policies laid down by the Assembly.

Relations between the ISA and individual contractors are governed by a separate Annex, entitled *Basic Conditions of Prospecting, Exploration and Exploitation.*[9] This Annex lays out in great detail the rules designed to prevent discrimination among entities competing for contracts of exploration or exploitation and to ensure that seabed mining will not be heavily biased towards a particular geographical area or to entities belonging to the same social and economic system. This Annex also contains detailed provisions for the transfer of technology to the Authority. Its provisions on *reserved sites* give the Enterprise an important advantage over its competitors. According to these provisions, the Enterprise may reserve for itself half of the sites claimed by individual contractors. On these *reserved sites*, the Enterprise is given the option to conduct activities directly or through joint arrangements with qualified seabed miners. Financial arrangements between the ISA and individual contractors may consist, at the contractors choice, of a single system based on a combination of production charges and a share of net proceeds. Production charges are fixed at a percentage of the market value of the processed metal produced from the nodules extracted from the contract area. During the first ten years of commercial production, these charges will be fixed at 8 per cent, thereafter, the charge will be increased to 13.5 per cent. If the financial contribution is made through the flexible system, the production charge is reduced to 2 per cent and 5 per cent for the first and second period of commercial production. In this scheme, the ISA's share of net proceeds will be 45 per cent and 65 per cent of attributable net proceeds for the first and second periods of commercial production. Attributable net proceeds are equal to 35 per cent of the common contractor's net proceeds.

The organization envisaged by the ICNT reveals the enormous effort and ingenuity displayed by seabed negotiators in accommodating the various interests of the states participating in the Conference. The experience gained by the evolution of the United Nations system and the practice of many other international organizations have undoubtedly been taken into account in the process of drafting the provisions of the ICNT. Some of the most frequent obstacles affecting the work of international organizations have been explicitly considered by the ICNT. Thus, the Assembly monitors every major decision of the organization, but some safeguards have been introduced in order to prevent it from creating unnecessary delays. The composition of the Council ensures that all major interest groups are given an adequate hearing. Finally, the Enterprise enjoys a large measure of autonomy within its technical sphere of activity. The ICNT reveals very clearly its aim of striking a reasonable balance between the principles of equal representation and operational efficiency.

It is not possible, in the context of this paper, to undertake a thorough evaluation of the provisions of the negotiating text. However, on the basis of the information available about the structure of the ISA, and from the perspective of an outsider to the Conference, I will suggest some general points concerning the nature of the compromise and its relation to the initial negotiating position of the two sides.

The proposed system of parallel exploitation seems to stand halfway between the original position of the two opposing sides. The system is defined as parallel because it provides for the coexistence of two regimes of seabed mining: one run by the ISA and the other by individual contractors. On paper there appears a perfect symmetry between the two factors making up the compromise. The parallel system of exploitation does not, however, require that seabed mining should be equally divided between the ISA and other contractors. Indeed, absolute equality in the relative allocation of mining sites is neither an objective of the Third World negotiation nor something which could be determined before actual mining begins. However, it is fair to suppose that those Third World officials who accepted the parallel system as a compromise solution might have expected that the ISA would control either the majority of the available sites or at least a proportion roughly equal to one-half of the total. If this interpretation of the reasons underlying the Third World's acceptance of the compromise formula is correct, it is necessary then to examine whether the ideal of equality underlying the compromise formula has any chance of becoming reality. In other words, will the equality of opportunity envisaged by the formula actually materialize in the real world of seabed mining.

It is not possible to predict how the ISA might evolve in practice. Yet, it may be interesting to examine two problems that the ISA will have to confront, given the general outline of the proposed organization. This exercise may be useful because the compromise formula is still in the process of negotiation and because, as we know, very often a compromise, which on paper may appear reasonable and fair, turns out to be quite the opposite after the fine points of detail have been introduced. This could happen to the seabed compromise, at least with regard to the provisions dealing with technology and those dealing with the allocation of power to the principal organs of the ISA.

The provisions on transfer of technology are long and have been very carefully drafted. They require that independent contractors making a bid for a mining site must make available to the ISA information about the technology they intend to use. This duty to reveal technological know-how is reinforced by the obligation to actually supply the technology to the Enterprise on fair and reasonable commercial terms. If we assume that seabed technology will be concentrated in the hands of a few large private consortia and protected by a watertight system of national and international property rights, it is easier to envisage ways in which these provisions on technology will be circumvented than how they will be honoured. It is, of course, possible, for the sake of argument, to assume that multinationals and nation-states will comply in good faith with these provisions, even though they are bound to raise some difficult domestic constitutional issues concerning the protection of property.

A more fundamental problem arising from the provisions on the transfer of technology concerns the division of labour, which they seem to take as given. Indeed, these provisions take for granted that the ISA will always buy technology that is generated and further developed elsewhere.

This implies that, even assuming the good faith of all parties involved, the ISA will be condemned to perpetual dependency on seabed technology. This dependency is bound to handicap permanently its mining activities. There are probably many compelling technical reasons why no serious consideration has been given to the idea of setting up a massive fund in order to allow the Enterprise to develop its own technology. There are certainly some very obvious political reasons explaining why (inter)nationalizing the existing technology has never been seriously considered. None the less, if the Enterprise is not allowed from the start to stand on its feet in order to compete with other miners, it may be forever condemned to play the role of a marginal producer, if it ever gets that far.

While the Enterprise may confront serious problems in assuming its roles as an international mining agency, the Council may well find that its Executive powers could be severely undermined by the Assembly. Although great care has been taken to prevent the Assembly from interfering with the technical aspects of the day-to-day administration of the organization, this may still occur because there is a substantial amount of overlap in the powers delegated to the principal organs of the ISA. The Assembly could, in theory, intervene in the sphere of competence reserved to the Enterprise. Here again, reality may prove these fears to be ill-founded. Indeed, the practice of the organization may demonstrate that the good disposition of the member states may resolve any logical or legal inconsistency which on paper appears intractable. There is little evidence, however, that the organization as envisaged by the seabed negotiators will be equipped with the powers necessary to fulfil its functions. The ISA may be condemned to live in the worst of all worlds: it will not have any more powers than those of existing international organizations; yet its functions and responsibilities will be those of a supra-state. Given these circumstances, it is unlikely that the ISA will live up to the expectations of the Third World.

The eventual failure of the ISA will not necessarily violate the terms of the compromise formula. Indeed, under the terms of the compromise, the ISA has an excellent fall-back position. The ICNT provisions dealing with the relations between the ISA and individual contractors will constitute an excellent cushion if the ISA is eventually forced to confine the bulk of its activities to administering an international tax system. Thus, the compromise solution may in fact evolve into a neat division of labour in which nation-state regulation will play a leading role, thus leaving the field free to individual contractors.

This scenario may be unduly pessimistic, yet it is not inconceivable given the material constraints which will surround the launching of the ISA. If the ISA is not capable of establishing itself as an important factor in seabed mining the worst fears about the inherent inefficiencies of international bureaucracies will be proved right. Third World countries have invested too much political capital to the seabed negotiations to risk establishing an international mechanism which may not live up to their expectations. Such failure will severely undermine Third World solidarity. The current deadlock in the negotiations provides everyone concerned with a good opportunity to re-appraise their position.

NOTES AND REFERENCES

1   For a survey of the main issues involved in the seabed negotiations, see R.L. Friedheim and W.J. Durch, 'The International Seabed Resources Agency Negotiations and the New International Economic Order' in *International Organization*, XXXI (1977), 343–84. A good summary discussion of the most controversial questions before the United Nations Conference on the law of the Sea Conference is to be found in *Report of the Committees and Negotiating Groups on Negotiations at the Seventh Session . . .*, GE. 78–85880 (1978).

2   A good introduction to seabed technology is found in Flipse, 'Deep Ocean Mining Technology and its Impact on the Law of the Sea' in F.T. Christy *et al.*, *Law of the Sea: Caracas and Beyond* (1975), Ballinger, Cambridge, Mass., 325–41.

3   For a reappraisal of the interests of the United States see, Knight 'Consequences of Non-Agreement at the Third U.N. Law of the Sea Conference', *American Society of International Law, Studies in Transnational Legal Policy* No. 11 (1976) and Darman, 'The Law of the Sea: Rethinking U.S. Interests', *Foreign Affairs* (January 1978), 373–95.

4   See generally: M. Hardy, 'The Implications of Alternative Solutions in Regulating the Exploitation of Seabed Minerals', in *International Organization* Vol., XXXI (1977), 313–42; J.J. Charney 'The International Regime for the Deep Seabed: Past Conflicts and Proposals for Progress', *Harvard Journal of International Law*, Vol. XVII (1976), 1–50; A.O. Adede, 'The System for Exploitation of the "Common Heritage of Mankind" at the Caracas Conference', *American Journal of International Law*, Vol. LXIX (1975), 31–49.

5   For a good summary of the international legal issues involved in the seabed debate, see Burton, 'Freedom of the Seas: International Law Applicable to Deep Seabed Mining', *Stanford Law Review*, Vol. XXIX (1977), 1135–80.

6   See, for example, J. Sweeney, R.D. Tollison and T.D. Willett, 'Market Failure, the Common Pool Problem, and Ocean Resource Exploitation', *Journal of Law and Economics*, Vol. XVII (1974), 179–92; Eckert, 'Exploitation of Deep Ocean Minerals: Regulatory Mechanisms and United States Policy', ibid., 143–77; Logue, Sweeney and Petrov, 'The Economics of Alternative Seabed Regimes', *Marine Technology Society Journal*, Vol. IX (April-May 1975), 9–16.

7   A very helpful interpretation of the economic interests of developing countries is found in D.M. Leipziger and J.L. Mudge, *Seabed Mineral Resources and the Economic Interests of Developing Countries* (1976), Ballinger, Cambridge, Mass.

8   United Nations Conference on the Law of the Sea, *Informal Composite Negotiating Text/Rev. I*, A/Conf. 62/WP. 10/Rev. 1(1979).
9   Ibid., Annex II.

14 Aspects of NIEO in the Third U.N. Conference on the Law of the Sea: Exclusive Economic Zone and the Continental Shelf

*Hugo Caminos**

Equitable distribution of ocean resources and of benefits derived there-from is an aspect of the new international economic order which features prominently in the Third UN Conference on the Law of the Sea (LOS Conference). A discussion of this aspect would embrace: the international seabed, the exclusive economic zone and the continental shelf. As the international seabed is being covered by the other papers, I will limit myself to the other two areas: the exclusive economic zone and the continental shelf.

These two subjects are related to marine areas under national jurisdiction. One is the exclusive economic zone. The other is the continental shelf. Without delving deeper into the history of the exclusive economic zone, it may nevertheless be useful to examine the view taken by some that the idea of the creation of the exclusive economic zone has not been conducive to a better distribution of ocean resources among developing countries. This idea is based on the assumption that the major beneficiaries of the concept of an exclusive economic zone are some of the most developed countries in the world. If we look, however, at the process that led to the adoption of the exclusive economic zone, we would conclude that basically it came as a reaction against unrestricted access of distant-water fishing by developed countries which exploited, and in some cases depleted, the living resources of some areas of the oceans adjacent to the coasts of developing states.

The first of the two problems to be discussed here is the question of the right of access of land-locked and geographically disadvantaged States in a subregion or region to the exploitation of the living resources

*Third UN Law of the Sea Conference.

of the exclusive economic zone. This matter has been discussed since the days of the Seabed Committee. There were different approaches to it: at one extreme, there was, for example, a proposal to allow access on the basis of agreements with coastal States, and at the other, there was the suggestion urging creation of regional economic zones that would give coastal, land-locked, and geographically disadvantaged States equal rights to exploit the living resources within these regional economic zones. In the *Informal Composite Negotiating Text* (ICNT) issued at the end of the Sixth Session of the Third UN Conference on the Law of the Sea, there are two provisions providing for the right of access of land-locked and geographically disadvantaged States to the exploitation of the living resources of the exclusive economic zones of the same subregion or region. The matter has been one of those considered as hard-core issues by the Plenary of the Conference at its Seventh Session. As a result, it has been the subject of negotiations in one of the negotiating groups (Negotiating Group 4) established by the Conference for the purpose of facilitating a compromise solution.

One of the main difficulties was that according to the group of land-locked and geographically disadvantaged States, the access to the living resources should be on a preferential basis. On this point, the new text, which was proposed by the Chairman of Negotiating Group 4 and which practically can be considered as a product of the present state of negotiations, gives a kind of preferential right, without calling it preferential, in the case of the developing States. Thus, when a coastal State contemplates the access of third States to the exploitation of the living resources in its exclusive economic zone, special consideration should be given to those land-locked and geographically disadvantaged States which are developing countries.

Another problem was that in the ICNT the right of access to the exploitation of these living resources is essentially on the surplus. Under the regime of the exclusive economic zone, the coastal State has the right to determine the total allowable catch in its exclusive economic zone as well as its own capacity to harvest those resources. The objective would be optimum utilization. If the coastal State did not have the capacity to harvest 100 per cent of the total allowable catch, then it would have to give other States access to the surplus of the allowable catch. The question was then raised: what happens in a non-surplus situation? After lengthy negotiations the Chairman of Negotiating Group 4, suggested a compromise provision in the following terms;

When the harvesting capacity of a coastal State approaches a point which would enable it to harvest the entire allowable catch of the living resources in its exclusive economic zone the coastal State and other States concerned shall co-operate in the establishment of equitable arrangements on bilateral, subregional or regional basis to allow for participation of developing States with special geographical characteristics of the same subregion or region in the exploitation of the living resources of the exclusive economic zones of coastal States of the subregion or region as may be appropriate in the circumstances and on terms satisfactory to all parties. In the implementation of this provision, the factors mentioned in paragraph two shall also be taken into account.

The factors include: the need to avoid effects detrimental to fishing communities or fishing industries of the coastal State; the extent to which the land-locked State or the State with special geographical characteristics, as the case may be, is participating or is entitled to participate under existing arrangements in the exploitation of living resources of the exclusive economic zones of other States; the extent to which other land-locked States and States with special geographical characteristics are participating in the exploitation of the living resources of the exclusive economic zone of the coastal State and the need to avoid a particular burden for any single coastal State or part of it; the nutritional needs of the population of the respective States. The merit of the suggested provision is that it might succeed in bringing a consensus among the delegations most directly interested. And that, of course, is the main objective of the whole exercise.

Another problem which has been mentioned is the distinction between developing and developed land-locked and geographically disadvantaged States. In fact, the ICNT provides that developed land-locked States shall only have access to the exclusive economic zones belonging to developed States.

Finally, in his report on the work of Negotiating Group 4 during the first part of the Seventh Session, the Chairman refers to some difficulties on terminology and definition. One of them relates to the use of the expression 'geographically disadvantaged State'. Incidentally, the draft suggested by the Chairman of Negotiating Group 4, eliminates this expression and replaces it with the term 'States with special geographical characteristics'. The group of land-locked and geographically disadvantaged States which has fifty-three members, is not quite happy with this change because the old expression had a special significance throughout these negotiations.

Among the relevant factors to be taken into consideration by the coastal State in giving access to its exclusive economic zone to other States, the ICNT mentions: the significance of the living resources to its economy and its other material interests, the rights of land-locked States and States with special geographical characteristics, the requirements of developing countries in the subregion or region in harvesting part of the surplus and the need to minimize dislocation in States whose nationals have habitually fished in the zone or which have made substantial efforts in research and identification of stocks.

The provision dealing with the utilization of the living resources in the exclusive economic zone contains a non-exhaustive list of matters that can be the subject of regulation by the coastal State. In the case of developing coastal States special mention is made of financing, equipment and technology relating to the fishing industry as means of compensation for the granting of licences to nationals of other States. Joint ventures and other similar arrangements are also mentioned. A great number of bilateral agreements between developing and developed countries in the last few years, based on the regime on fisheries emerging from UNCLOS III negotiations, contain interesting provisions on financial and economic co-operation, transfer of technology, development of the fishery industry, training of personnel, co-operation in the field of scientific research and marketing. There is also a trend to establish joint ventures between developing countries and enterprises from developed countries. These arrangements are intended to facilitate the development of exclusive economic zones of developing countries, with the necessary co-operation of traditional fishing countries. No doubt, important principles of the new international economic order are involved in this new regime of fisheries.

Although the debate on the access of land-locked States and States with special geographical characteristics to the exploitation of the living resources is related to a more equitable distribution of resources, which is one of the objectives of the new international economic order, it cannot be characterized as a North–South negotiation. Among the members of the group of land-locked and geographically disadvantaged States we find countries with varying degrees of development, for example, the Federal Republic of Germany, Uganda, the Netherlands, Switzerland, Cameroon.

The latter comment is also true of the second item I wish to touch upon briefly: the system of revenue sharing in the exploitation of the continental shelf beyond 200 miles. Here also the most directly interested countries have established the so-called group of 'margineers'. These are the countries which possess broad continental shelves and this interest group includes States such as Pakistan and Mauritius along with the United States and Canada. Therefore, we cannot identify this group with either of the two parties in the North–South negotiations.

The ICNT provides for a system of revenue sharing on the exploitation of the continental shelf beyond 200 miles and the debate on this subject can be summarized as follows: on the question of what is to be shared, that is to say if it is going to be a share of the profits or in all production, the ICNT has chosen the sharing of gross revenues.

On the question of figures, there is a five year grace period and payments of 1 per cent per year up to a maximum of 5 per cent. Probably these figures cannot be considered definite and further negotiations will be required on this matter.

The next question is who are going to be the contributors to this system of revenue sharing? Would all 'margineers' be included? At first, there was a proposal excluding all developing countries but at a later stage in the negotiations the exception has been restricted to those developing countries that are net importers of a mineral resource produced from its continental shelf beyond 200 miles.

Finally, there is the question of who would be the recipient of the contributions and how would the benefits be distributed. The ICNT establishes that payments or contributions shall be made to State parties on the basis of equitable sharing criteria, taking into account the interests and needs of developing countries, particularly the least developed and the land-locked amongst them. This would seem the most reasonable solution.

I would like to add that the LOS Conference has had a healthy influence in the present trend of unilateral legislation because it has driven most national laws towards the exclusive economic zone or fisheries zone approach rather than to the territorial sea approach, and this includes many Latin American States.

15 Equitable Solutions in the International Law of the Sea: Some Problems

*Kamal Hossain**

I

For a whole range of problems involving the international law of the sea, equitable solutions have been urged. The International Court of Justice resorted to such solutions in the *North Sea Continental Shelf* cases in respect of the problem of the delimitation of lateral boundaries of continental shelves,[1] and in the *Fisheries Jurisdiction* cases in respect of the unilateral extension of its fisheries limits by a coastal state asserting preferential rights to fish in the seas around its coasts against states which claimed historic rights to fish in those seas.[2] In the Informal Single Negotiating Text,[3] which emerged from the Geneva session of the UN Law of the Sea Conference nearly a dozen provisions propose some form of equitable solution to the problems which are sought to be dealt with. Thus, Articles 9 and 23 envisage 'equitable sharing' of the benefits to be derived from activities in the seabed, beyond the limits of national jurisdiction. Article 47 provides that in cases where the convention does not attribute rights or jurisdiction to the coastal state or to other states within the exclusive economic zones, and a conflict arises between the interests of the coastal state and any other state or states, the conflict should be resolved 'on the basis of equity, and in the light of all relevant circumstances, taking into account the respective importance of the interests involved to the parties as well as to the international community as a whole.' Article 57 invests 'land-locked states' with the right to participate in the exploitation of the living resources of the exclusive economic zones of adjoining coastal states 'on an equitable basis, taking into account

*Centre for Research on the New International Economic Order.

the relevant economic and geographical circumstances of all the states concerned.' It is further provided that the terms and conditions of such participation shall be determined by the states concerned through bilateral, sub-regional or regional agreements. Article 58 makes a similar provision with regard to 'geographically disadvantaged states'. Thus, it is provided that 'developing coastal states which are situated in a subregion or region whose geographical peculiarities make such states peculiarly dependent for the satisfaction of the nutritional needs of their populations on the exploitation of the living resources in the economic zones of their neighbouring states' and 'developing coastal states which can claim no exclusive economic zone of their own' shall have a right to participate 'on an equitable basis' in the exclusive economic zones of other states in a sub-region or region. The terms and conditions of such participation are to be determined 'by the states concerned through bilateral, sub-regional or regional agreements, taking into account the relevant economic and geographic circumstances of all the states concerned, including the need to avoid effects detrimental to the fishing communities or to the fishing industries of the states in whose zones the right of participation is exercised.' Article 61 provides that the delimitation of exclusive economic zones between adjacent or opposite states shall be effected by agreement, in accordance with 'equitable principles, employing where appropriate the median or equidistance principle and taking into account all the relevant circumstances.' Article 70 makes a similar provision for the delimitation of continental shelf boundaries. Article 69 envisages payment of contributions to the International Seabed Authority in respect of the development of non-living resources beyond the 200-mile economic zone, and provides that the Authority shall distribute the contributions so received among states on the basis of 'equitable sharing criteria'.

Inherent in all these problems are questions of distribution or apportionment of resources, or the benefits arising from the exploitation of resources, among competing claimants. Even in the *North Sea Continental Shelf* cases, while the Court affirmed that its task related 'essentially to the delimitation and not the apportionment of the areas concerned', and that 'delimitation in an equitable manner is one thing, but not the same thing as awarding a just and equitable share of a previously undelimited area', it conceded that 'in a number of cases the results may be comparable, or even identical', and further went on to admit (an admission which it is submitted is noteworthy) that: 'any dispute about boundaries must involve that there is a disputed marginal or fringe area, to which both parties are laying claim so that any delimitation of it which does not leave it wholly to one of the parties will in practice divide it between them in certain shares, or operate as if such a division had been made.'[4] Indeed, a boundary delimitation problem, viewed in practical terms, may be seen as the problem of apportionment of the area that falls between the different boundary lines proposed. The nearer to the line proposed by a party a boundary is located the greater is likely to be its gain and greater the corresponding loss to the other party: gains and losses which would have a significant economic value in terms of mineral deposits and other resources which might be found in the area affected by the delimitation.

The Court's characterization of the problem and its formulation of the equitable solution to it in the *North Sea Continental Shelf* cases was no doubt influenced by the sound judicial policy of playing down the legislative or innovative aspect of its functions. Thus, the Court declared:

> When mention is made of a court dispensing justice or declaring the law, what is meant is that the decision finds its objective justification in considerations lying not outside but within the rules, and in this field it is precisely a rule of law that calls for the application of *equitable principles*. There is consequently no question in this case of any decision *ex aequo et bono*, such as would only be possible under the conditions prescribed by Article 38, paragraph 2, of the Court's statute.[5]

The above formulation appears to suggest that there are ascertainable 'equitable principles' with a substantive content which would provide precise criteria for determination of what would be equitable in a given situation. On analysis, however, it will be seen that there are no such criteria to be found: although a practical procedure for dealing with the problem and arriving at an acceptable solution can be spelt out from the approach delineated by the Court.

A number of critiques of the North Sea judgment have reflected the views expressed by Judge Tanaka in his Dissenting Opinion, thus: 'the Court admits in favour of the Federal Republic an appeal to higher ideas of law such as justice, equity or equitableness, and reasonableness, which are self-evident, but which owing to their abstract or general character are unable to furnish any concrete criteria for delimitation. Reference to the equitable principle is nothing else but begging the question.'[6] Grisel observes that the two basic ideas governing lateral boundary delimitation, namely that they should be in accordance with equitable principles, and that the continental shelf is the natural prolongation of the state's territory, do not as such provide any practical method for drawing of boundary lines. They are somewhat question-begging and in fact leave open the two issues which will arise in each case: Where does the 'most equitable' frontier line lie, and what are the areas which appertain to each of the countries concerned? In other words, the basic ideas formulate the goal to be achieved rather than the means to achieve it.[7]

Munkman is critical of writers who 'have seen the concept of "equity" as affording appropriate criteria for judicial legislation'. In her view:

They have . . . failed to elaborate the content of equity sufficiently to make it serviceable to resolve concrete disputes. It is plain, for example, that such concepts as general notions of good faith, the maxims of English equity, or 'general principles of law' and 'objective justice' are either inadequate or unhelpful. The notion of 'equity' as requiring that all the surrounding circumstances, including economic and political factors and 'expediency' be taken into account, is nearer the mark. But again, this is insufficiently elaborate to provide a set of criteria for the resolution of particular disputes.[8]

Another criticism of the North Sea judgment is directed against the alleged arbitrariness of the Court in singling out the disadvantage (for purposes of delimiting lateral boundaries) to a state resulting from the concavity of its coastline, while ignoring other disadvantageous geographical circumstances. Thus Friedmann finds it difficult 'to comprehend the rationale of the philosophy which regards inequalities caused by the differences between coastal states and land-locked states, or between coasts with long and short coastlines, as facts of nature which have to be accepted, while the fact that one state's coastline is straight or convex, and another's concave is "unnatural".' Friedmann concludes with the following observations:[9]

Certainly the International Court was not empowered to undertake such a re-distribution of resources, even between the three states concerned. But then the most equitable alternative would appear to have been to recognise the relatively limited inequality stemming from the concave curvature of the coast of West Germany as one of the thousands of inequalities of nature, that have been magnified by the division of the planet into some one hundred and thirty sovereign national states of unequal type and wealth. It cannot even be said that the correction of this particular accident of nature was a kind of Robin Hood justice. For the Court's delimitation benefited as it happened, the biggest and wealthiest of the three states concerned. The

North Sea case illustrates the impossibility of an equitable allocation of the sea resources on the basis of competing sovereignties.

The weakness of this criticism is manifest from the fact that the Court did not itself lay down any rigid criteria, or carry out a delimitation. It defined a procedure for dealing with the issues involved in delimitation, and in fact rejected an approach which would involve a mechanical application of a single method, that is, the equidistance method. There is perhaps an element of substance in the point that the Court was arbitrary in laying special emphasis on such a feature as concavity of the coastline, but Friedmann's assertion that 'the most equitable alternative would appear to have been to recognise the relatively limited inequality stemming from the concave curvature of the coast as one of the thousands of inequalities of nature' is equally subjective and arbitrary. Friedmann's error stems from his inability to appreciate that the complex issues involved in delimitation, namely the weight or value to be attached to different geographical, geological and other features, cannot be resolved by reference to a set of precise criteria. The Court's approach reflects an awareness of this complexity, and the need for adopting appropriate procedures for dealing with such a problem. Thus, the Court while enumerating in the *dispositif*, factors to be taken into account, clearly indicated that the enumeration was not exhaustive. It expressly laid down that:

> In fact there is no legal limit to the considerations which states may take into account for the purpose of making sure that they apply equitable procedures, and more often than not it is the balancing up of all such considerations that will produce this result rather than reliance on one to the exclusion of all others. The problem of relative weight to be accorded to the different considerations naturally varies with the circumstances of each case. In balancing the factors in question, it would appear that various aspects must be taken into account. Some are related to the geological, others to the geographical aspects of the situation, others again to the idea of unity of deposits. These criteria though not entirely precise, can provide adequate bases for decisions adapted to the factual situation.[10]

The Court also laid down that there need be no restriction on the method to be used nor indeed for parties to be restricted to one single method; thus, it held that:

> If for the above reasons (where geographical circumstances would make its application inequitable), equity excludes the use of the equidistance method . . . as the sole method of delimitation, the question arises

whether there is any necessity to employ only one method, for the purposes of a given limitation. There is no logical basis for this, and no objection need be felt to the idea of effecting a delimitation of adjoining continental shelf areas by the concurrent use of various methods . . . The international law of continental shelf delimitation does not involve any imperative rule and permits resort to various principles and methods, or a combination of them, provided that, by the application of equitable principles, a reasonable result is arrived at.[11]

What lies at the root of the approach of the Court is a recognition that the delimitation of continental shelf boundaries involves an element of distribution or apportionment, whereby one party will get more or less, depending on where the boundary line is located. There is also a recognition that 'the share' of one claimant can be enhanced or reduced depending on whether value, or weight, is given to certain factors in defining the boundary line. The protagonists of delimitation by the equidistance method in conceding that the presence of 'special circumstances' justify a departure from that method, in effect concede that it is not right, or just, or 'equitable' for one side to gain a larger 'share' by relying on certain features. Thus for example it is conceded that unless rocks or islets situated in the middle of a semi-enclosed sea are ignored in drawing an equidistance line, these 'islands have the effect of displacing (assuming a position near midpoint on an opposite situation) the boundary approximately a quarter of the width of the body of the water . . . The inequity would be obvious.'[12] The issue at root is thus one of justifying a claim to a larger share by reference to a feature, which the opposing claimant would maintain should not be taken into account. Since no precise definition of 'special circumstances' or an exhaustive enumeration of them exists, or is likely to be agreed upon, the fundamental problem remains the impossibility of achieving 'an objective order of special circumstances'. In the absence of an agreed exhaustive enumeration of special circumstances, there is no formal limit which can be imposed upon the considerations which can be urged to justify a particular boundary-line. The limits are in fact set by the demands of prudence, good sense and reasonableness, so that parties involved in negotiations, to the extent to which a boundary settlement is a common objective, would not take up utterly unreasonable, or inflexible, positions. This is not to say that such negotiations may not be facilitated by the development of specific criteria to which reference could be made to deal with certain types of features. Exercises such as Hodgson's 'Islands: Normal and Special Circumstances',[13] which seek to develop certain criteria by reference to which the effect that should be allowed to islands in boundary delimitation may be assessed, would be helpful to negotiators, or to an arbitrator who is called upon to decide a delimitation question *ex aequo et bono*. An 'equitable solution' in this context, however, is one which is a 'mutually acceptable' solution, which is the result of an agreement reached through negotiations, or the award of an arbitrator deciding the case *ex aequo et bono*. This is implicit in the dicta of the Court that, 'As the operation of delimiting is a matter of determining areas appertaining to different jurisdictions, it is a truism to say that the delimitation is equitable: rather it is the problem above all of defining the means whereby the delimitation can be carried out in such a way as to be *recognized* as equitable.'[14]

The resort to 'equity' and to equitable solutions by the International Court in dealing with essentially distributive questions as were involved in the *North Sea* cases and in the *Fisheries Jurisdiction* cases, should be seen as a judicial technique whereby the Court, once it characterizes the question before it as one involving distribution or apportionment, in an area, where there are no precise, objective criteria by reference to which such an apportionment can be made, declares it to be a question to which only an 'equitable solution' is possible (or more obliquely as one which can be settled only by the application of 'equitable principles'). The Court itself cannot adjudicate on the issue − it therefore directs that the appropriate method to be adopted in such a case is negotiations in good faith aimed at arriving at an agreement. The Court could also logically urge that failing agreement, the appropriate method for settlement would be an arbitration *ex aequo et bono*.

Thus, as regards the *Fisheries Jurisdiction* cases, without commenting on the criticism that the Court went beyond the terms of the submission made before it, it can be argued that once the Court took the view that the essential issue underlying the dispute related to a distribution of resources among competing claimants, it was justified in treating it as one to which an 'equitable solution' would have to be sought in the manner outlined above. The form in which the reasons in support of the judgment have been set out, as in the Separate Opinion of Judge Dillard can be misleading. For after citing Judge Hudson's dicta in the *Diversion of Waters of the River Meuse* case that 'what are widely known as principles of equity have long been considered to constitute a part of international law', he proceeds to state that those principles 'are particularly relevant when the issues focus on the common use of limited resources and the applicable norm of international law is couched in the form of a standard.'[15]

This is misleading as it suggests that just as Judge Hudson was able to draw upon a general principle such as 'equality is equity' to hold that a state seeking the interpretation of a treaty must itself have completely fulfilled the obligations of that treaty, a Court faced with a question of distribution could draw upon established 'principles of equity' by reference to which it could effect an equitable apportionment. Indeed it would appear from Judge Castro's separate opinion, that he has been just so misled, for he has taken the view that:

> It is open to the Court to take the initiative and examine *proprio motu* the factual elements in the case. By making orders for the conduct of the case it can entrust qualified individuals or commissions with the task of carrying out enquiries or giving expert opinion, before or after the oral stage of the proceedings, the Court would be able to balance the interests involved and decide according to *principles of equity*.[16]

Clearly this is something the Court could not do, since it would find that there are no 'principles of equity' which furnished precise criteria by reference to which it could 'balance the interests'. The Court could only assume this task if the parties agreed in the manner contemplated by Article 38, paragraph 2, of the Court's statute to a decision of the case *ex aequo et bono*.

Judge Gros in his dissenting opinion recognizes the complexity of the issues involved in effecting a distribution of resources, thus:

> To hold the balance between the economic survival of a people and the interests of the fishing industry of other states raises a problem of the balanced economic development of all, according to economic criteria, in which fishing is only one of the elements to be taken into account, and of which the bases are international interdependence and solidarity. The concepts of rate of economic growth, industrial diversification, vulnerability of an economy faced with 'caprices of nature', population structure and growth, use of energy, investment needs, development of external markets for fish products, regularization of such markets, foreign participation in Icelandic undertakings, industrial development funds, among many others define the economic interests which are not the concern of the Court. But the Court cannot make them disappear by refusing to see anything but a conservation problem . . .[17]

Judge Gros is right in pointing out the multiplicity of factors that may be relevant in effecting an equitable apportionment of fishery resources.[18] The validity of his assertion that the 'economic interests are not the concern of the Court' is, however, questionable. The Court is certainly justified in taking cognizance of the relevant economic interests involved, though having done so, it may be compelled to reach the conclusion that the problem is one which is not appropriate for judicial settlement, but is one for which an equitable solution must be sought – through agreement or arbitration *ex aequo et bono*. The Informal Single Negotiating Text recognises that the appropriate method for effecting an apportionment of fishery resources (where provision is made for apportionment), is through agreements (bilateral, sub-regional, or regional) to be arrived at through negotiations in which 'all relevant geographic and economic circumstances must be taken into account.'

Thus it is evident from the foregoing analysis that where problems of distribution are involved, and precise criteria for apportionment are not available, the only appropriate course is to seek an 'equitable solution'. The factors and considerations that are relevant will vary. The inherent complexity of the issues involved become manifest once we turn to examine some specific problems for which equitable solutions are considered appropriate.

II

Three specific problems that we shall examine are:

(a) Sharing of benefits arising out of the exploitation of the resources of the seabed, beyond the limits of national jurisdiction;
(b) Unity of mineral deposits, extending across boundaries;
(c) Equitable participation in the exploitation of living resources in certain economic zones by land-locked and geographically disadvantaged states.

(a) Sharing of benefits arising from exploitation of resources of the seabed beyond the limits of national jurisdiction

The Informal Single Negotiating Text provides for equitable sharing of the benefits derived from the exploitation of the resources of the seabed beyond the limits of national jurisdiction. This calls for the working out of sharing formulae, which would equitably distribute the benefits among some 155 states. A specific formula proposed in the Conference proposes that the net annual revenue should be distributed as follows: 10 per cent to a price stabilization fund, 35 per cent to all developing countries, 23½ per cent among land-locked states, 12 per cent among disadvantaged states and 20 per cent among all states. Of these all except the first and last categories are to be distributed according to the following formula based upon population and per capita income:

$$\frac{\text{Population of state}}{\text{Global population}} \times \frac{\text{Global per capita income}}{\text{Per capita income of the state}}$$

The question is raised whether 'the "thin spread" of revenues which would result from the formula is more beneficial than the distribution of revenues on a more selective basis, perhaps giving a substantial proportion of a "year's profits" for the funding of some regional projects.'[19] Indeed one can conceive of a whole range of alternative formulae which it could be argued were more 'equitable'. The choice of one from among these alternatives is not likely to be determined by abstract principles of equity, but through a process of negotiations, so that the formula which is ultimately adopted will be the one which is 'recognized to be equitable' by a consensus of the states concerned.

(b) Unity of mineral deposits extending across boundaries

The problem of mineral deposits extending across submarine boundaries received early attention from those who dealt with the problem of boundary-delimitation. M. Gidel in the 1950 Report on the Continental Shelf to the International Law Commission observed that the primary concern in the case of potential petroleum deposits should be directed to the 'preservation of the unity of the deposit'.[20] Mouton urged that where an oil-pool might be divided by a line drawn in accordance with the principle of equidistance 'account must be taken of the essential unity of the deposit'![21] A view was expressed that insistence on the preservation of the unity of the deposit implied that 'no offshore petroleum deposit would be allowed to be divided by international boundaries',[22] while another held that a solution could be found to the problem by parties arriving at 'an accommodation between themselves'.[23] A variety of solutions were devised to deal with the two basic problems that were presented, namely the effective exploitation of the common reservoir and a basis for apportionment of the benefits arising from such exploitation. An early solution proposed was that of 'establishing a protective perimeter' so that no drilling would be permitted in a defined area on each side of the boundary, without prior agreement.[24] This solution was adopted in the Continental Shelf Delimitation Agreement between Qatar and Iran of 7 May 1971, in which Article 2 provides:

> If any single geological or petroleum structure or petroleum field, or any single geological structure or field of any other mineral deposit, extends across the boundary line . . . and part of such structure or field which is situated on one side of that boundary line could be exploited wholly or in part by directional drilling from the other side of the boundary line, then
> (a) no well shall be drilled on either side of the boundary line so that any producing section thereof is less than 125 metres from the said boundary line, except by mutual agreement between two Governments . . .

A similar provision was included in the Bahrain-Iran Delimitation Agreement of 17 June 1971.

A type of solution adopted in some agreements in the Gulf, provided for joint exploitation and a fifty-fifty sharing of income (the Saudi Arabia-Bahrain Agreement of 22 May 1958) while one provided for a fifty-fifty division of recoverable oil.

Inevitably, the concept of 'equitable sharing' would commend itself to those seeking a solution to this type of problem.[25] Thus, in a series of Delimitation Agreements involving Indonesia (the Australia-Indonesia Seabed Boundaries Agreement of 18 May 1971, the Indonesia-Malaysia Delimitation Agreement of 27 October 1969 and the Australia-Indonesia Agreement of 9 October 1972), a provision is included in the following terms:

> If any single accumulation of liquid hydrocarbons or natural gas, or if any other mineral deposit beneath the seabed, extends across any of (the agreed boundary-lines) and part of such accumulation or deposit that is situated on one side of the line is irrecoverable in fluid form wholly or in part from the other side of the line, the two Governments will seek an agreement on the manner in which the accumulation or deposit shall be most effectively exploited and on equitable sharing of the benefits arising from such exploitation.

A number of agreements simply provide for effective exploitation and apportionment of the proceeds from such exploitation to be determined by agreement (the Canada-Denmark Delimitation Agreement of 17 December 1973, the Denmark-United Kingdom Agreement of 25 November 1971, and the India-Sri Lanka Agreement of 26 June 1974), while others such as the United Kingdom-Germany Agreement of 25 November 1971 provides for exploitation and apportionment to be governed by an agreement, but in default of agreement, provision is made for the manner of exploitation and the apportionment of proceeds to be determined by a sole Arbitrator.

A different solution is elaborated in the Argentina-Uruguay Treaty concerning the La Plata River and its Maritime Limits of 19 November 1973. It provides that in case of a deposit which extends across a lateral boundary 'each party shall be free to conduct exploitation, provided this does not cause substantial detriment to the other party and is in compliance with the requirements for an integral and rational utilization of the resource' and that 'the resources extracted from the said field will be allocated to the parties in proportion to the volume located respectively on either side of the boundary.'

A combination of these approaches, with a significant refinement, is found in the Delimitation Treaties between the Federal Republic of Germany and Denmark and the Netherlands respectively, both of 28 January 1971 (concluded following the decision in the North Sea cases). Article 2 in each of the treaties provides for exploitation and the apportionment of proceeds to be determined by agreement, and in default of agreement by an arbitral tribunal, which would be empowered to decide *ex aequo et bono*.

Equitable solutions have thus been developed to deal with the problem of mineral deposits extending across submarine boundaries. The unity of deposits have not been preserved in the physical sense, but the aim has been to provide for effective joint exploitation and apportionment of the benefits from exploitation, on the basis of agreement, with a provision in a number of cases that failing agreement, the matter would be determined by arbitration *ex aequo et bono*.

(c) Equitable participation in the exploitation of living resources in certain economic zones by land-locked and geographically-disadvantaged states

The Informal Single Negotiating Text contains specific provisions which invest land-locked and geographically-disadvantaged states with the right to participate 'on an equitable basis' in certain 'neighbouring' economic zones. The complexity of the issues involved in working out equitable arrangements for such participation are well brought out by Alexander and Hodgson in their examination of these provisions in the context of what they describe as 'the new ethic of equity being applied with respect to the sea'.[26] The problems are sharply focused in their examination of a concrete situation in Africa, thus:

The geographical obstacles, for example, in allocating to Niger access to the living resources of adjacent states, appear insuperable. Niger is bound by the coastal states of Algeria, Libya, Dahomey and Nigeria. Will Niger be granted access to each of the four economic zones or will Dahomey be exempt since it too is a GDS (geographically disadvantaged state)? How may Niger gain access across the Sahara to Libyan and Algerian economic zones? If this right proves too expensive to exercise, will Niger concentrate its activities only in the zone of Nigeria? How will these rights be apportioned among Dahomey, Niger and Nigeria? The answers seem fraught with potential conflicts creating more problems than they may actually solve.[27]

It might be argued that the problem of working out an arrangement may not prove as difficult as the above analysis suggests, if the states concerned seek an 'equitable solution' through an agreement in which what they would aim at is not a fine determination of each of the issues referred to above, but a practical basis for sharing benefits from a scheme for exploitation of living resources.

III

Thus 'equitable solutions' are increasingly sought to problems involving the law of the sea in relation to such matters as distribution, and apportionment, of resources. It will not do for international lawyers to avoid facing up to these problems by adopting a position such as Judge Sorensen did in his Dissenting Opinion in the *North Sea* judgement: 'The idea of *justitia distributiva*, however meritorious it may be as a moral or political principle, has not become part of international law, as will be seen from a cursory glance at the established international order with its patent factual inequalities between states.'[28] One might say that a cursory glance at the current global environment reveals that pressures have built up for a change in the established order. There is no dearth of evidence of a growing recognition of the need for equitable distribution of resources, and as provisions in favour of land-locked, geographically-disadvantaged, and developing states show, this concern extends to redressing some of the factual 'inequalities' that are seen to exist.

'Equitable solutions' to problems of distribution are thus to be sought by adopting procedures which will enable competing claims and interests to be reconciled in agreements arrived at through negotiations, and failing agreement through arbitration *ex aequo et bono*. The lawyers' contribution to this process would be the more effective if they were more widely and deeply informed of all the relevant economic, geographic and other considerations to which the competing claimants attach value or weight when they put forward their alternative solutions, while declaring that their common objective is to find one which is 'just' and 'equitable'.

NOTES AND REFERENCES

1   ICJ, *Reports* (1969), p. 4.
2   ICJ, *Reports* (1974), p. 4.
3   *International Legal Materials*, Vol. 14 (1975), p. 710.
4   ICJ, *Reports* (1969), p. 22, para. 20; see A.L.W. Munkman, 'Adjudication and Adjustment — International Judicial Decision and the Settlement of Territorial and Boundary Disputes', 1972–73, *British Yearbook of International Law*, Vol. 47, p. 1 at pp. 87 and 115.
5   Ibid., p. 48, para. 88.
6   Ibid., pp. 196–7.
7   E. Grisel, 'The Lateral Boundaries of the Continental Shelf and the Judgment of the International Court of Justice in the North Sea Continental Shelf Cases', *American Journal of International Law*, Vol. 64 (1970), p. 562 at p. 589.
8   Munkman, 'Adjudication and Adjustment', p. 19.
9   W. Friedmann, 'The North Sea Continental Shelf Cases — A Critique', *American Journal of International Law*, Vol. 64 (1970), p. 229 at pp. 239–40; see also, T. Rothpfeffer, 'Equity in the *North Sea Continental Shelf* cases', *Nordisk Tidsskrift for International Ret*, (Acta Scandinavica Juris Gentium), Vol. 42 (1972), p. 81 at pp. 114–15.
10   ICJ, *Reports* (1969), p. 50, para. 93.
11   Ibid., p. 49, para. 90.
12   R.D. Hodgson, 'Islands: Normal and Special Circumstances' in J.K. Gamble and G. Pontecorvo, eds., *Law of the Sea: The Emerging Regime of the Oceans*, 1974, Cambridge, Mass., Ballinger, p. 137 at p. 188.
13   Ibid.
14   ICJ, *Reports*, (1969) p. 50, para. 92.
15   ICJ, *Reports* (1974), p. 62.
16   Ibid., p. 103.
17   Ibid., p. 147.
18   Some of the complex issues involved in determining whether a coastal state is in 'a position of special dependence' on coastal fisheries so as to be entitled to claim preferential rights are spelt out in R.R. Churchill's 'The Fisheries Jurisdiction Cases: The Contribution of the International Court of Justice to the Debate on Coastal States' Fisheries Rights', *International and Comparative Law Quarterly* Vol. 24 (1975), p. 82 at p. 97.
19   A.V. Lowe, 'The International Seabed and the Single Negotiating Test', *San Diego Law Review*, Vol. 13 (1976), p. 489 at p. 523.
20   *Yearbook of the International Law Commission*, 1950, Vol. II, New York, United Nations, p. 112.
21   M.W. Mouton, 'The Continental Shelf', *Hague Receuil de Cours*, Vol. I (1954), p. 347 at p. 421.
22   W.T. Onorato, 'Apportionment of an International Common Petroleum Deposit', *International and Comparative Law Quarterly*, Vol. 17 (1968), p. 85, at p. 86.

23 D.J. Padwa, 'Submarine Boundaries', *International and Comparative Law Quarterly*, Vol. 9 (1960), p. 628 at p. 645.

24 Mouton, 'The Continental Shelf', p. 421.

25 Onorato, 'Apportionment', p. 85; also, J.E. Horigan, 'Unitization of Reservoirs Extending Across Sub-sea Boundaries of Bordering States in the North Sea', *Natural Resources Lawyer*, Vol. 7 (1974), p. 67.

26 L.M. Alexander and R.D. Hodgson, 'The Role of the Geographically-Disadvantaged States in the Law of the Sea', *San Diego Law Review*, Vol. 13 (1976), p. 558.

27 Ibid., p. 581.

28 ICJ, *Reports* (1969), pp. 255–6.

Part IV

PERMANENT SOVEREIGNTY OVER NATURAL RESOURCES

16 Sovereignty over Natural Resources and The Search for a New International Order

*Hasan S. Zakariya**

INTRODUCTION

I

It is to be recalled that the heated controversy arising out of the sudden, major increase in the price of crude oil announced by the oil exporters late in 1973 and the mounting spirit of confrontation that followed, manifested, for example, in the Washington meeting of the big oil consumers in March 1974, was the immediate cause of the call for the Sixth Special Session of the General Assembly of the United Nations on raw material and development. The primary aim of that Special Session held in April 1974 was, of course, to air the collective grievances of the developing countries and to put forward their own counterclaims. The aim was also to defuse the tension and put an end to mutual recriminations with a view to introducing a new and more balanced formula for future international economic co-operation, generally acceptable to the various components of the world community.

The Sixth Special Session did contribute significantly towards the subsequent relaxation of tension and the subsidence of the mounting confrontation. Unfortunately, neither that Session, nor any of the international meetings which have been convened in its wake, notably the Conference on International Economic Co-operation (CIEC) — the so-called North–South Conference — have been successful in forging conclusively a concrete and mutually acceptable formula for future economic co-operation. All present indications would suggest that the global debate

*United Nations.

on the final shape of any such formula will continue to be with us for many years to come.

One important aspect of that global debate has been the question of state sovereignty over natural resources. This was logical enough. After all, it was petroleum, the natural resource *par excellence*, which kindled the big controversy in the first place. Thus both the Declaration on the Establishment of a New International Economic Order (resolution 3201 (S–VI)) and the Programme of Action thereon (resolution 3202 (S–VI)) reaffirm the crucial place of natural resources, and the manner in which they ought to be developed and disposed of both for the benefit of the producing countries and in the interests of the world community at large.

II

It may be said that the call for a new international economic order, as far as natural resources are concerned did not actually start with the Sixth Special Session, but was first made almost a quarter of a century earlier, during the early, formative years of the United Nations.

It is now almost three decades since the United Nations first took up the question of permanent sovereignty over natural resources. It was in 1952 when a certain developing country (Chile) raised this question during the debate on the Draft International Covenants on Human Rights.[1] The General Assembly had decided to include the right of all peoples and nations to self-determination as part of the Human Rights Covenants and called upon the Commission to prepare a draft on the subject. It was in the context of the debate on the right of self-determination that the economic and social, in addition to the political, aspects of this right were invoked. The debate which started in the Human Rights Commission in 1952 continued unabated in various forums of the United Nations until it culminated in the landmark resolution 1803 (XVII) of 14 December 1962. In subsequent years, the ideas enunciated in that Resolution were repeatedly reaffirmed, and at times elaborated on by the General Assembly itself or by other UN bodies.[2]

III

The adoption of the United Nations resolution 1803, and its repeated reaffirmation with such a remarkable degree of consensus attest not only to the deep-seated validity of the doctrine of permanent sovereignty but also to the wisdom and sense of fairness and statesmanship on the part of all those who eventually accepted the compromise from both developed and the developing countries.

It is to be remembered, however, that the invocation and the conceptual progress of the doctrine within the United Nations was due to the initiative of the developing countries themselves; it was, at once, a summation of the experience and accomplishments of these countries over the years preceding the birth of the United Nations, and an expression of the aspirations which were yet to be fulfilled.

The battle for economic self-determination and permanent sovereignty over natural resources was fought simultaneously in the post-World War II era on two fronts: concrete political and economic action by some of the developing nations individually or collectively, and the theoretical refinement of the underlying legal concepts and principles within the United Nations system. Any progress and success achieved on one front was bound to influence, if not determine the outcome of the other.

Without going as far as ascribing to the United Nations resolutions on sovereignty over natural resources a 'cause and effect' impact on subsequent major events in the developing countries, such as the major oil exporters, it is not to be denied that these resolutions were for them a rich source of inspiration, self-confidence and moral support. Those, for example, who were pleading the case of the petroleum exporters and arguing its merits, were keenly aware at the time of the salutary implications of these resolutions. Consequently, they did not fail to cite them again and again in demonstrating the legitimacy and justice of that case. Without these resolutions it would have been more difficult to realize such basic objectives, as, for example, the equitable sharing of benefits, a fair price for crude oil to reflect not only its depleting nature and replacement value but also its unique impact on social and economic development, effective state participation in the ownership and management of operations, renegotiation and readjustment of terms in light of changed circumstances, and the supremacy of national jurisdiction for the settlement of disputes.

It follows from the above that as far as this group of developing countries is concerned, and probably certain others who are relatively more advantaged economically, the standards and principles endorsed in the resolutions have become, to a great extent, a living reality; their achievements represent a major, if at times partial, fulfilment of those standards and principles.

Unfortunately, the same does not hold true for the rest of the developing countries which are economically less fortunate and to whom sovereignty over natural resources is, by and large, an ideal still to be pursued and a theory yet to be transformed into concrete action. This group of countries is the main concern of this paper.

THE LESS DEVELOPED COUNTRIES AND THE EXPLORATION AND DEVELOPMENT OF PETROLEUM RESOURCES

We propose now to deal with the case of the less developed countries from the special standpoint of the exploration for petroleum resources. The particular attention given to this group among the developing countries, and to petroleum among natural resources, is justified not only by paragraph (4-c) of the Declaration of the Sixth Special Session which emphasized the particular needs of these countries, but also by the fact that petroleum is now the most crucial raw material, and as such has the greatest impact on economic development.

As is well known, petroleum has been for many years now the main source of energy throughout the world. All present forecasts indicate that it will remain so for many years. The future availability and price of petroleum are two of the main concerns of the world community today. Since petroleum deposits are finite, the need for their rational utilization is becoming more and more urgent. Equally urgent is the development of alternative, or at least supplementary sources of energy so that this unique and wonderful gift of nature may be available to mankind for many generations to come.

The drive to locate new petroleum reserves in various parts of the world is, by and large, continuing with full force. However, this process is not evenly shared by all. The developing countries in general, and more particularly the non-producers of oil, appear to be getting less than their fair share of the exploration activities. What is most disturbing, however, is that when they do get it, the terms and conditions attached, more often than not, fall short of the standards established by the United Nations resolutions on Permanent Sovereignty.

It is common knowledge that most of the developing countries in this category (which, for lack of a shorter or better term, are referred to as the less developed countries, LDCs) have been for a few years now in a financially precarious position. They have been under double jeopardy, burdened by larger bills not only for imported oil, but also for other imported commodities as a result of sustained worldwide inflation. For those lucky enough to possess other exploitable minerals, such as copper and iron, the recent depressed market and frequent price fluctuations of some of these minerals represent no doubt a third jeopardy. For these countries the possible discovery of indigenous petroleum deposits in payable quantities could mean a fantastic dream come true, even if any such discovery means merely self-sufficiency.

Unfortunately, most, if not all of these countries are not able to meet the enormous costs of petroleum exploration on their own. Consequently, the task has been, and will have to continue to be, carried out with outside assistance. This assistance can be sought either from the international private sector, the international public sector, bilateral arrangements with other countries or a combination of two or more of the above.

International Private Sector

(a) Privately-owned oil companies:

These companies whose base is one or more of the major industrialized countries in Europe and North America, in addition to Japan, predominate in the international private sector. Included in this group are those few companies, like BP and CFP, in which their home government is a major share-holder. These private companies, whose role has been dominant for so long, still represent, as far as the LDCs are concerned, the main source of the kind of investments and technology needed for any decisive exploration. Needless to say, these companies are 'in business', and as such, are motivated mainly by profit making — the bigger the profit, the better! They are accountable, if at all, only to their own share holders who, in turn, are private individuals and institutions whose own notions of success and failure are naturally focused on the size of the profit earned.

For such private companies, the principles and standards of permanent sovereignty are *metaphysics*: incomprehensible or, at least, irrelevant to the type of work in which they are engaged. In the past, they fought fiercely against any attempt, by developing countries, to encroach upon what they profoundly considered to be their legal rights under their respective agreements. They never gave in voluntarily. Any compromise or retreat on their part was always the result either of a bold sovereign act by one individual state, by the collective action of a group of countries with similar interests or by a fundamental change of circumstances which shattered the order of things they tried so desperately to perpetuate.

Hence, it is very unrealistic to expect that in dealing with the LDCs for the first time, now or in the future, these private companies would subscribe voluntarily to or observe spontaneously the standards embodied in the UN resolutions. They have to be persuaded, pressured or coerced into observing these standards.

The problem is that in their initial dealings with the LDCs, at least, the private companies are in a much stronger bargaining position than the governments. Because of their preponderant position worldwide and the relative lack of other sources of assistance from the international public sector, the deals the companies offer to the governments of the LDCs are often on the basis of take it or leave it — in the fashion of the *Contrat d'adhésion* in which one of the parties has little or no power to negotiate the terms. This is the real dilemma confronting these governments.

In formulating the deal they offer to any particular LDC, the private oil companies are not only motivated by securing the largest margin of profit and the recovery of total investments within the shortest possible time but also by such additional considerations as the cost of unsuccessful operations elsewhere, and the need to hedge against political risks, real or imaginary, involved in each case.

What has just been said should not be interpreted as an attempt to deny the important role the private international sector has played so far in locating and developing petroleum resources worldwide, or the very useful role it can still play in this regard. What is to be emphasized is that, initially at least, the price for co-operation with these companies can sometimes be unreasonably high and not in strict conformity with the UN resolutions on permanent sovereignty over natural resources.

(b) State-owned Oil Companies:

There are several such companies which have been very active in petroleum exploration and development worldwide, alongside the older and more financially powerful ones — the major private companies. Historically, these state-owned companies, mostly European, have been created to fulfil the national policy of their respective governments, mainly to achieve some degree of security of supply from foreign sources and also to obtain in the process economic and financial advantages. Although they were, and of course still are mandated to operate in accordance with the usual norms of business and trade, some of these state companies, for reasons of their own, did offer some developing countries in the fifties and sixties terms which were somewhat better than those offered by the privately-owned companies and hence somewhat more consonant with the principles of state sovereignty over natural resources. However, as far as the type of deals offered at present to the governments of the LDCs are concerned, one can scarcely discern any tangible difference between those offered now by the privately-owned and the state-owned oil companies.

International Public Sector

The well-entrenched position of the private oil companies in the field of petroleum exploration worldwide, the considerable funds needed for such exploration and the high financial risks involved have no doubt contributed very significantly to inhibiting the availability of international public funds for financing such operations in the more disadvantaged countries and in limiting the useful role which international institutions might otherwise have played.

1. *The United Nations System:*

Although, for nearly two decades now, the United Nations Development Programme (UNDP) has been an important source of funds for exploration activities in developing countries, the bulk of these activities has been for hard minerals only; exploration drilling for petroleum was rarely included.[3]

The Revolving Fund for the Exploration of Natural Resources was established in 1973 (General Assembly resolution 3167 (XXVIII) of 17 December 1973) in recognition of the need to extend and intensify the activities of the United Nations system in the field of exploration for natural resources in the developing countries. Although the Fund was originally conceived to apply to all natural resources, the Governing Council of the Fund decided that it should concentrate its initial operations on solid minerals, thus excluding, among others, all petroleum resources. The reasoning behind this decision is thought to lie in the high cost of oil and gas exploration as compared to the level of resources which the Fund might reasonably be expected to attract at the outset of its operations.[4]

2. *Regional Development Banks:*

On the whole, the attitude of the regional development banks, such as the Inter-American Development Bank and the Asian Development Bank, to petroleum exploration in the developing countries has been, so far, similar to those of the World Bank (to be discussed next), i.e. refraining from providing loans for exploration projects. There are indications, however, that some of these Banks are contemplating new policies for involvement in some aspects of exploration.[5]

3. *The World Bank:*

Until recently, the Bank policy was to refuse to provide loans for financing petroleum production projects. In July 1977, however, the Bank decided to start lending for such projects on an experimental and limited basis. This new policy was no doubt prompted by the changed economics of energy worldwide in recent years.

Eighteen months after taking that initial step, the Bank decided to expand the scope of this new facility to include risk funds for petroleum exploration. On 16 January 1979, the Board of Directors of the Bank approved a $3 billion loan programme for a proposed plan for oil and gas development in non-Opec developing countries. Only a small part of this amount — about $500 million — will be devoted to exploration. The bulk will be devoted to developing proven oil and gas reserves and the introduction and installation of secondary recovery techniques in countries with declining recoverable reserves.

This latest step has been taken by the Bank in response to the requests by, among others, the United Nations and the Bonn Summit of 17 July 1978, that the Bank, and other international agencies, expand their assistance to the developing countries in this sector.

In spite of its belatedness, this new policy of the World Bank should, of course, be viewed on the whole as commendable and welcome. Although it is perhaps too early to assess the real impact this will have on the drive to locate and develop new petroleum resources in the developing countries, there are certain aspects of the Bank's new policy which are ambiguous at best, and rather disappointing at worst. More definitely, as far as one can tell from the official reports of the Bank itself, the new policy does not seem to have been designed to promote in any particular way the adherence of the international private sector to the standards and principles proclaimed in the UN resolutions on permanent sovereignty over natural resources. Let us consider the following:

1. The Bank funds available for risk exploration in non-Opec developing countries are rather meagre compared to the immensity of the task at hand. They are envisaged mainly to assist some of these countries to meet their exploration costs in association with private foreign companies. In countries where such companies are unwilling to invest capital in

exploration, the Bank would consider providing ten-year credit to cover the costs incurred by them.

2.   The loans are expected to be extended on normal World Bank terms — 7 per cent interest, 15-20 year maturity, three to four year grace periods — and will require a government guarantee from the recipient country. As was made abundantly clear by a Bank spokesman: 'The Bank is not taking the risk of getting nothing back on its investment. The country is taking the risk of getting nothing back on its investments.'[6]

3.   It is to be pointed out that, the financial burden of unsuccessful exploration for petroleum deposits (the risk investments) has so far been uniformly borne solely by the professional gamblers — the foreign oil companies. This has been the rule of the game for a long while. Under the Bank's new policy, the role of those companies in the field of exploration would continue to be dominant. In making the developing country share the financial burden of such a risky venture, it is not clear what price the Bank will exact, or urge the country concerned to exact from the companies concerned in return for this departure from the established norm. Will this potential sacrifice on the part of the developing country be matched by a corresponding improvement in the terms of the deal usually offered by these companies? Would this lessening of the risk burden of the companies mean a better application of and wider adherence to the principles of UN resolutions on permanent sovereignty? The legal and moral responsibility of the Bank in this regard cannot be over-emphasized. It is not just another commercial bank. It is an international institution with a salutary public purpose. It is therefore incumbent upon the Bank to declare its preference for the type of contractual terms it would wish to see consummated between the country receiving its assistance and prospective private oil companies.

SUMMARY AND CONCLUSIONS

1.   More than a decade before the United Nations Sixth Special Session was convened in 1974 to consider the problem of raw materials and development, the United Nations made a definite attempt to regulate world co-operation in the field of natural resources. The UN resolutions on permanent sovereignty over natural resources, notably that of December 1962 (1803) may be said to represent the first call for a new international economic order as far as natural resources are concerned.

2. Although adopted with a remarkable degree of consensus, the UN resolution 1803 and all other similar resolutions that subsequently either reaffirmed it or articulated some of its principles, were introduced and keenly pursued by the developing countries themselves, to serve as a summation of their experience and achievements and as an expression of aspirations not yet fulfilled. It is important to bear this fact in mind during any interpretation and application of these resolutions.

3. While some developing countries, particularly the petroleum exporters, have made great strides towards translating the norms and principles of the resolutions into a living reality, for most of the others, particularly the less developed ones (LDCs), these resolutions still represent little more than an abstract ideal. Regrettably, they have a long way to go before this ideal is realized.

4. It is submitted that the norms and principles embodied in these resolutions are, by and large, still adequate to provide the general legal framework for future, equitable international co-operation in the field of natural resources. What is urgently needed, however, especially in the case of the LDCs, is not so much their adoption in the national legislation of each of these countries, as the material conditions and practical means for their effective and faithful implementation, without which these norms and principles will remain irrelevant to the concrete experience of these countries.

5. It goes without saying that before any country can exercise sovereignty over its natural resources, these resources must first be located and developed. Since most, if not all, of the LDCs are not in a position to do so without the financial and technological assistance of outsiders, the problem, if not the dilemma, for these countries, is not only how to obtain such assistance but also, and more importantly, how to ensure that its terms conform to the spirit of the above-mentioned UN resolutions.

6. Due to the continued importance of petroleum deposits as a raw material, source of energy and generator of foreign exchange so essential for any accelerated economic development, the LDCs are faced with the particularly urgent need to locate and develop whatever petroleum there is within their territorial jurisdiction. The need for outside assistance is also particularly acute in this case.

7. So far, the international private sector has been the main source of such assistance. In providing their services to the LDCs, the main and immediate concern of the international private sector, as represented

by the oil companies, is not how to help these countries on the road to economic development but how to reap the largest profit possible, as soon as possible. Confronted alone by these private companies, the LDCs are, initially at least, in a much weaker bargaining position. They either have to accept the deals offered to them by the companies *in toto*, or leave their potential resources untapped for many years to come — hardly a comfortable choice!

8. The international public sector has so far been generally reluctant to provide effective assistance to the LDCs in the field of mineral exploration, particularly for petroleum. Although of late there have been a few faint indications that this long-held attitude is beginning to change (witness the new policy of the World Bank, for example), this change is very limited in scope and not designed, of course, to replace the traditional role of the international private sector, which will continue to be dominant.

9. The international public sector is called upon to assume a larger and more decisive role in assisting the LDCs to locate and develop their potential petroleum resources. One of the main purposes of such an expanded role is to dispense with the services of the private companies as far as possible, or at least to enable the governments of the LDCs to demand, and obtain from these companies, terms and conditions which are more in conformity with the standards of the UN resolutions on permanent sovereignty.

10. The developed industrialized countries can, and should play a more positive role in this process. Apart from increasing their direct aid to the LDCs, those developed countries which have well-established and internationally active state-owned companies, should not only direct these national companies of theirs to offer financial and technical services to more LDCs, but they should also be most scrupulous in observing the UN standards in dealing with them.

As sole shareholders of state oil companies, these industrialized countries are presumed to be largely motivated not by profit-making but by a national public purpose. They can afford the privilege, if not the distinction, of being motivated in their dealings with the LDCs by an international public purpose.

NOTES AND REFERENCES

1   Eighth Session of the Human Rights Commission, in pursuance of General Assembly resolution 545 (VI) of February 1952.

2   For example, resolutions 2158 (XXI) of 25 November 1966; 2386 (XXIII) of 19 November 1968; 2692 (XXV) of 11 December 1970; and 3016 (XXVII) of 18 December 1972.

3   For more details, see *Development and International Co-operation*, Report of the Secretary-General (United Nations), A/33/256 of 16 October 1978, pp. 19–20.

4   The Fund's current resources amount to only £23 million, ibid., p. 21.

5   Ibid., p. 22.

6   Quoted in the *Middle East Economic Survey*, 29 January 1979, p. 8.

17 Application of the Rules of State Responsibility to the Nationalization of Foreign-Owned Property

*Eduardo Jimenez de Arechaga**

The rules concerning State responsibility apply in a special way in the case of nationalization or expropriation of foreign-owned property. Contemporary international law recognizes the right of every State to nationalize foreign-owned property, even if a predecessor State or a previous government engaged itself, by treaty or by a contract, not to do so. This is a corollary of the principle of permanent sovereignty of a State over all its wealth, natural resources and economic activities, as proclaimed in successive General Assembly resolutions and particularly in Article 2, paragraph I, of Chapter II of the Charter of Economic Rights and Duties of States. The description of this sovereignty as *permanent* signifies that the territorial State can never lose its legal capacity to change the destination or the method of exploitation of those resources, whatever arrangements have been made for their exploitation and administration.

Traditional international law considered any interference by a State with foreign-owned property a violation of acquired rights, which were internationally protected, and thus an international unlawful act. Today any measure of nationalization or expropriation constitutes the exercise of a sovereign right of the State and is consequently entirely lawful. This fundamental change of approach has significant consequences in respect of the application of the rules of State responsibility, particularly in regard to the existence and scope of the duty to compensate the aliens affected by the nationalization measures.

*International Court of Justice.

APPROACHES TO THE QUESTION OF COMPENSATION

The traditional doctrine considered that since the act of nationalization or expropriation was in violation of acquired rights, the normal principles of State responsibility for unlawful acts should apply. Consequently, a secondary duty was imposed upon the nationalizing State to eliminate all the damaging consequences of its unlawful act. This was to be achieved by restitution of the expropriated undertaking, and, if restitution was not possible, by the 'payment of a sum corresponding to the value which a restitution in kind would bear', plus the award of 'damages for loss sustained which would not be covered by restitution in kind or payment in place of it'.[1] On the strength of this judicial pronouncement the classical doctrine claimed that the indemnity in case of expropriation or nationalization should be determined on the basis of the full market value of an undertaking, as a 'going concern' plus the future earning prospects (*lucrum cessans*) and the goodwill it had developed as well as other intangible assets. This claim was synthesized in the formula, still defended by many industrialized States, of a 'just' or 'adequate' compensation, which should, furthermore, be 'prompt and effective'. This means that the payment ought to be made at the time of dispossession or shortly thereafter and in a convertible and freely transferable currency.[2]

The very basis of this traditional doctrine, which is the assumption of the existence of an unlawful act, is removed once it is realized that the acquired right to private property, in particular private ownership of the means of industrial production, is no longer protected by contemporary international law. Different economic systems coexist peacefully in the world of today and there is a growing recognition of the right of each State to organize as it chooses its economic structure and to introduce all the economic and social changes which the government of the day deems desirable. As provided in Article 1 of Chapter II of the Charter of Economic Rights and Duties of States 'every State has the sovereign and inalienable right to choose its economic system'.

Once the measures of nationalization are not *per se* unlawful, but, on the contrary, constitute the exercise of a sovereign right, the general rules of State responsibility in respect of unlawful acts can no longer apply. To assert, for instance, that there is a duty of restitution of a nationalized undertaking would be tantamount to a denial of the right to nationalize: this in turn deprives of relevance the principle proclaimed by the Permanent Court that the amount of compensation should correspond as closely as possible to the economic benefit which the foreign owner would gain from restitution.

A second and opposed approach to the question of compensation, is to contend that there is no duty to pay compensation in the event of nationalizations which have been adopted in furtherance of a general programme of economic and social reform, particularly when no such indemnity is paid to the affected national owners.

However, such a contention cannot be based upon the practice actually followed by States. That practice, particularly the experience of widespread nationalizations after the Second World War, shows that compensation has been generally granted to alien owners, often in the form of global compensation agreements between the nationalizing State and the States whose subjects were affected by the nationalization measures: the so-called 'lump-sum' agreements. Even Socialist States whose economic policies are based on the national ownership of means of production, have made and have accepted *inter-se* claims for compensation in respect of properties belonging to their nationals which had been nationalized in other socialist countries.[3] These examples show that the legal foundation of the payment of compensation in the event of nationalization must be looked for in certain legal principles different from the classical doctrine of an internationally protected acquired right of property.

(1) The Doctrine of Unjust Enrichment

The doctrine which constitutes the legal foundation of the conduct actually followed by States is the principle of unjust enrichment. If the nationalizing State were to grant no compensation when nationalizing alien property, it would enrich itself without justification at the expense of a foreign State considered as a distinct political, economic and social unity. Through the exercise of its sovereign right to nationalize, that State would be depriving an alien community of the wealth represented by the investments it has made on foreign soil: it would be taking undue advantage of the fact that economic resources originating in another State had penetrated its territorial domain.

This principle signifies that it is not the loss or impoverishment of the expropriated individual owner, in all its elements, which must be taken into account, but the enrichment, the beneficial gain which has been obtained by the nationalizing State. The measures which bring about a transfer of wealth in favour of the nationalizing State or one of its agencies are those which give rise to a duty to compensate. Measures such as the total suppression, for reasons of general policy, of a detrimental or inconvenient industrial or commercial activity, are not subject to compensation. The reason is that in those cases no enrichment is gained by the nationalizing State, even if a loss has been experienced by the foreign owner. Similarly, goodwill will not be a ground for compensation when the abolition of free market conditions of competition nullifies the value of this intangible asset.

However, the municipal law principle of unjust enrichment, in all its aspects, cannot be mechanically transplanted to the sphere of international law. Lord McNair wisely advised that international law does not import private law rules and institutions 'lock, stock and barrel' but regards them 'as an indication of policy and principles'.[4] What makes the principle of unjust enrichment highly relevant in the field of nationalizations is its equitable foundation, which makes it necessary to take into account all the circumstances of each specific situation and to balance the claims of the dispossessed alien with the undue advantages that he may have enjoyed prior to nationalization.

Thus, the principle of unjust enrichment works both ways. It also requires that the undue enrichment acquired by foreign companies during a period of monopoly or of highly privileged economic position, as, for instance, during a period of colonial domination, should be taken into account.

(2) The Charter of Economic Rights and Duties of States

Article 2, paragraph 2, litt. c, of Chapter II of the Charter of Economic Rights and Duties of States proclaims that each State has the right:

> to nationalize, expropriate or transfer ownership of foreign property, in which case appropriate compensation should be paid by the State adopting such measures, taking into account its relevant laws and regulations and all circumstances that the State considers gives rise to controversy, it shall be settled under the domestic law of the nationalizing State and by its tribunals, unless it is freely and mutually agreed by all States concerned that other peaceful means be sought on the basis of the sovereign equality of States and in accordance with the principle of free choice of means.

The question arises as to which of the various approaches to the question of compensation the above provision corresponds. It is obvious that it does not correspond to the doctrine of 'adequate, prompt and effective compensation'. In the early stages of the drafting of the Charter the industrialized States insisted that such were the requirements of existing international law. A vast majority of States categorically rejected the proposal to refer to 'adequate, prompt and effective compensation', thus demonstrating that the alleged customary rule lacked the necessary generality and uniformity. Consequently, one of the facts evidenced by the process of elaboration of this instrument is that the classical doctrine does not represent the general consensus of States and consequently cannot be considered as a rule of customary law.

The *travaux préparatoires* of the Charter of Economic Rights and Duties of States also show that the provision of Article 2 (c) is not based on the negative position which denies the existence of any obligation to pay compensation. It is true that such was the position originally adopted by the working group which drafted the Charter but this position was abandoned during discussion of the instrument.

The text originally presented to the General Assembly stated that compensation was to be paid 'provided that' 'all pertinent circumstances so require'. This text clearly avoided imposing the duty to compensate and left such payment to the discretion of the expropriating State.

It was only a few days before the vote that the Group of 77 changed its position and proposed to revise the text by inserting a provision imposing the obligation to pay 'appropriate compensation'. The text as finally adopted not only imposes the duty to pay 'appropriate compensation'; it also provides that such compensations shall be determined 'taking into account all circumstances that the State considers pertinent'.

The elaboration of the Charter provides useful guidance as to which of the pertinent circumstances are to be taken into account. One is the time during which the expropriated undertaking has exploited a public service or the nationalized resources; another is whether it has recovered or not the initial investment; if there has been undue enrichment as a result of a colonial situation; if the profits obtained have been excessive; the contribution of the enterprise to the economic and social development of the country; its respect for labour laws; its reinvestment policies, etc. That unpaid taxes are due is not a factor which determines in itself the amount of compensation due, but they represent a credit of the expropriating State *vis-à-vis* the expropriated company which may be set off at the moment of payment. For this reason or similar ones, there may be cases where, in fact, the indemnity is minimal, none or even negative. But this does not signify, legally, the non-payment of compensation.[5]

It is for these reasons that the Charter employs the term 'appropriate' instead of 'just' or 'adequate' since it conveys better the complex circumstances which may be pertinent in each case.[6]

The basic features of the provision adopted – the recognition of an international duty to pay compensation, the determination of the amount due in the light of the particular circumstances of each case which are in turn based on equitable considerations – all point to the provision's being based on the principle of unjust enrichment. As has been pointed out: 'The notion of appropriate compensation is flexible enough to allow the decision-maker, whether domestic or international, to take into account elements of unjust enrichment in the background of the investment in determining which under the circumstances constitutes appropriate compensation.'[7]

(3) Criticisms Made of the Provisions of the Charter of Economic Rights and Duties of States

However, this is not an interpretation of the Charter provision which is generally accepted, in particular by writers from industrialized countries. The main criticism addressed against this provision in the Charter is 'the absence of any references in Article 2 to the applicability of international law to the treatment of foreign investment',[8] what is described as 'the utter rejection of international law' in respect of nationalization or expropriation measures. The Charter is thus interpreted as pronouncing for the exclusive jurisdiction of the territorial State and 'so conceived national law itself would place within the hands of the State all available means to circumvent the obligation it provides'.[9] It is observed that the only obligation 'is to grant such compensation, if any, as it is subjectively thought to be appropriate, considering only local law and "circumstances" to which international law is not necessarily "pertinent" '.[10]

It must be recognized that the drafting of Article 2, paragraph 2, in Chapter II, the result of a compromise between differing views, is so vague and ambiguous as to lend support to such a reading of the provision. However, a reading of the full text of the Article in its context, taking into account other parts of the instrument considered as a whole as well as basic principles of international law, leads to a different interpretation.

It is true that Article 2, paragraph 2 (c), does not contain the provision which appeared in General Assembly resolution 1803 of 1962 which provided that in case of nationalization or expropriation, the owner should be paid appropriate compensation 'in accordance with rules in force in the State taking such measures in the exercise of its sovereignty and *in accordance with international law*'. The elimination of this phrase was caused by the insistence of the developed countries in asserting that international customary law provided for 'adequate, prompt and effective compensation'. This originated in Third World countries' 'suspicions as to what Western countries expected from international law'. However, once it was manifest that the alleged customary rule of 'immediate, adequate and effective' compensation was no longer accepted by the vast majority of the international community, the reference to a non-existent rule of general international law lost the meaning intended by the developed countries.

It is also true that the provision of the Charter refers to the application by the expropriating State of its laws and regulations and to its appreciation of all pertinent circumstances. To accept this determination as the one to be made in the first instance is perfectly legitimate since under the local remedies rule national law and local remedies must be applied and exhausted. But the host State remains under Article 2, paragraph 2 (c), still obliged to pay what is described as an 'appropriate compensation'. Thus if a nationalizing State, in application of its laws and in its appreciation of the circumstances, were to offer compensation which is not considered by the other interested State (and not just by the individual party) as an appropriate one, the subjective determination by the host State would not be final and would not constitute the end of the matter. The State of nationality of the expropriated owner would become authorized under the existing rules of international law to take up the case of its national and to make a claim on its behalf, on the ground that the international duty of paying an 'appropriate compensation' as provided in the Charter, has not been complied with. In the event, an international controversy would arise between the two States, as is expressly recognized in Article 2 (c), of the Charter of Economic Rights and Duties of States.

(4) The Settlement of Investment Disputes

The industrialized States proposed that if an international controversy were to arise out of measures of nationalization or expropriation, then, after national laws and remedies had been exhausted, the dispute should be submitted to compulsory adjudication or arbitration.

While not denying the existence of an international controversy in these cases, the Group of 77 was of the view that this type of investment dispute should not be treated differently from other international disputes and should be governed by the same general rules of international law on the subject.

Their basic argument was that these disputes, being of a legal character, are not different from other legal disputes. Although the Charter of the United Nations provides in Article 36, paragraph 3, that legal disputes should 'as a general rule be referred to the International Court of Justice', a different principle has come to prevail in actual practice. This is the principle described in the 1970 Declaration of Principles of Friendly Relations as that of the 'free choice of means', namely that a manifestation of the sovereignty of each State is that no one of them is bound to accept a particular method of settlement except on the basis of its own consent.

Consequently, compulsory adjudication or an obligation to submit to third-party settlement only exists when that method has been agreed upon by both interested States, either on an *ad hoc* basis or by means of a pre-existing treaty or agreement.

This is the case, for instance, when States have accepted either the compulsory jurisdiction of the Court in respect of all legal disputes or are parties to the World Bank arbitration agreement. But unless there is such agreement, there is no rule of general international law compelling States to solve their investment disputes by recourse to international judicial settlement or to arbitration. This is in substance what is established in Article 2, paragraph 2 (c) *in fine*.

However, by recognizing the existence of an international controversy in the event of disagreements as to the appropriateness of a unilaterally determined compensation, and by referring in its final words to the 'sovereign equality of States' and to 'the principle of free choice of means', Article 2, paragraph 2 (c), of the Charter of Economic Rights and Duties of States brings in Article 33 of the United Nations Charter. The dispute may remain unsettled but it continues to be an international controversy. One of the basic rules of international law, a corollary both of the principle of sovereign equality of States and that of free choice of means is that an international dispute cannot be settled unilaterally by any one of the parties, not even by its municipal tribunals.

It follows that it is not entirely accurate to say that international law has been 'utterly rejected' by the Charter of Economic Rights and Duties of States. Though expelled through the door because of its alleged identification with the doctrine of 'adequate, prompt and effective compensation', it has come back through the window in the garb of an equitable principle which takes into account the specific circumstances of each case and is, in such a way, more likely to assist in the settlement of investment disputes through negotiation or, if the parties so agree, through adjudication.

THE QUESTION OF INVESTMENT AGREEMENTS BETWEEN STATES AND PRIVATE PERSONS OR COMPANIES

The question of the legal status of investment agreements between States and private companies constituted the chief stumbling block in the intense diplomatic efforts to achieve a consensus on the terms of the Charter of Economic Rights and Duties of States.[11]

The industrialized States were in favour of referring expressly to these agreements in the text of the Charter, emphasizing the obligation of States to fulfil them in good faith and of respecting the procedures for arbitration they sometimes provide for. In support of this position they argued that General Assembly resolution 1803 of 1962 provides that 'agreements freely entered into *by* or *between* sovereign States shall be faithfully observed'. This text places on the same footing inter-State agreements and those concluded by a State with private foreign companies.

The countries of the Group of 77, while not denying the general duty of all States to fulfil their obligations in good faith, considered that such agreements were not international agreements, since they were not concluded between States and were therefore governed by the domestic law of the State concerned. They did not have international status, because private companies are not subjects of international law. Consequently, the developing countries refused to accept the proposals of the industrialized countries because they felt that it would be tantamount to conferring international status on such companies and making the legal bond between the company and the State a bond of international law. Disagreement on this issue was radical.[12] This opposition is justified by the Court's position in the *Anglo-Iranian Oil Co.* case. The Court could not accept the view that a concessionary contract signed between a government and a foreign private corporation could be considered to be an international treaty.[13]

Consequently, the cancellation of a concession of this nature, before the expiry of its term, as a consequence of a measure of nationalization, cannot be considered a breach of an international treaty. But this does not mean that an anticipated cancellation would have no legal consequences. The rights represented by a concession or a contract are no more exempt from expropriation than a mine or a factory. The agreement and the expectancies thereunder represent property interests subject to the eminent domain of the territorial State. The measure would thus constitute the expropriation of the contractual rights of a foreign company: consequently, its legitimacy would be subject to the payment of 'appropriate compensation' in accordance with Article 2, paragraph 2 (c), of the Charter.

If the concession contains an arbitration clause, such agreed method of determining the appropriate compensation would not be affected by the cancellation of the contract, in accordance with the established principle of the autonomy or independence of the compromissory clause of a contract. The arbitration clause stands on its own and is separable from the contract: if that were not the case the purpose of having such a clause in a contract would be defeated. Consequently, the contracting State would be subject to the obligation to fulfil the arbitration agreement and to pay the compensation which the tribunal finds appropriate. But this is not an obligation resulting from an international treaty; it derives from the contract itself and constitutes an obligation based on the general principles of law, particularly the one requiring a State to observe all its obligations in good faith.

The Washington Convention sponsored by the World Bank provides a binding arbitration procedure for investment agreements: in this case, the obligation to comply with this method of settlement results from the consent given by the States parties to the Convention. The opposition of the Group of 77 to the proposals of the industrialized States on this subject was based on the fear that their incorporation in the Charter might give a character of general international law to the solution sponsored by the World Bank. In the view of some Latin American States which have accepted without reservations the compulsory jurisdiction of the International Court of Justice, this Convention is an expedient devised by capital exporting countries to remedy the lack of judicial guarantees resulting, for these countries, from their own reluctance to accept without crippling reservations the compulsory jurisdiction of the Court in respect of investment disputes. For this reason a dispute concerning the appropriate character of a given compensation, instead of being decided in litigation between the interested States, is to be determined by an arbitration which places the private company and the developing State on the same level of adversary proceedings.

STABILIZATION CLAUSES AND INTERNATIONAL LAW

What is the situation if the concession or contract contains an express stabilization clause providing, for instance, that the contract will not be altered during its term except with the consent of both parties? Professor Weil, in very penetrating studies on this subject reaches the conclusion that such clauses deprive the host State of the power to put an end to the concession except with the private party's consent. However, this conclusion runs counter to the fundamental concept and purpose of the permanent sovereignty of a State over its natural resources and wealth proclaimed in the Charter and in other General Assembly resolutions.

This does not mean that such stabilization clauses have no legal effect and may be considered as unwritten. An anticipated cancellation in violation of a contractual stipulation of such a nature would give rise to a special right to compensation; the amount of the indemnity would have to be much higher than in normal cases since the existence of such a clause constitutes a most pertinent circumstance which must be taken into account in determining the appropriate compensation. For instance, there would be a duty to compensate also for the prospective gains (*lucrum cessans*) to be obtained by the private party during the period that the concession still has to run.

Professor Weil bases his conclusions on the ground that the contracts containing a stabilization clause are not subject to the law of the contracting State but to international law. We do not believe that there is an international law of contracts, but even if it were so, international law contains the fundamental and overriding principle of the permanent sovereignty of State over all its wealth and natural resources.[14] In this respect, stipulations have been inserted into contracts of this type providing that the contract will be governed by international law or by the general principles of international law.[15] This is designed to make the contract escape from the municipal law of the host State, thus obtaining a sort of indirect or disguised stabilization clause. In my view, such a stipulation, which is often resisted by developing States, does not achieve the purpose of stabilization which is pursued and is in other respects unnecessary and even counter-productive.

It does not achieve the function of a real stabilization clause because international law does not forbid a nationalization, nor the resulting cancellation of the contract, provided appropriate compensation is paid. It is unnecessary because international law is always applicable to the situation resulting from the cancellation of the contract or the nationalization of the enterprise without appropriate compensation. There would be in the event international responsibility for expropriation of contractual rights, enforced by diplomatic protection, after the exhaustion of local remedies, just as in the case of any other expropriation not accompanied by an appropriate indemnity. To reach that result it is not necessary to stipulate that the contract will be governed by international law. It is not the contract as such, but the situation as a whole which is governed by international law, whether or not the parties have so stipulated.

Finally, the stipulation may be counter-productive because international law does not possess adequate rules governing contracts of this nature. Some of these long-term contracts — for instance, the oil concessions of the thirties — had to be adjusted to new circumstances when it became evident that the original conditions were too favourable for the companies. This process of readjustment was conducted on the basis of institutions of municipal contractual law such as the doctrine of frustration of contract or that of administrative contracts. Such a process would have been much more difficult if the strict conditions governing the change of circumstances in the field of treaties had failed to be applied. The exclusion of the flexible methods for contractual adjustment which have been elaborated by the various systems of municipal law, and their replacement by the rigidity of international law, may lead in practice to the complete breakdown of the contractual link, a situation which is neither favourable to the maintenance of the rule of law, nor in the interest of the private party itself.

GOOD FAITH AND CONTRACTUAL AGREEMENTS BETWEEN STATES AND COMPANIES OR INDIVIDUALS

In certain cases these contracts contain a stipulation providing that the private party agrees not to call upon his State of nationality in any issues arising out of the contract (Calvo clause). The developed and industrialized States have often disputed the validity of this clause as involving a waiver by the private party of an inalienable right of the State, that of protecting its citizens abroad. However, a Calvo clause, by which the private party agrees not to request the diplomatic protection of his State of nationality must be complied with on the basis of the principle of good faith, as much as the governmental party is expected to observe the arbitration or the stabilization clauses contained in the contract. This is confirmed by the recognition in important arbitral awards of the validity of the Calvo clause with respect to any matter connected with the contract, provided naturally that the governmental party also complied with the agreement.[16]

The principle of good faith binds both parties equally. As described by the International Court of Justice, it constitutes 'one of the basic principles governing the creation and performance of legal obligations whatever their source.'[17] The critics of the Charter of Economic Rights and Duties of States emphasize the refusal to accept a proposal from the industrialized States to refer expressly and in the context of contracts between States and private parties, to the principle of good faith.[18]

However, the developing countries maintained that this general principle applies to all State obligations. To insert it specifically in connection with the duties enumerated in Article 2 would have unbalanced the situation in respect of other obligations of States also enumerated in the Charter, such as the duty to avoid the use of coercion and that of non-intervention. The non-insertion of the principle of good faith at this particular juncture does not mean that the duty to perform contractual obligations in good faith has been excluded from the Charter. This results from Chapter 1, No. 1 (litt. j) of the instrument, which˙applies to all obligations dealt with therein, including those of Article 2, and reads: 'Econonˉic as well as political and other relations among States shall be governed, *inter alia*, by the following principles . . . (1) Fulfilment in good faith of international obligations.' Article 33 (2) of the Charter of Economic Rights and Duties of States further provides that: 'In their interpretation and application, the provisions of the present Charter are inter-related and each provision should be construed in the context of the other provisions.'

In conclusion Ambassador Castaneda has remarked, confirming with his experience as Chairman of the drafting group the interpretation of the relevant provisions of the Charter advanced here, that

> the Charter accepts that international law may act as a factor limiting the freedom of the State when the interests of aliens are affected, even if Article 2 does not say so expressly. From a legal point of view this follows from the provisions contained in other articles of the Charter which must be interpreted and applied jointly with Article 2.[19]

NOTES AND REFERENCES

1   *Chorzow Factory (Merits)* case, PCIJ, Series A/B, No. 17, p. 47.
2   In the terms of the Hickenlooper amendment, what is required, according to this doctrine, is 'speedy compensation for such property in convertible foreign exchange equivalent to the full value thereof'.
3   See for example Czechoslovakia's agreements with Yugoslavia (1956), Poland (1958) and Roumania (1961) and agreement between Yugoslavia and Hungary (1956).
4   *International Status of South West Africa*, Advisory Opinion, ICJ *Reports* (1950), p. 148.
5   J. Castaneda, 'Justice économique internationale', *Contributions à L'Etude de la Charte*, ed. Gallimard, p. 105.
6   Richard A. Falk, 'The New States and International Legal Order', *Recueil des Cours*, Vol. 118 (1966), p. 29.
7   Statement by the delegate of Canada in *Official Records*, General Assembly, 29th Session, 2nd Committee, p. 446, para. 47.
8   G.·Feuer, 'Reflexions, sur la charte des droits et devoirs économiques', *Revue Générale de Droit International Public*, Vol. 79 (1975), p. 195.

9   C.N. Brower and J.P. Tepe, 'The Charter of Economic Rights and Duties of States. A Reflection or Rejection of International Law?' *International Lawyer*, Vol. 9 (1975), p. 304.

10 De Waart, P., 'Permanent Sovereignty over Natural Resources as a Cornerstone for International Rights and Duties', in H. Meijers and E.W. Vendag, eds., *Essays on International Law in Honour of Professor Tammes*, London, 1975, p. 313.

11 Statement by the President of the Working Group, Ambassador Castaneda, in *Official Records*, General Assembly, 2nd Committee, 1638th Meeting, 25 November 1974, p. 383, para. 6.

12 Ambassador Castaneda, ibid., para. 7.

13 ICJ *Reports* (1952), p. 112.

14 P. Weil, 'Les clauses de stabilisation ou d'intangibilité inserées dans les accords de développement économique', *Melanges Rousseau*, pp. 301-28 and 'Problèmes relatifs aux contrats passés entre un Etat et un particulier', *Recueil des Cours*.

15 See Van Hecke, 'Les accords entre un Etat et une personne privée étrangère', *Annuaire de l'Institut de Droit International*, Vol. 57, tome 1, pp. 192 ff.

16 M. Sorenson, ed., *Manual of Public International Law*, London, 1968, pp. 591-93.

17 ICJ *Reports* (1974), p. 473.

18 Cf. for instance G. White, *Virginia Law Quarterly*, Vol. 16 (1976), p. 331.

19 J. Castaneda, 'La charte de droits et devoirs économiques des états', *Annuaire Française de Droit International*, Vol. 20 (1974), p. 54.

18 The Concept of Stability of Contractual Relations in the Transnational Investment Process

*Samuel K.B. Asante**

Within our own generation no less than seventy countries have attained political independence and joined the international community of nation States. Third World countries now command a preponderant majority in the United Nations and other world bodies, yet it is trite knowledge that the attainment of political independence and the proliferation of nation States in the Third World has had little impact on the world economic power structure. Access to the corridors of the United Nations and other international bodies has not necessarily assured effective participation in the shaping and restructuring of the world economic system.[1] After the first flush of exhilaration over political independence, developing countries have now grasped the sobering fact that sovereignty is not synonymous with economic self-sufficiency or development and that the rich industrialized countries still substantially control the production and distribution of the world's resources. An analysis of European direct investment in Africa shows that by the end of 1967 the former metropolitan powers still dominated investments in their former colonies. The percentage of the total investments in the respective African countries held by the former imperial powers is shown in Table 1.

This realization is now being translated into a determined and sustained onslaught on the international economic order and the hegemony of the industrialized countries over such a system. The attempts of OPEC countries to reverse the old pattern in the production and distribution of petroleum through collective measures are well known to you. Within the past few years the chambers of the United Nations have echoed with persistent demands by the developing countries for the inauguration

*UN Centre of Transnational Corporations.

Table 1 *Percentage of Total Investment in Various African Countries Held by Former Imperial Powers*

Investment by United Kingdom		Investment by France		Investment by Belgium		Investment by Italy	
Swaziland	96.6	Niger	95.7	Zaire	87.8	Somalia	83.3
Malawi	92.7	Central African Rep.	91.8	Rwanda	86.8	Tunisia	28.5
Botswana	88.0	Senegal	87.4	Burundi	84.5		
Rhodesia	83.3	Chad	80.4				
Zambia	79.6	Mali	76.9				
Kenya	78.8	Cameroon	75.1				
Sudan	74.9	Gabon	73.4				
Ghana	59.1	Algeria	71.7				
Nigeria	53.8						

Source: Multinational Corporations in World Development, New York, United Nations, 1973.

of more equitable arrangements with regard to the pricing and supply of basic raw materials, the sharing of technology and the distribution of the world's food resources. More explicitly and precisely, less developed countries have pressed for a just price for oil, the unqualified assertion by each state of permanent sovereignty over natural resources, the imposition of limits on monopolistic or oligopolistic practices in the global economic system, the conclusion of stable and fair commodity agreements to assure a fair and reliable return on commodities produced in the Third World, a tighter regulation of contracts for the purchase of technology and, what is more relevant to our purposes, a more effective control over transnational corporations and foreign investment. These are some of the elements of the New International Economic Order proclaimed by the General Assembly of the United Nations[2] and actively pursued in such international forums as UNCTAD, the United Nations Commission on Transnational Corporations, the North–South Dialogue, the Commonwealth Prime Ministers' Conference, and so on.

In calling for the establishment of a more equitable international economic order, and the effective control of their respective economic resources, developing countries have invoked various general philosphical, juristic and pragmatic ideas such as equality, the concept of human needs, the principle of historic entitlement, the claim of the rectification of past injustice and the goals of self-reliance and economic development.[3] The debate has the familiar ring of the anti-colonial compaign which preceded the era of political independence. Here I must hasten to register a disclaimer. The object of these lectures is not to rehash the rhetoric which has characterized the demand for the restructuring of the world economic order. Nor will I presume to unravel the intricacies of the inequities of the economic relations between North and South. I will leave that to competent economic experts. My object is a less ambitious one. I propose to dwell on some aspects of the rather circumscribed area of the legal infrastructure of these economic relations in order to demonstrate the extent to which certain basic legal values, concepts and institutions in traditional transnational law serve as the fundamental underpinnings of the old international economic order. My concern here is to demonstrate that the system which has been the object of much rhetoric at the United Nations and other international forums is supported by a formidable and highly sophisticated armoury of legal and commercial concepts and values which require a radical revision if the international economic order is to be restructured to promote the development goals of the Third World. I will also consider the extent to which the revised legal arrangements in this regard have been successful in eliminating the essential incidents of the old economic order or in advancing the professed economic goals of developing countries.

In short, this is an exercise in 'professional particularism'. That is to say, while our politicians and diplomats thunder and inveigh against the inequities of the prevailing international economic order with the characteristic flamboyance which captures the headlines, professional men such as lawyers, accountants, engineers, valuers and the like should focus on the more prosaic but equally vital aspects; more precisely, we should unravel the full technical implications of the legal, accounting, financial or engineering concepts usually associated with this system in order to pave the way for a meaningful restructuring of North–South economic relations.

Before discussing some of these legal concepts which I have classified as traditional concepts, a few words of warning would seem to be in order. First, concepts such as ownership, contract, corporate personality of affiliates and subsidiaries, and holder in due course in negotiable instruments, which appear quite innocuous within the context of a municipal legal system, may have grave implications when transplanted into the sphere of transnational transactions. Thus, in questioning the propriety or feasibility of some of these concepts in the transnational investment process, I should not be understood to be launching a general attack on these concepts as they operate within a particular municipal law. Second, it is customary for the adherents to the positivist school in Europe and America to refer to these legal concepts as colourless or value-neutral ingredients of a legal system. Yet any perceptive observer familiar with the history of the evolution of these concepts and the role they have played in various societies in Europe and America would concede that these concepts sometimes denote discreet value systems of a distinct individualistic bias which are often manifestly inimical to the aspirations and development goals of new nations. It is therefore appropriate to remind ourselves that these concepts do not enjoy the status of immutable and universal postulates and that they should therefore be subjected to a rigorous reappraisal in the light of development strategies.

STABILITY OF CONTRACTUAL RELATIONS

The relations between developing countries and transnational corporations are often embodied in long-term agreements which may be concessions, economic development agreements, management agreements, joint ventures, service contracts, sales or purchasing contracts, production sharing agreements, financing arrangements, licensing agreements, technical assistance agreements and the like. Conceptually, each of these agreements is classified by Western jurists as a species of a private contract, and therefore subject to all the traditional folk-lore on this subject, notwithstanding the fact that such transactions are concluded with governments and may involve the exploitation of a major natural resource or the use of a vital national utility, such as electric power or telecommunications, which is bound up with the development strategies of the country concerned. The critical question here is whether the traditional concepts and rules applicable to a private contract are admissible in respect of these special arrangements between governments and transnational corporations.

To answer this, let us first consider the philosophical, economic and sociological bases of the modern idea of contract. We are assured by Professor Kessler, a distinguished Yale Law School professor, that, in the Anglo-American conception, a contract is the most convenient tool of capitalism, inspired by a proud spirit of *laissez-faire* individualism. The classical idea of a contract is a private bargain struck by parties of equal bargaining strength and firmly rooted in the free will of the parties. It is an institution of the market place in every day capitalist society — indeed, an indispensable instrument of the entrepreneur. With the development of a free enterprise system based on division of labour, capitalist society needed a highly elastic legal institution to safeguard the exchange of goods and services on the market. Since a contract is the result of free bargaining of parties who are brought together by the interplay of the market forces and who meet each other on a footing of social and approximate economic equality, there is no danger that freedom of contract will be a threat to the social order as a whole. The highest philosophical manifestation of this theory is that rational behaviour within the context of Western culture is only possible if agreements are respected. Oppressive bargains can be avoided by careful shopping around since everyone has complete freedom of choice with regard to his partner.

Such a concept of contract clearly militates against the idea of judicial intervention in contractual arrangements. Courts are extremely hesitant to declare contracts void as against public policy or to readjust the bargain struck by the parties because it is in the supreme interest of the social order that men of full age and competent understanding shall have the utmost liberty of contracting, and that their contracts when entered into freely and voluntarily shall be held sacred and enforced by the courts of justice.

Tracing the evolution of the Will Theory of Contract in the nineteenth century,[4] Professor Atiyah of Oxford had this to say:

Contractual obligations came to be treated as being almost exclusively about promises, agreements, intentions and acts of will. The function of the law came to be seen as that of merely giving effect to the private autonomy of contracting parties to make legal arrangements. It is of course well known, indeed has become part of modern orthodoxy that the private autonomy, this extreme freedom of contract came to be abused by parties with greater bargaining power, and has been curtailed in a variety of ways both by legislative activity and by the judges.

[Yet,] despite the increasing attacks on freedom of contract the conceptual apparatus which still dominates legal thinking on these issues is the apparatus of the nineteenth century. It goes indeed far beyond the law itself. Our very processes of thought, our language in political, moral or philosophical debate, is still dominated by this nineteenth century heritage . . .

I want to suggest further that this conceptual apparatus is not based on any objective truths, it does not derive from any eternal verities. It is the result quite specifically of a nineteenth century heritage, an amalgam of classical economics, of Benthamite radicalism, of liberal political ideals of the law, itself created and moulded in the shadow of these movements. The result is that our basic conceptual apparatus, the fundamental characteristics and divisions we impose on the phenomena with which we deal do not reflect the values of our own times, but those of the last century.

In this connection it is worth remembering that the Anglo-American theory of contract has not remained static or fossilized over the years. Professor Horowitz of Harvard Law School[5] has pointed out that the modern Will Theory of Contract, that is, the robustly individualistic idea, did not appear until the eighteenth century and early nineteenth century when the spread of markets forced jurists to attack equitable concepts of exchange. Prior to that, the courts applied an objective theory of contract which enabled them to intervene actively to rectify contractual provisions on grounds of equity. In more recent years, we have witnessed a pronounced legislative intervention to cure the excesses of standard or adhesion contracts on the same theory. Professor Kessler has ably demonstrated that such intervention makes nonsense of the Will Theory of Freedom of Contract. It follows that there is no immutable doctrine of contract, and that developing countries are perfectly entitled to invoke ideas of fairness and equity in reviewing contracts which are inimical to the national interest.

The philosophical ideas and concepts of contract of the nineteenth century have nevertheless provided a basis for a formidable array of traditional legal and business concepts which have been applied in their pristine purity to transnational transactions. These concepts will be thrown into sharp relief in the discussion of stability and renegotiation of contracts.

However, the barest acquaintance with the actual circumstances surrounding the conclusion of concessions between metropolitan companies and African chiefs or investment agreement or transnational contracts between transnational corporations and governments of developing countries will dispose of these individualistic assumptions. The hollowness of the pretence that colonial transactions with illiterate chiefs are freely negotiated transactions between parties of equal bargaining strength will be evident to all of you. Even the modern variant of these transactions, which is the investment agreement between the government of an underdeveloped country and a multinational corporation, cannot be truly described as an arms-length transaction rooted in the free will of parties of equal bargaining power, because of the superior negotiating skills, knowledge and more favourable bargaining position which the multinational corporation usually commands at the inception of the relationship. Thus, in the negotiations between Ghana and Kaiser and Reynolds of America in respect of the Volta River Project of Ghana in the early sixties, President Nkrumah is reported to have been so anxious to conclude a deal that, while urging his officials to negotiate for the best terms, he firmly directed them to come to some terms at all costs.

This, not surprisingly, gave the foreign companies a superior negotiating position.

In any case, less developed country governments would certainly dismiss *laissez-faire* ideas as totally inappropriate to this category of transactions. A long-term investment agreement spelling out comprehensively the relations between the government and the corporation in respect of the development and marketing of a natural resource and specifying all relevant fiscal arrangements is anything but a private contract — an institution of the market place. Governments of less developed countries quite properly regard these agreements as major instruments of public policy — a prominent feature of their development strategies, hardly distinguishable from a development plan. These transactions are a framework for a joint public enterprise in which the government and the foreign partner are engaged in the development of a strategic public resource or the operation of a vital public utility. In short, they lie more in the domain of public law than in the province of private contract, and consequently the traditional individualistic doctrines as well as the speculative rules devised for the exchange of fungible commodities in a market regime are clearly inapplicable to them. It follows that these transactions cannot be insulated from the pressures which impinge on public institutions such as political changes in the country, changed economic conditions and the general expectations of the public. Furthermore, having regard to the peculiar nature of these transactions, there is no reason why they should not be governed by the objective theory of contract which admits of the rectification of contractual provisions on the grounds that they are unfair or inequitable to one of the parties.

RENEGOTIATION

A major source of conflict between host governments of developing countries and transnational corporations derives from the preoccupation of transnational corporations with stability and predictability in contractual relations on the one hand, and the persistent demands of host governments for a more flexible contractual regime on the other.

In their quest for certainty and stability of contractual provisions, transnational corporations have invoked traditional legal doctrines and concepts. First, as I have already pointed out, the investment agreement between a host government and a transnational corporation is classified as a species of traditional contract rooted in the free will of the parties.

One of the consequences of this approach is that the transnational corporation regards such a transaction as a static model representing a definitive 'deal' — a fixed regime of obligations, rights, impositions and
benefits which does not admit of variation or modification throughout
the term of the agreement. Any departure from such a transaction is
deemed repugnant to 'sanctity of contract'. The conception of an investment agreement as a static model derives from the bargaining traditions
associated with a market exchange. In colloquial language, once a party
has made his 'kill' in a deal, the transaction cannot be re-opened. The
operative word here is the 'kill', because it denotes that a good bargain
struck at a particular time represents a set of advantages and benefits
which must be preserved and adhered to. Inadequacy of consideration
is no basis for upsetting the bargain, and the fact that such an investment agreement is concluded with a State, has a duration of thirty or
forty or even eighty years and is in respect of a major natural resource
should not detract from the integrity of the deal. In short, an investment
agreement is not a general relationship which admits of a process of
accommodation and adjustment of the benefits and impositions but a
definitive bargain in which one party 'wins' and the other 'loses'.

Secondly, to immunize such a fixed contractual regime from possible
variation by the municipal law of the host State, some jurists from capital-
exporting countries have argued that the peculiar features of an investment
agreement between a government and a foreign company make it analogous to an international agreement and therefore subject to such international legal doctrines as *pacta sunt servanda* — agreements must be
kept at all costs.[6] The legal consequence of this reasoning is that a state
is not entitled unilaterally to modify or abrogate contracts to which
aliens are parties. The practical effect of this theory would be to exclude
the renegotiation or review of investment agreements or other transnational contracts at the instance of the host government. Another variant
of this doctrine is that the contractual interest of the alien constitutes
an acquired right which cannot be invaded by the state even upon the
payment of prompt, adequate and effective compensation.[7] Others
seek to insulate the investment agreement from the operation of the
law of the host state by classifying the investment agreement as an independent and self-sufficient system of law regulating the entire range
of relations between the host government and the foreign company
without reference to any municipal law. In effect the investment agreement creates a separate, self-contained and coherent body of legal
principles which exclusively governs relations between the host State
and the transnational corporation. Other writers, while stopping short

of assimilating the transnational contract to the class of international agreements, would still argue that unilateral modification or abrogation of such agreements consitutes an international delict imposed by international law irrespective of the effect of private international law on the contract.[8]

All these theories share the common characteristic that they employ traditional international or municipal legal concepts essentially deriving from the nineteenth-century Will Theory of Contract and resulting in the construction of a rigid conceptual apparatus which does not admit of variation on grounds of equity of changed circumstances.

Other writers, particularly jurists representing host governments, have countered these doctrinal and conceptual arguments as follows: an agreement between a host State and a private corporation, albeit a transnational corporation, does not enjoy the status of an international agreement and on well-settled principles of private international law, such an agreement should be governed by the law of the host State and not public international law. It follows that analytically it is inadmissable to characterize subsequent changes in the law of the host State which modify the agreement as a breach of contract.[9] However, assuming that such an agreement were subject to public international law, the doctrine of *pacta sunt servanda* would be effectively qualified by the equally well-established international legal principle, *clausula rebus sic stantibus*, which sanctions the revision of international agreements on the basis of a fundamental change of circumstances. Thus, it is argued that international law does not ordain absolute immutability of agreements.

As to the theory that the investment agreement creates an independent, exclusive and self-sufficient legal system, this is dismissed as patently untenable on the grounds that the validity of every agreement must itself be derived from some external legal order — be it international or municipal. It follows that the concepts of immutability implicit in this theory cannot be sustained without reference to some legal system.

It is finally argued that inasmuch as reliance is placed on general principles of law in the representative legal systems, sanctity of contract has never been treated as an absolute and an unqualified principle in any of the major legal systems.[10] The French doctrine of *imprévision* the corresponding doctrine of *Wegfall der Geschafts Grundlagen* in German law and the concept of good faith in other civilian systems, all provide for the revision of contracts in appropriate cases by reference to objective criteria not traceable to the will of the parties. According to the civilian doctrine of imprevision, an alteration in contractual rights between a state and foreign company can take place upon the occurrence of a subsequent event not foreseen by the parties which have rendered the obligation of one party so onerous that it may be assumed that if he had it in contemplation all the time, he would not have made the contract. With particular reference to agreements concluded with governments and public authorities, the civil and common law systems all recognize the principle that such contracts may not only be renegotiated at the instance of the government, in appropriate cases, but may even be unilaterally modified by the government in certain circumstances by virtue of the government's sovereign rights.

With regard to renegotiation, Professor Oscar Schachter has pointed out that

> renegotiation may be justifiable on the grounds that excessive or windfall profits have been obtained in the carrying out of a government contract. This is widely accepted by the industrialized countries; witness the renegotiation procedures under United States law (which have been applied to cases of alleged excess profits on overseas investment). There is no reason why renegotiation on a similar basis should not be accepted in contractual arrangements between foreign companies and developing governments, provided that adequate procedures are available for a fair determination.[11]

It is submitted, however, that most juristic writing in this area has suffered from excess of formalism and has failed to address itself to the crucial issues of a practical and functional character which beset the economic and legal relations between host governments and transnational corporations. A basic flaw in the approach of many jurists derives from the valiant attempt to analyse the intricate problems posed by the transnational contract, a highly complex phenomenon, by reference to some tidy and simplistic doctrine of international law or municipal law which has little or no relevance to such a transaction. Thus a blind insistence on the application of *pacta sunt servanda* to such transnational contracts, betrays a lack of sophisticated appreciation of the nature and origin of such transactions, the inherent instability in such long-term arrangements, and the formidable difficulties posed by their administration. Equally, a bold assertion of an unqualified sovereign right to unilaterally abrogate or modify such agreements, while plausible as an effective rejoinder to a right doctrine of *pacta sunt servanda* and a powerful inducement for renegotiation, cannot provide a viable basis for a meaningful economic relationship between a host government and a transnational corporation. The commercial implications of such a posture in our independent world would be obvious to you. Again, by reason of the qualifications attached to them, even the more flexible doctrines of *rebus sic stantibus* or *imprevision* hardly suffice as a comprehensive conceptual framework which adequately covers the many issues which plague government-investor relations.[12]

The proper approach, I would suggest, is that we should embark on a functional analysis of the causes of the inherent instability of these special agreements untrammelled by any *a priori* concepts or tidy solutions, and then proceed to prescribe meaningful formulae for resolving the conflict.

First, the colonial factor. As I have already pointed out, a number of transnational contracts were concluded as incidents of the colonial system in which metropolitan companies were offered privileged investment interests in the colonies and accordingly given such grotesquely favourable terms as could hardly survive the collapse of colonialism. It is a patent fallacy to characterize such interests as grounded on contracts freely negotiated by parties of equal bargaining strength. The circumstances surrounding the conclusion of these transactions belie all the classical theories of freedom of contract. In these circumstances, host governments of newly independent countries consider renegotiation or restructuring of these arrangements as a legitimate part of the decolonization process. It is now generally recognized that 'colonial concessions or agreements' may be rearranged. But this concession is a function of economic and political realism, not the consequence of any universally accepted traditional legal doctrine. A newly independent country which invoked the mere fact of political independence as a juristic basis for repudiating such agreements would almost certainly be confronted by a formidable array of such well-known traditional doctrines as *pacta sunt servanda*, sanctity of contract, acquired rights, state succession — doctrines which are likely to be upheld by most international and indeed some traditionally oriented domestic tribunals. It is not without significance that the restructuring of colonial agreements was achieved not immediately upon independence but after a decent interval of say five to ten or fifteen years. Yet, despite this armoury of traditional doctrines, foreign companies and governments actuated by a shrewd sense of realism, if not equity, have come to accept the renegotiation or restructuring of colonial agreements. This development represents a triumph of common sense and equity over formal doctrine. The critical question is whether this sense of realism and fairness will also characterize the attitude of investors and home governments to the renegotiation of the modern type of transnational contracts to which we now turn.

Transnational agreements are not purged of their inherent instability by reason of only the fact that they were concluded with governments of independent countries. A functional analysis of such arrangements, in particular long-term agreements relating to natural resources or public utilities replete with elaborate fiscal regimes, ownership and control arrangements irresistibly points to the inevitability of review, renegotiation or readjustment from time to time. Let us start our analysis by considering the concerns of transnational corporations in this area. Transnational corporations insist on stability and predictability as an essential prerequisite to prudent investment. Before committing substantial resources to such long-term agreements as concessions, joint ventures, service contracts, sale contracts, power contracts and the like, transnational corporations carry out elaborate financial projections and cash flow analysis in order to determine the expected return on their investment. In making these projections and calculations, they demand that governments unequivocally spell out the full range of fiscal impositions such as tax, royalties, duties, rents, bonus consideration to be stipulated on the transaction for the entire duration of the agreement. They contend further that bankers and other financial institutions will not provide them financing for their projects unless they present to them definitive long-term contracts concluded with host governments which spell out in great detail the entire fiscal package, and contain cast-iron guarantees from the host governments regarding these financial arrangements.

A familiar mechanism for ensuring such guarantees is the stipulation of stability clauses. That is, stipulations designed to stabilize or freeze the essential provisions of the agreement by strictly prohibiting any legislative or administrative act which derogates from or is otherwise inconsistent with the provisions of the agreement or the legal environment of the transaction. Stability clauses are in particular directed against:

(1) The raising of taxes beyond the rates operating at the time of the agreement or otherwise stipulated in the agreement;
(2) The imposition of any fiscal changes in the general industrial or commercial sectors in excess of the fiscal charges provided in the agreement;
(3) The amendment of the laws such as corporate and tax laws, which were in force on the date of the agreement. The Valco Agreement of Ghana provides that the proper law of the agreement shall be the law of Ghana as at the time of the agreement (1962);
(4) Expropriation, nationalization and any other form of intervention in the enterprise.

After the conclusion of such elaborate arrangements, transnational corporations are naturally precoccupied with securing the basic integrity of the entire deal against any variation or revision which would substantially diminish their expected financial returns or radically alter the basic ground rules of the transaction mid-stream. They, therefore, do not welcome the prospect of renegotiation or review involving such vital matters as a change in any aspect of the fiscal regime, participation by the host government in the equity or management of the undertaking or a reduction in the terms of the contract. They maintain further that such revision is disruptive of elaborate financing arrangements made with third parties, that is, banks and financial institutions which are predicated on the assumption that the enterprise will yield a certain return over a prescribed period for the purpose of repaying the loans. In their conception, therefore, the recent spate of renegotiations represents a serious crisis in the investment climate.

With particular reference to natural resource agreements, the concerns of transnational corporations are accentuated by the peculiar problems of the extractive industry. In many cases, transnational corporations expend vast sums in survey work, exploration and prospecting for several years — five to ten years, that is, the lead time before achieving successful production. Having regard to the size of the risk capital involved, and the conditions stipulated by their financiers, transnational corporations insist, as a matter of prudent investment, on definitive long-term guarantees as to the fiscal package from host governments even before embarking on the preliminary phases of survey, exploration and prospecting. They maintain that such projects cannot be mounted without solid financial backing from banks and other institutions, and that such institutions will not provide financing in the absence of unequivocal guarantees from host governments in respect of the financial package for the entire duration of the agreement.

But understandable as the financial concerns of transnational corporations may be, the very nature of such long-term assurances poses acute problems for the developing country. In the nature of things, governments of developing countries are expected to determine the price of the ore or the fuel, the tax payable, the royalty and other impositions chargeable and all the elements of the fiscal regime over a ten, fifteen or thirty-year period even before the government has the vaguest idea of the size of the ore body or other national resource or the economic prospects of such resource. The feasibility study for the project, which should properly be the basis of any fiscal regime, is prepared not before but *after* the conclusion of the long-term contract. Thus, a government which is anxious to attract an investor is compelled by its weak bargaining position and the insistence of transnational corporations and their banks to conclude long-term fiscal arrangements without the benefit of all the facts essential to the determination of the components of that package — the price of the ore, tax, the royalty rent consideration and other fiscal impositions. The result is that these transactions are invariably lopsided and highly advantageous to the investor. In the course of time, the bargaining position changes. The feasibility report is prepared, the government has a better appreciation of the size of the ore body and the economic prospects of the undertaking. The venture turns out to be much more profitable than was vaguely anticipated, and the company is in full production, realizing a high return, if not excessive profits. In these circumstances, whatever the theorists may say about *pacta sunt servanda*, the government is bound to call for a renegotiation of the agreements either on its own initiative or in response to overwhelming political pressure. One of the tragic effects of the artificial conceptualism which is reflected in tradition juristic analysis in this area is to characterize such a demand for renegotiation on the ground of equity and fairness as delinquent conduct or breach of contract on the part of the state. It is worth pointing out that legitimate concern of governments to amend, in the public interest, fiscal regimes in respect of the exploitation of natural resources, is by no means confined to developing countries. The United Kingdom and Norway recently had recourse to such measures in order to ensure effective participation by their respective governments in the excess profits realized by the petroleum companies exploiting the North Sea oil. As Mike Faber and Roland Brown have said in a penetrating study of this problem, 'Much of the instability in operating conditions about which the companies are complaining is either inherent in the nature of the mining business or a consequence of the way in which mining investment has to be fitted into a rigid contractual framework from a very early stage in the life of a project. It has very little to do with anything which could normally be described as politics.'[13]

I need hardly point out that the doctrines of *pacta sunt servanda* and sanctity of contract reinforced by such devices as stability clauses fly in the face of global developments as well as the highly fluid situation in developing countries. It requires no prophet to pronounce that rigid fiscal or other arrangements cannot realistically persist in the face of the dynamic economic changes at the global and national level for over ten years. Yet, the conceptual framework of these transnational agreements does not acknowledge the possibility of change as a normal feature of transnational business. We have just witnessed the major disruption of economic expectations by virtue of the world energy crisis. It is well known that many petroleum companies renegotiated their supply contracts with public utilities in Europe and America in consequence of this crisis. That same sense of realism should induce them to review their contracts with host governments.

The concerns of the investor in this area are understandable, but they are hardly tenable. Far from undermining the stability of agreements, renegotiation provides a sort of insurance against that kind of explosive reaction generated by the bitter realization that the investment agreement itself emphatically rules out any rational process of revision. There would be little inclination to abrogate an agreement or nationalize an undertaking, if the terms of an investment agreement could be re-opened say, every five years. If periodical review is recognized as a realistic feature of the investment process, financiers could take it into account in determining the financing arrangements and the renegotiation could be so timed as to coincide with the year in which the investor would have recouped his investment. Thereafter, both parties could agree on a reasonable rate of return which the investor may expect, and the renegotiated terms could make appropriate provision for this.

The investor's preference for *ad hoc* renegotiation is hardly surprising. The absence of express provision for revision puts the investor in an advantageous position when the government of a developing country requests a renegotiation. The investor is thus enabled to proceed from a position of strength because he is under no legal obligation to renegotiate, and he may rebuff the government's initial approaches on the ground that there is no legitimate economic or other basis for renegotiation. In this regard, it is worthy of note that the renegotiation of the power rate stipulated in the Valco power contract of 1962, which has a thiry-year term, has dragged on for nearly ten years. The initial approach to Valco was made by VRA in 1967. After five years of renegotiations, the original rate of US $2.75 million was abandoned on 26 October 1972. Further negotiations continued and, pending the conclusion of the negotiations, an interim price of US $3.125 million was agreed with effect from 26 November 1973. The two parties then retained a Canadian consulting firm to review the entire tariff structure and make appropriate recommendations. The consultants submitted their recommendations in 1975, and the final round of negotiations commenced in January 1976 and were not concluded until 1977. These protracted proceedings would have been unnecessary if a renegotiation clause had been expressly stipulated in the agreement.

Why is it necessary to provide for renegotiation? The reasons are not hard to find. As I have already intimated, changed economic conditions may render the entire package deal patently inequitable. During the negotiations between the Ghana Government and Shell for the On-Shore Petroleum Prospecting and Production Agreements, the fiscal impositions agreed earlier in the first part of 1973 were virtually nullified by the energy crisis in the latter part of that year and we had to renegotiate the entire fiscal arrangements. After this experience, Shell was persuaded to accept a renegotiation clause to the effect that the terms of the agreement would be reviewed if the fundamental economic bases of the agreement changed, having regard to the world market prices in the petroleum industry and all other relevant economic factors. Renegotiation may also become imperative by reason of the fact that the multinational corporation concerned has concluded a series of much more liberal agreements with neighbouring countries. In such a situation, a sort of most favoured nation clause comes into operation. Nigeria invoked this principle when the oil companies renegotiated their contracts with the Arab states. Sometimes a change of government bringing in a new regime which is more ideologically committed to the control of the strategic sectors of the country's economy would result in negotiations for equity participation in the foreign-owned undertaking. The country may also be confronted with dire economic difficulties, which may compel the government to turn to the foreign enterprise as a source of increased revenue. This is what happened in Jamaica recently as regards the bauxite concessions held by various American and Canadian companies. In a famous statement on this crisis, the Prime Minister of Jamaica declared that sanctity of contract could not be allowed to override the impelling demands of economic necessity. Again, a general review of fiscal policies of a country may make it virtually impossible to exclude the foreign investor with special concessions from the ambit of the new measures. Sometimes technical reasons, such as the obsolescence of the technical formula for determining a rate, would be a legitimate ground for renegotiation.

Renegotiation should therefore be acknowledged as an integral feature of the foreign investment process. In this regard, OPEC has declared that changed economic circumstances provide a legitimate basis for host governments to renegotiate petroleum agreements. In Resolution No. XVI.90 of 1968, OPEC declared that governments have a right to renegotiate contracts when transnational corporations serving as operators receive 'excessively high net earnings after taxes'. Such renegotiation shall apply to the financial terms of the agreement. Concrete rules have been prescribed by OPEC to determine excessive profits and also the criteria to be used for such renegotiations.

Some of the more realistic investors, such as the foreign partners in the Lamco Project have now abandoned the idea that an investment agreement constitutes an inflexible structure which must be rigorously enforced to the letter, and have humorously suggested that a concession agreement may be described as an agreement to make concessions!

Recent international pronouncements provide considerable support to the case for reviewing or negotiating agreements between host governments and transnational corporations. The Group of Eminent Persons appointed by the Secretary-General of the United Nations to study the impact of multinational corporations on development and international relations, specifically addressed themselves to this issue in their report as follows:

> While a clear understanding on various issues at the time of entry is vital, it has to be recognized that conditions change, and what may seem to have been adequate and fair at the time of entry may prove unsatisfactory to either party over time.
>
> A large number of agreements made in the past lack comprehensiveness and contain no provision for renegotiation. Developing countries have, of course, the power, through legislation, to modify the terms of agreements. But sometimes such actions, if carried out unilaterally, entail disproprotionately high costs in terms of the future flow of investments. A willingness on both sides to renegotiate agreements which have been in force for more than, say, 10 years, could help to avoid recourse to extreme measures. The *Group recommends* that in the initial agreement with multinational corporations host countries should consider making provision for the review, at the request of either side, after suitable intervals, of various clauses of the agreement.[14]

In recent years, the Secretary-General of the International Centre for Settlement of Investment Disputes has advocated the adoption of renegotiation and review clauses in investment agreements as a mechanism for avoiding or containing conflict and investment disputes.[15] In its Programme of Action on the Establishment of a New International Economic Order, the General Assembly expressly stipulated that one of the five major objectives of a code of conduct on transnational corporations is to facilitate, as necessary, the review and revision of previously concluded arrangements.

The Ad Hoc Inter-Governmental Working Group of the United Nations Commission on Transnational Corporations has before it a formulation on renegotiation of contracts in the following terms:

> As parties to contracts freely entered into, transnational corporations should respect and adhere to such contracts. In the absence of

contractual clauses providing for review or renegotiation, transnational corporations should respond positively to requests for review or renegotiation of contracts concluded with Governments or governmental agencies in circumstances marked by duress, or clear inequality between the parties, or where the conditions upon which such a contract was based have fundamentally changed, causing thereby unforeseen major distortions in the relations between the parties and thus rendering the contract unfair or oppressive to either of the parties. Aiming at ensuring fairness to all parties concerned, review or renegotiation in such situations should be undertaken with due regard to applicable legal principles and generally recognized legal practices.[16]

RECENT RENEGOTIATIONS

Whatever the doctrinal or theoretical position may be, renegotiation or revision of agreements is by no means a mere academic proposition. During the past fifteen years, the relations between host governments and transnational corporations have been marked by numerous revisions of contractual arrangements, especially in respect of natural resources, partly by legislation by the host States and partly by renegotiations with transnational corporations. Sometimes, renegotiation has taken place at the request of transnational corporations, in circumstances where insistence on the original contractual terms would have caused considerable hardship to the corporation.[17] A survey of 170 cases of relations between host governments and United States subsidiaries indicates that host governments have increasingly resorted to renegotiation as a means of changing the terms of investment, and that such a method is preferred to outright nationalization when the basic motivation is economic.

Between 1968 and 1974, the OPEC member states made considerable progress in securing control and the revision of fiscal provisions. They have sought to achieve effective sovereignty over their petroleum resources by participating in the control of the operating companies. The New York agreement of 1972 and subsequent OPEC declarations called for a timetable, within which host State participation would rise from 25 to 51 per cent from 1973 to 1982. These targets have generally been realized and, in many countries, home State participation has been advanced and accelerated above the rates and time schedules set by the New York agreement (see Table 2).

Subsequently, participation arrangements were extended to downstream operations, particularly refining, shipping, marketing and distribution.

Table 2 *Illustrative cases of changes in relationships, including renegotiation in the petroleum sector*

Country	Transnational Corporation	Year	Result
Algeria	Getty Oil	1968	51% Sonatrach-participation.
Algeria	CFP/ERAP	1971	51% Sonatrach-participation. (1971: Petroleum majority Code: State participation obligatory, state company Sonatrach as holder of concession/licenses.)
Algeria	ERAP	1975	100% state ownership, severing of relations.
Algeria	CFP	1975	51% state participation, renewed contract until 1980.
Colombia		1975	Concessions cancelled. Renegotiation into association and service
Ecuador*	Texaco-Gulf (et al.)	1973/74	25% participation by CEPE (state company).
Ecuador	Texaco-Gulf	1977	100% state ownership.
Indonesia		1974	Excess profits tax for contractors of PERTAMINA (by statute and renegotiation).
		1976	New agreement: share of net operating income, 85% for the government and 15% for the foreign firms.
Iran	'Consortium' (Gulf, Mobil, Exxon, Texaco, BP, ARCO, CPF, Standard Oil of Calif. et al)	1973	Consortium agreement of 1954 abrogated. Full management and control taken over by NIOC Sales and Purchase Agreement with Consortium (5 years).
Kuwait	Kuwait Oil Company	1972	25% state participation.

Kuwait	Kuwait Oil Company	1974	60% state participation.
Kuwait	Kuwait Oil Company	1976	100% state ownership (retroactive from 1975).
Kuwait	BP/Gulf	1975	Supply contract (5 years) for transnational corporation. 100% state ownership
Libyan Arab Jamahiriya	Exxon *et al.*	1973/74	51% participation.
		1977	100% state ownership.
Nigeria	Shell/BP	1973	Participation schedule: 35% to 51% in 1981.
		1974	55% immediately.
		1976	60% government, 20% Shell and 20% BP.
Qatar	QGPC, QPC *et al.*	1974	60% state participation.
Qatar	QGPC, QPC *et al.*	1976	100% state ownership; service contract for transnational corporations.
Saudi Arabia	ARAMCO	1974	60% participation: long-term supply, technical assistance contract.
Saudi Arabia	ARAMCO	1976	100% state ownership; maintain ARAMCO as operating entity (service contract).
United Arab Emirates	Abu Dhabi Oil Company	1974	60% state participation.
United Arab Emirates	Abu Dhabi Oil Company	1976	100% state ownership of all gas, both associated and non-associated, formalized by decree.
Venezuela†		1975	Takeover of oil companies, replacement by oil sales agreements (2 years, renewable), technical assistance agreements (3 years).

Source: United Nations Centre on Transnational Corporations, based on national sources.

* Starting 1977, in addition to the national oil company, CEPE, a consortium was organized with 62.5 per cent share by CEPE and 37.5 per cent share by Texaco.

† Since 1975, government is trying to expand and diversify its sale of oil to new consumers independently of the foreign oil companies.

Renegotiation of oil concessions resulting in participation by host governments has not entirely eliminated the role of transnational corporations; they still continue to' deal with the host States under new arrangements such as long-term sales contracts on rather favourable terms and long-term technical assistance agreements. However, even here a tendency towards shorter durations for such arrangements can be observed. The renegotiated terms have had a strong influence on newly negotiated contracts, which tend to reflect the standards and objectives already achieved by host countries in their renegotiations, and vice versa.

It is interesting to note that previously existing joint ventures and service contracts have remained largely unmodified by renegotiation, in so far as the host State's participation and control is concerned. This fact may suggest that companies which opted for more flexible agreements, and conceded a larger share of partnership and control to the host State, have achieved a higher degree of stability in their contractual terms and conditions.

Agreements between host governments and transnational corporations in the hard mineral sector have also been substantially revised by renegotiation, supplemented in certain cases by legislation. The main objects of such revision have been participation of host states in the ownership and operation of the mining undertaking, improvement of the fiscal regime in favour of host States, the stipulation of economic linkages in the renegotiated agreements, and the conclusion of new contractual arrangements such as technical assistance agreements, service contracts, management and joint venture agreements with transnational corporations (see Table 3).

In the manufacturing and service sectors, there have also been cases of renegotiation. Thus, the 1962 power contract for the sale of electric power by the Volta River authority of Ghana to an aluminium smelter owned by a subsidiary of Kaiser and Reynolds was renegotiated in 1977 before the expiration of its thirty-year term, the essential features of the revised terms being a substantial increase in the price of power and the stipulation of a new escalation clause. The agreement between Liberia and Firestone in respect of the manufacture of tyres was renegotiated in 1976, resulting in a substantial revision of the fiscal regime in favour of the Liberian Government.

Developing countries and transnational corporations have come to the realization that, in the course of renegotiations, not every type of contract and every generally recognized objective can be adopted. Much depends on the level of development, the market structure and the specific bargaining power of the host country. Accordingly, an array of various types of contractual regimes is evolving through experience rather than in reference to a model contract. Such a learning curve is illustrated by four major agreements in Liberia (LAMCO, LISCO, Bong and Firestone). Between 1960 and 1977, these agreements have been the subject of at least four renegotiations, resulting in a gradual and systematic modification of the terms within the framework of the basic concessions. Renegotiation is thus a main feature of modern, large-scale and long-term investment contracts in natural resources. The renegotiation pattern and the results reflect the sophistication achieved by the host country in developing the basic abilities to exercise control over its natural resources.[18]

RENEGOTIATION AND REVIEW CLAUSES

The recent renegotiation and review of contractual arrangements between host governments and transnational corporations has given rise to attempts to establish a mechanism for such an exercise. A growing number of investment agreements now expressly stipulate various formulae for the review of renegotiation of investment agreements to ensure greater predictability of conditions under which renegotiation may take place.

For example, some investment agreements contain general review and renegotiation clauses which affect the entire substance of such agreements. They prescribe conditions under which the entire bargain may be reopened. Thus, the agreement between the Government of Papua New Guinea and Bougainville Copper Limited in 1974 in respect of the renegotiation of the Bougainville Copper Agreement provided as follows: 'That the parties would meet at intervals of seven years to consider in good faith whether the Agreement was operating fairly to each of them and, if not, to use their best endeavours to agree upon such changes to the Agreement as may be requisite in that regard.'[19]

Similarly, the On-Shore (Voltaian Basin) Petroleum Production Agreement of 1974 between the Government of Ghana and Shell Exploration and Production Company of Ghana Limited, a subsidiary of Shell International Limited, contains the following provision:

It is hereby agreed that if during the term of this Agreement there should occur such changes in the financial and economic circumstances relating to the petroleum industry, operating conditions in Ghana and marketing conditions generally as to materially affect the fundamental economic and financial basis of this Agreement, then the provisions of this Agreement may be reviewed or renegotiated with a

Table 3 *Illustrative cases of changes in relationships, including renegotiation in the non-fuel mineral sector*

Country	Transnational Corporation	Year	Result
Gabon/Mauritania (Iron ore)	Miferma/Somifer	1974	Partial/complete takeover, marketing arrangements, entry of Japanese trading companies.
Ghana (Gold)	Lonrho	1973	55% equity interest in reorganized Gold Mine, with 5-year management contract for Lonrho. 6% royalty plus mineral duty and tax at 50%.
Ghana (Diamonds)	CAST	1973	55% equity interest in reorganized Diamond Mine, with 5-year management contract for CAST. 6% royalty plus mineral duty and tax at 50%.
Ghana (Aluminium)	Kaiser (VALCO) and Reynolds	1977	Substantial increase of rates for purchase of electric power.
Indonesia (Copper)	Freeport Minerals	1974/75	Reduction of tax holidays.
Jamaica (Bauxite)	Kaiser, Reynolds ALCOA, ALCAN (Heads of Agreements/ Final Agreements)	1974/76/ 77	Super-royalty: Imposition of a tax based on a percentage of the final ingot price (7.5% to 8.5%). 51% participation of Jamaica. Programme to increase processing of bauxite into alumina in Jamaica: long-term supply agreement (40 years); 7-year management contract.
Liberia (Iron and Steel)	LAMCO	1974	Increase in use of company's transportation system, localization of employment, minor increase of fiscal revenues.
Liberia (Iron and Steel)	Dt. Exploration and Bergbau (Bong Mining Company)	1974	Minor increase in revenue, stronger provisions for localization, creation of technical committee to increase national control.

Country (commodity)	Company	Year	
Liberia (Iron and Steel)	LISCO	1975	Payments for deferral of exploitation, liability to taxes of general application.
Liberia (Rubber)	Firestone	1976	Subjection to general laws, modernization of agreement, increase in revenue.
Papua New Guinea (Copper/Bougainville)	Rio Tinto Zinc	1974	Excess profits tax (sliding tax) and other tax changes. Mutual review of agreement every 7 years, other adjustment provisions.
Senegal (phosphate)	Taiba	1974	50% government participation, increase of tax receipts.
Sierra Leone (Diamonds)	Consolidated African Selection Trust Ltd	1970	51% equity interest for government and compensation of £2.55 million paid by government bonds at 5.5 interest over 8 years; management contract for transnational corporation.
Venezuela (Iron ore)	US Steel Bethlehem Steel	1974	Negotiated takeover followed by management agreement with another United States company.
Zambia (Copper)	Roan/AMAX	1969	51% state participation, management and sales contract for transnational corporation.
	Roan/AMAX	1974	Increase of national control over management via the newly created state company.

Source: United Nations Centre on Transnational Corporations based on United Nations Economic and Social Council, *Permanent Sovereignty over Natural Resources* (E/C.7/53, A/9716 and E/C.7/66 31 January, 1975, 20 September, 1974 and 1 March 1977; N. Girvan *Corporate Imperialism: Conflict and Expropriation. Transnational Corporations and Economic Nationalism in the Third World* White Plains, Indiana:: M.E. Sharpe, 1976 and other sources.

view to making such adjustments and modifications as may be reasonable having regard to the Operator's capital employed and the risks incurred by him, always provided that no such adjustments or modificiations shall be made within 5 years after the commencement of production of Petroleum in Commercial Quantities from the Production Area and that they shall have no retroactive effect.[20]

In some cases, transnational corporations have secured most favoured company treatment in their agreements with host governments. Thus, in its Aluminium Smelter Agreement of 1966 with Swiss Aluminium Limited, the Government of Iceland undertook not to 'offer any foreign producer of aluminium a power price more favourable for an aluminium smelter located in Iceland than the price and conditions set forth in the Power Contract.'[21] However, modern trends indicate a reversal of this pattern and host governments are now insisting upon the stipulation of most favoured country clauses. The object of these provisions is to enable host governments to benefit from more favourable terms which transnational corporations subsequently concede to other countries. However, since such concessions cannot be mechanically determined, the ultimate effect of most favoured nation clauses is to set in motion a renegotiation of the entire agreement when the requisite conditions have been satisfied. In some cases, the most favoured country clauses are confined to a particular region, such as Africa or the Middle East.[22] Nigeria invoked a most favoured African nation clause in 1967 in securing a general review of its petroleum agreements with transnational corporations in consonance with the terms which had been conceded by such transnational corporations in Libya.[23]

Some agreements have stipulated precise formulae for automatic adjustments in the financial and fiscal aspects of the agreement. Examples of such mechanisms are an escalation clause for varying the price of the commodity or the production and a graduated fiscal scheme in which the tax, royalties and other fiscal impositions increase at a certain level of production. Such provisions hardly involve any renegotiation since the expected changes are quantifiable and therefore automatic.

OVERVIEW

Although, as indicated above, some investment agreements have adopted the mechanism of expressly providing for review or renegotiation, this trend is by no means general. The impact of the exhortations of the

Secretary-General of the International Centre for Settlement of Investment Disputes in this regard is yet to be felt. In the first place, while many transnational corporations have generally manifested considerable readiness in accepting renegotiation at the instance of host governments, they have, on the whole, preferred to treat each invitation to renegotiate on an *ad hoc* basis, without committing themselves to a general principle of renegotiation according to a predetermined formula. The concept of an agreement as constituting a definitive bargain excluding subsequent review or modification is still prevalent, and many transnational corporations regard express renegotiation or review mechanisms as unnecessary or burdensome. In the second place, some host governments consider express renegotiation clauses as unduly restrictive, since they exclude review until certain specified conditions, such as a lapse of five or seven years, have been satisfied. Some host governments would therefore prefer to reserve their sovereign prerogative to call for renegotiations when political and economic exigencies so demand.

My critique of the conceptual structure of investment agreement as a species of private contract points to several alternative arrangements. Instead of a contract in the traditional sense, an investment agreement could be regarded as no more than a broad framework in which the government and the transnational corporation declare their basic commitment to a particular undertaking or project; but a framework which admits of a continuous process of the revision and redefinition of their relations when circumstances require. As a commentator has remarked, the investment agreement would then be regarded as a mere invitation to the ball, with the substance of the terms being determined according to the tune of the particular number![24]

In short, a long-term transnational agreement can only provide a basis for a viable and enduring relationship between a host government and a transnational corporation if it is regarded as a broad framework of business relationship which admits of a continuous process of accommodation and adjustment between the parties, rather than a body of fixed rights and obligations impervious to political, economic and social changes. Such an approach would, of course, constitute a radical departure from traditional doctrine, but, as has already been pointed out, the Anglo-American theory of contract has not always remained fossilized and inflexible. A departure from current traditional doctrine is therefore not necessarily inimical to the common interest of both investors and host governments.

From the practical point of view, flexibility could be further ensured by recourse to in-built mechanisms in the agreements which provide for systematic or programmed changes. As previously mentioned, the stipulation of review clauses is one such mechanism. Another device is to insert 'fade-out' provisions whereby the equity or other interest of the transnational corporation is reduced, with a corresponding increase in the interest of the host government, in accordance with an agreed programme. 'Fade-out' arrangements could also be made applicable to the number of expatriates employed by the transnational corporation. This would involve a programme for increasing the number of local personnel in respect of designated positions within a prescribed period.

Another mechanism for ensuring flexibility is to provide for shorter terms of the agreement. The renewal of such short terms would then provide an opportunity for an appropriate revision.

Many commentators and indeed transnational corporations would acknowledge the essential validity of the case for renegotiation but would contend that renegotiation or review clauses would be more equitable and fair if they provided for reference to third party arbitrament in the event of a dispute between the host government and the transnational corporation as to the terms of the revision. Distinguished jurists such as Shawcross[25] and Hyde[26] have indeed suggested the establishment of an international adjudicatory body fully invested with jurisdiction to review transnational contracts in the light of all relevant factors. Such a jurisdiction would go substantially further than that of many international tribunals which is limited to the adjudication of disputes arising from the interpretation and enforcement but not the review of contractual arrangements. An obvious consequence of such third party arbitrament would be to exclude the unilateral action by the host government as a last resort on the basis of its sovereign rights.

The feasibility of such a system would obviously depend on the confidence which both parties, particularly the host government, have in the competence, fair-mindedness and philosophical outlook of the panel and the extent to which the basic ground rules applicable to such review are acceptable to host governments in view of their disenchantment with the principles of traditional transnational law.

In view of the controversy which has raged over various theories of contracts, it may well be that another possibility in regulating the relations between host governments and transnational corporations is to dispense with the investment agreement or its equivalent altogether. This would mean that the transnational corporation and its operations would be brought under the normal regime of the municipal law of the host country, subject of course to such concessions as would be appropriate in the circumstances. This would dispose of any pretensions of the transnational corporation to a little legal enclave fortified by traditional legal and commercial concepts. It is to be noted in this connection that developed countries do not entertain such long-term transnational agreements with transnational corporations. The interests of such corporations are regulated by the general law.

NOTES AND REFERENCES

1   See paragraphs 1 and 2 of Declaration on a New International Economic Order, General Assembly resolution 3201 (S–VI).
2   Resolutions of the Sixth and Seventh Special Sessions of the General Assembly; namely, the Declaration and Programme of Action in the Establishment of a New International Economic Order — resolutions 3201 (S–VI) and 3203 (S–VI); The Charter of Economic Rights and Duties of States — resolution 3281 (XXIX); and resolution 3362 (S–VI) on Development and International Economic Cooperation.
3   See generally Oscar Schachter, *Sharing the World's Resources*, New York, Columbia University Press, 1977.
4   P.S. Atiyah, 'Contracts, Promises and The Law of Obligations', *Law Quarterly Review*, Vol. 94 (1978), p. 193.
5   Morton J. Horowitz, *Harvard Law Review*, Vol. 87 (1973–74), p. 1.
6   For example, Louis B. Sohn and R.R. Baxter, 'Responsibility of States for Injuries to the Economic Interests of Aliens', *American Journal of International Law*, Vol 55 (1961).
7   Lord Shawcross, 'The Problems of Foreign Investment in International Law', *Receuil des Cours*, Vol. 102 (1961), pp. 339–63.
8   R.Y. Jennings, 'State Contracts in International Law', *British Yearbook of International Law*, Vol. 37 (1961), p. 156.
9   F.A. Mann, 'State Contracts and State Responsibility', *American Journal of International Law*, Vol. 54 (1966), p. 581. See also Fatouros, 'Government Guarantees to Foreign Investors', 1962, and R. Brown, 'Choice of Law Provisions in Concession and Related Contracts', *Modern Law Review*, Vol. 39 (1974), p. 625.
10 R. Geiger, 'The Unilateral Change of Economic Development Agreements', *International and Comparative Law Quarterly*, Vol. 23 (1974), p. 73.
11 Oscar Schachter: *Sharing the World's Resources*, New York, Columbia University Press, 1977, p. 128. The relevant United States law is the US Negotiation Act of 1951, as amended.
12 Shawcross, 'The Problems of Foreign Investment in International Law'.
13 M. Faber and R. Brown, '*Changing the Rules of the Game*', paper submitted to the Workshop on Mining Legislation and Mineral Resource Agreements, Botswana, 1978, p. 12.
14 *Report* of the Group of Eminent Persons to study the Impact of Multinational Corporations on Development and on International Relations: United Nations Document E/5500/Rev.1.ST/ESA/6 of 1974, p. 38.
15 For example, *Annual Report* of the Secretary-General to the Administrative Council in 1974 and 1975.
16 Paragraph 5 of the Chairman's formulation of the Basic Principles in the Code of Conduct for Transnational Corporations.
17 E.g., the renegotiation of the Shashe Project in Botswana.

18   An internal paper prepared for the United Nations Centre on Transnational Corporations by T. Walde.

19   Item IDV of the Heads of Agreement of 6 June 1974.

20   Section 47(b) of the Agreement.

21   Article 36 of Master Agreement *re* Aluminium Smelter between Iceland and Swiss Aluminium Limited, 28 March 1966.

22   See, for example, Section 47(a) of the above-mentioned On-Shore (Voltaian Basin) Petroleum Production Agreement between Ghana and Shell.

23   D.N. Smith and L.T. Wells, Jr., *Negotiating Third World Mineral Agreements, Promises as Prologue*, 1975, Cambridge, Mass., Ballinger, p. 137.

24   Powell-Lamco Project: Proceedings of American Society of International Law, 1967.

25   Shawcross, 'The Problems of Foreign Investment in International Law'.

26   James N. Hyde, 'Economic Development Agreements', *Receuil des Cours*, Vol. 105 (1962), pp. 271–369.

19 Changed Circumstances and the Continued Validity of Mineral Development Contracts

Hasan S. Zakariya*

INTRODUCTION

I

In their attempt to renegotiate the inequitable terms of some outdated mineral agreements concluded with foreign concession companies, some developing countries have sought in recent years to justify their demand for modification on the principle of changed circumstances. Thus, for example, the Declaratory Statement of Policy adopted by the Organization of Petroleum Exporting Countries (OPEC) in June 1968 (Resolution XVI, 90), in calling for several readjustments of the contractual relationship prevailing between individual OPEC countries and oil companies at that time, pointed out that such a process is warranted by changed circumstances.[1] In their public statements the concession companies denied then, and probably would still deny, the legal validity of that doctrine arguing the inviolability of contractual relationships.

This paper is an attempt to demonstrate that the principle of 'changed circumstances' is not merely a matter of expediency, but has, as its basis, the solid foundation of legal theory and practice.

II

Before turning to the main task, certain preliminary observations which might appear self-evident, must nevertheless be made.

*United Nations.

Freedom of contract:

It is universally recognized that persons, natural or juridical, can enter into contracts with a view to regulating the manner in which their present or future relationship is to be governed. Hence the maxim that 'the contract is the law of the contracting parties'.

It is equally recognized however that the autonomous will of the contracting parties is not absolute; it is subject to certain conditions and limitations laid down by law within the context of which the contract has been made. Some of these conditions relate to the *ab initio* validity, such as the capacity to enter into a binding contract (age limit, state of mind, marital status, . . . etc.), and a proper declaration of will not vitiated by fraud, mistake or duress. Other conditions are designed to bring the contractual terms into harmony with the general standards of morality and public policy.

Once the contract is thus validly conceived and born, the law normally will give it its blessing and allow it to run its normal course with little or no hindrance. However, under certain circumstances, during the execution of the contractual provisions, the law may sometimes intervene, with a view to adjusting the contractual relationship in order to restore the contractual balance, thus making it more equitable and just.

The effect of 'changed circumstances' upon the continued validity of the contractual provisions belongs to this particular stage in which the law and the contract cross paths.

Nature of mineral development contracts and the applicable law:

It is useful to mention at the outset that all mineral development contracts are normally made between the state or one of its agencies, and private parties, individuals or corporate entities. Since the element of public interest is overwhelming in all of them, these contracts must be regarded as *contracts of public law*; the specific name which may be conferred upon them under various systems of law, be it 'state contract', 'administrative contract' or 'contract of public authorities', is in fact of little practical consequence.

It follows therefore, and perhaps it need not even be said, that if the other party to the contract happens to be a foreign subject, this should not alter the nature of the mineral development contract so as to remove it from the jurisdiction of the contracting State and make it subject to another system of law, such as, for example, international law.

It is axiomatic now, to say, that only *States* can be subject to international law.[2]

THE VALIDITY OF THE PRINCIPLE OF CHANGED CIRCUMSTANCES

Those who deny that changed circumstances should have any effect on the continued validity of contractual relationships normally contend that it has not been accepted in international law and has never been applied in any case by an international court or tribunal. They also maintain that no legal system provides a sound basis for the argument that the principle of the sanctity of contracts should be qualified by the principle of changed circumstances.

This position is in fact untenable. There follows some of the evidence which would demonstrate its untenability from the standpoint of (1) international law, (2) leading systems of national law, (3) ethics, philosophy and general theory of law.

1. International Law/Law of Treaties

Before discussing the impact of changed circumstances on the continued validity of treaties in international law, it is necessary to stress once more the fact that mineral development contracts are not subject to international law. International law is cited here not only because of the close affinity of the law of treaties with the law of contracts under private law — a considerable part of the former has been borrowed from the latter[3] — but also because international law reflects the general trend of legal thinking on this matter in the world community.

As has been observed, the doctrine *conventio omnis intellegitur rebus sic stantibus* (which hereafter will be referred to simply as *rebus sic santibus*) is originally a private law doctrine which dates back to the Roman Glossatores and found its way later into international law through private law.[4]

While it is true that the precise meaning of the doctrine has not been strictly defined in any international judgment, most writers on international law seem to agree that, according to the doctrine, there is in every treaty an implied clause which provides that the treaty is to be binding only so long as things remain the same. Basic changes in circumstances which were taken for granted by the contracting parties at the conclusion of the treaty may entitle the party against whom the change operates to suspend or denounce the treaty.[5]

For the purpose of the discussion at hand there is no need, we feel, to deal at length now with the scope and the precise conditions for the application of this doctrine in international law. Our immediate concern here is to show that, contrary to what the mineral development companies contend, this doctrine has long been accepted in international law.

The following is only some of the evidence in support of this conclusion:

Writers on International Law:

Almost all writers on international law refer to the doctrine, and numerous articles and special treatises on the subject have appeared since the time of Grotius who mentioned it in his treatise on the law of war and peace.[6] A great number of jurists have, in one form or another, approved the doctrine but in general they seem to have restricted themselves to a mere repetition of what their predecessors said before them.[7]

Some of the early writers on international law, particularly Kluber and later German writers, such as Heffter, Hartman and Holtzendorff, believed that the validity of treaties ends 'at the time of the essential change of such and such circumstances whose existence was supposed necessary by the two parties . . .' Whether this condition was stipulated expressly or not, it results from the very nature of the treaty.[8]

Among the more recent writers one can site Oppenheim who held that:

> Vital changes of circumstances may be of such a kind as to justify a party in demanding to be released from the obligation of a treaty which cannot be abrogated by unilateral notice. Many writers defend the principle . . . and assert that all treaties are concluded under the tacit condition *rebus sic stantibus*. In substance — although it has on occasions been abused by providing a cloak for lawless violation of the treaties — the doctrine *rebus sic stantibus*, when kept within proper limits, embodies a general principle of law as expressed in the doctrines of frustration, or supervening impossibility of performance, or the like.[9]

Sir John Fisher Williams wrote:

> There has been a general acquiescence in the doctrine that an essential change of conditions involved the obsolescence, that is to say the supervening invalidity, of treaty obligations contracted with a view to the conditions so changed, so far as those obligations remain executory. The doctrine has commended itself as we shall see to lawyers as to philosophers . . . The good sense of mankind supports it; an analogous doctrine of English municipal law may be vouched in its favour.[10]

Schwarzenberger, who in his 'Treatise on International Law' refers to this doctrine as 'the highly dynamic principle of treaty interpretation', has this to say: 'The maxim . . . *rebus sic stantibus* has a sound basis in experience. In every consensual engagement a number of basic assumptions are made, and frequently taken for granted, by both parties. If, subsequent to the conclusion of a treaty, these conditions cease to be fulfilled, the treaty may be thought to have lost its raison d'être.'[11]

Rousseau may be quoted (translation from the French):

73 — Radical and Unforeseeable Changes in Circumstances.
Theory of the clause *rebus sic stantibus.*

The doctrine of *rebus sic stantibus* is the theory according to which an essential change in circumstances, in light of which a treaty was concluded, can cause such a treaty to be annulled, or at least affect its binding force. In other words, the rule according to which treaties are to be concluded on condition that circumstances remain the same — *rebus sic stantibus* — implies that a treaty can cease to be binding if the conditions which existed when it was signed were later subject to changes of fundamental significance to the relationship between the contracting parties.

Introduced at an early stage into the legal writings on International Law, this theory is accepted today by the majority of authors.[12]

O'Connell, in discussing this doctrine, considers it not as an implied condition in all treaties, but rather as a rule of law. He says:

One is entitled to conclude that the notion of *rebus sic stantibus* has a place in international law, though it is much more limited than earlier writers suspected. The basis of the doctrine still, however, remains obscure. It can be regarded as a formulation of the rule of obsolescence or that of impossibility of performance, and as such a mode of termination of treaty, or it can be regarded as a right to revision. It can be considered as a rule of law operating objectively to affect the treaty or as no more than an implied term for the realization of the parties intentions . . .

It is preferable to view the matter as one of treaty revision rather than one of treaty termination . . . , and a rule of law rather than an implied term.[13]

State Practice:

It is to be noted that the doctrine of *rebus sic stantibus* has been invoked on several occasions in modern times by various states, including some of the Western democracies.[14]

It is to be admitted that the doctrine may at times be abused and become an excuse for breaches of treaty as in the case of the German violation of Belgian neutrality in 1914. But apart from this flagrant example, as Friedmann pointed out, there are several undisputed occasions on which leading Western powers seem to have invoked the doctrine with greater justification to obtain release from a treaty obligation. He cites several examples which he firmly believes constitute an implicit recognition of the doctrine of *rebus sic stantibus*, among them the successive revisions of the Treaty of Versailles and the more recent example of the consent of the three Western allied powers — contrary to the inter-allied agreements of Yalta and Potsdam with regard to the status and administration of Germany — to the establishment of the Federal Republic of Germany, the constitution of which was approved by them in May 1949, and the many subsequent acts of recognition of the *Bundesrepublik* not only by these Western powers, but also by the Soviet Union.[15]

There are several other occasions on which the doctrine has likewise been invoked in modern times: Russia in 1870, Austro-Hungary in 1908, the Ottoman Government in 1913, Norway in 1924, Soviet Union in 1924, China in 1927, Persia in 1927, France in 1929, Germany in 1936 and the United States in 1941.[16]

It is of particular interest to note that the United States resorted expressly to this doctrine in support of its unilateral abrogation of the International Load Line Convention. In his opinion of 28 July 1941, the then Acting Attorney General of the United States, in arguing that this Convention had ceased to be binding upon the United States, said: 'It is a well-established principle of international law, *rebus sic stantibus*, that a treaty ceases to be binding when the basic conditions upon which it was founded have essentially changed. Suspension of the Convention in such circumstances is the unquestioned right of the State adversely affected by such a change. . .'

The Proclamation of August 1941, issued thereafter by President Roosevelt suspending the Convention, re-iterated the same reasoning as that advanced by the Attorney General.[17]

Judicial Application:

It is to be admitted that comparatively few cases have arisen before judicial bodies, national or international, in which it has been necessary for them to define and apply the doctrine of *rebus sic stantibus* as a rule of international law.

In these few cases, however, not only was the validity of the doctrine accepted without question, but there is evidence, as we shall shortly show, that the only reason why it was not applied to the case at hand was that the particular facts involved did not warrant its application.[18]

(i) National courts: there are at least six reported cases since 1882 in which the doctrine was invoked and brought before various national courts: three before the Swiss Federal Tribunal, decided in 1882, 1923 and 1928 respectively; one before the American Court of Claims decided in 1887; one before the German Court (Reichsgericht) in 1925; and one before the Mixed Civil Court of Egypt in 1925.[19]

The conclusion which may be drawn from these cases is that the courts of Switzerland, United States, Germany and Egypt have recognized the existence of the doctrine of *rebus sic stantibus.*[20]

(ii) International Tribunals: while it may be true that this doctrine has not been applied as yet by any international tribunal, this fact should not be construed to mean that the doctrine itself has been rejected. The fact is that these tribunals never questioned its validity; they simply held that the particular facts in the cases brought before them and in which this doctrine was invoked by the claimant state, did not justify its application.[21]

A leading case in which the merits of the doctrine were before the Permanent Court of International Justice was the often-cited one between France and Switzerland regarding the Free Zones of Upper Savoy and Gex, in which France claimed that the provisions made after the Napoleonic Wars for the withdrawal of the French customs lines some distance behind the Franco–Swiss boundary should be held to have lapsed owing to changed circumstances.

According to Lauterpacht, the Court was prepared to recognize the principle although it refused to say to what extent the change of conditions may have an effect on the continuity of the treaty obligations.[22]

Codification Projects of International Law:

Most significantly, the doctrine of *rebus sic stantibus* has been recognized and adopted both in the Harvard Draft Convention on the Law of Treaties in 1929 and the draft articles on the Law of Treaties prepared by the United Nations International Law Commission in 1966. The Vienna Convention on the Law of Treaties which was based on the latter provides in Article 62 for changed circumstances.[23]

The Covenant of the League of Nations:

It is of considerable significance also that Article 19 of the Covenant of the League of Nations[24] permitted the revision or abrogation of a treaty which had become inapplicable because a new situation had arisen, thus confirming the validity of the doctrine *rebus sic stantibus*.[25]

2. Leading Systems of National Law

As has already been mentioned, the doctrine of *rebus sic stantibus* was originally a private law concept dating back to the Roman Glossatores.[26] Various writers on international law have analysed certain aspects of the law of contract under different systems of law in order to show that his doctrine is widely accepted, although sometimes under a different name, as a general principle of law to which contractual obligations are subject.[27]

There follow some illustrations of the application of the doctrine under some leading national systems of law:

Anglo-American Law:

Change of circumstances as a valid qualification on the operation of the principle of sanctity of contracts is well-recognized under English common law. Brierly[28], McNair,[29] Lauterpacht[30] and others have all referred in this connection to the English doctrine of frustration or supervening impossibility of performance of contracts developed by English courts since the latter half of the nineteenth century.

In his 'Sanctity of Contracts in English Law' (1959), Sir David Hughes Parry, has this to say:

1. Where there is a positive contract to do a thing, the contractor must perform it or pay damages for not doing so, although in consequence

of unforeseen accident the performance of his contract has become unexpectedly burdensome or even impossible. But during the last one hundred years the courts have been evolving a doctrine to the general effect that if there should occur some intervening event or change of circumstances so fundamental as to strike at the root of the agreement, the contract should be treated as brought to an end forthwith, quite apart from the expressed volition of the parties themselves.[31]

2. Consequently, other juristic justifications for the dissolution of certain contracts by impossibility have had to be explored. The conclusion I have reached is that the doctrine of the implied term has served a useful purpose; it has enabled the courts, as it were by a legal fiction, to assume the jurisdiction to modify or dissolve contractual obligations so as to dispense justice to the parties, having regard to fundamental changes in circumstances outside their control. The doctrine of frustration is now so well recognized and established that it no longer needs the fiction of an implied term to support it. So it is generally but gradually being displaced by the theory that a change in circumstances that fundamentally strikes at the root of a contract justifies the imposition by the court of a solution that is just and reasonable in the new circumstances. The truth is, as Lord *Wright* has written in one of his Essays, 'that the court or jury as a judge of fact decides the question in accordance with what seems to be just and reasonable in its eyes. The judge finds himself the criterion of what is reasonable. The court is in this sense making a contract for the parties, though it is almost blasphemy to say so'.[32]

The French Law:

Here again, the doctrine is well recognized under French administrative law, a fact which should be of particular significance in discussing the nature and characteristics of mineral development contracts. The theory which is known as *l'imprévision* was formulated and developed by the highest administrative court in France, the *Conseil d'Etat*, and expounded for the first time in the now famous case of *Gas de Bordeaux* (of 24 March 1916). According to this theory, re-adjustment of the obligations of the contracting parties to an administrative contract is allowed if unforeseen changes in circumstances occur during the life of the contract.

Bruzin explains the theory as follows:

A contract is made in view of an existing economic situation. It is applicable to this economic situation or to an analogous economic situation with all the favourable and unfavourable hazards that they may comport; but when they pass the maximum of foreseeable events we are confronted by extra-contractual circumstances, because the contract was made in view of these circumstances. The contractual lien may subsist but the contract is not enforceable under the new conditions. Insofar as this situation endures, the execution of the contract can be required only as regards the conditions that were foreseen.[33]

Comparing this doctrine with the doctrine of frustration under English law, Professor Mitchell made the following observation:

In its outline the theory has much similarity with the English doctrine of frustration, but there is one major difference. While the English theory recognizes the termination of the contract and adjusts the position of the parties in view of this fact, the doctrine of *imprévision* on the contrary is founded upon the continuation of the contract. It was designed, in the first place, as a means of surmounting temporary obstacles to the continuity of performance. The similarity of the two doctrines lies in the circumstances which give grants for their application. The French doctrine depends upon the existence of unforeseen circumstances which result in *'bouleversement de l'économie du contrat'*, a phrase which is very close to Lord Wright's phrase, – the 'frustration of the commercial purpose'.[34]

It might be of interest to mention here that the theory of *l'imprévision* has found its way into the private law of certain other countries which adopted it in their civil codes promulgated in recent years. One can cite, for example, Article 269 of the Polish Civil Code of 1932, Article 1467 of the Italian Civil Code of 1946 and Article 147 of the Egyptian Civil Code of 1948. This theory has likewise been adopted in the codes of other developing countries.

Other Western Systems:

The notion that in certain cases the law will refuse to continue to give effect to originally valid contracts after a change of circumstances seems to obtain also in other systems of law. Lauterpacht cites Article 939 of the Austrian Civil Code which stipulates that the agreement to conclude a contract in the future is binding only if the circumstances have not in the meantime changed so as to frustrate the express or implied object of the agreement.[35] He cites also Articles 323, 605, 775, and 542 of the German Civil Code permitting the termination of the contract before its fulfilment in consequence of unforeseen circumstances.[36]

Further illustrations are to be found in the practice of the German courts in abrogating or remodelling contracts vitally affected by change of circumstances, a practice which is described as wide and comprehensive. Among the leading cases which should be mentioned in this regard are those decided by the Reichsgericht of 7 June 1921 in which the court, in affirming its right to modify the terms of the contract, referred to the 'elastic adaptation of the law to the economic conditions' as a means of fulfilling its true function of meeting the requirements of the time.[37]

All this shows clearly, as Lauterpacht pointed out, that the law will recognize at times that the contract has, as a result of unforeseen circumstances, failed to realize the true will of the parties and that it therefore cannot be maintained wholly or in part.[38]

3. Justification of the doctrine in ethics, philosophy, and general theory of law

The doctrine of *rebus sic stantibus* is not only widely accepted in both international law and some leading municipal laws, but is also deeply steeped in philosophy and ethics to an extent that led a certain jurist to point out that this doctrine owes its existence to the moral conscience rather than to the legal one.[39]

In spite of their strict adherence to the idea of the 'sanctity of contracts', the Canon law and the fathers of the Christian Church have recognized the validity of the doctrine and advocated its application. Thus Thomas Aquinas (1225–74) who in principle maintained that contracts be upheld even with regard to enemies, also said that, if circumstances existing at the time of making the contract had changed, non-performance of the contract was excusable.[40]

Later on, Western philosophers, such as Spinoza (1632–77), maintained that treaties and contracts last as long as the cause which produced them. 'No one makes a contract for the future except on the hypothesis of certain preceding circumstances. But when these change, the reason underlying the whole position also changes; accordingly every contracting party retains the right to consult its own interests'.[41]

Several other justifications and rationalizations have been advanced in modern times by the exponents of the doctrine:

Some jurists trace its roots not only to the maxim that contractual obligations must be carried out in good faith, but also to the rule, expressed for example in Article 1135 of the French Civil Code, that the contract binds the parties not only to what is directly stated in it, but also to all the consequences of the obligations implied by equity, custom and law.[42]

Some others find its basis in the theory known as the 'enrichment without cause', which prevents one party from enriching itself unduly at the expense of the other.

Still other jurists justify the doctrine on the basis of the principle of the 'abuse of right', others, on the idea of gross inadequacy of consideration, whether *ab initio* or *a posteriori*.[43]

IS THE SANCTITY OF CONTRACTS IRRECONCILABLE WITH THE DOCTRINE OF CHANGED CIRCUMSTANCES?

There are some who seem to believe that the application of the doctrine of changed circumstances would undermine the other crucial doctrine of 'sanctity of contracts'. While nobody would deny the outstanding significance of the sanctity of contracts, *pacta sunt servanda*, and the enormous influence — ethical, religious and legal — which it has had since ancient times,[44] it is not, in fact, as absolute as some people would have us believe. There have been several limitations on the freedom of contract brought about by both statutes and courts in various countries over the years, and more particularly during the last hundred years or so, even in those countries which still adhere to the free enterprise system.[45]

Pacta sunt servanda should of course continue to enjoy the respect and adherence due to it as an essential vehicle of stability and security without which no legal order can properly be maintained. But legal order should equally ensure equity and justice. This can only be achieved through the rational application of such principles as *rebus sic stantibus*.

Pacta sunt servanda, both in international law and under various municipal laws, is a relative concept. All systems of law have long ceased to regard absolute freedom of contract as socially desirable. As Lauterpacht pointed out, there are contracts which the law forbids and which it would not enforce; there are contracts which the law will not enforce after certain events have taken place. The reason for this emanates from the need for either giving effect to the real will, expressed or implied, of the contracting parties, or for safeguarding certain social values relating to the public good. Both ideas are general principles of law and they are both inherent in the doctrine of changed circumstances.[46]

All this demonstrates that the two doctrines are not diametrically opposed as some would think. They can easily be reconciled, since they, in fact, complement each other like the two sides of a coin. *Rebus sic stantibus* tends to enhance the effectiveness of *pacta sunt servanda* since it tempers its rigidity, and renders its application more dynamic and equitable.

Modification of contracts, due to changed circumstances, especially those of long duration like mineral development agreements, is neither an exception to, nor in contradiction of the rule *pacta sunt servanda*. *Pacta sunt servanda* simply means that contracts which have legally come into existence and continue to be in force, must be observed. It means the inviolability, not unchangeability of contracts.[47]

The law of contracts, like the larger body of law itself, should be, if we may use the words of Lord McMillan in describing the common law of England: 'a living organism constantly readapting itself to its environment and it is in that power of constant readjustment that its supreme merit resides . . . .'[48]

NOTES AND REFERENCES

1 Two principles of that Declaratory Statement may be quoted for illustration: *Mode of Development*: 1.; 2; 3. 'In any event, the terms and conditions of such contracts shall be open to revision at predetermined intervals, as justified by *changing circumstances*. Such *changing circumstances* should call for the revision of existing concession agreements. *'Participation:'* Where provision for governmental participation in the ownership of the concession-holding company under any of the present petroleum contracts has not been made, the government may acquire a reasonable participation, on the grounds of the principle of *changing circumstances*. If such provision has actually been made but avoided by the operators concerned, the rate provided for shall serve as a minimum basis for the participation to be acquired.'

2 'Any contract which is not a contract between states in their capacity as subjects of international law is based on the municipal law of some country', Permanent Court of International Justice in the *Siberian Loans* case (1929) M.O. Hudson, ed., *World Court Reports*, Washington DC., Carnegie Endowment for International Peace, Vol. 2, p. 371.

3 For a comprehensive treatment of this subject, see H. Lauterpacht, *Private Law Sources and Analogies of International Law*, London (1929).

4 L. Oppenheim, *International Law*, 8th edn, 1955, London, Longmans and Green, p. 939, note 2. See also A.D. McNair, 'La Terminaison et la Dissolution des Traités', *Receuil des Cours*, Vol. 22 (1928), p. 469.

5 J.L. Brierly, *The Law of Nations*, 6th edn, 1963, Oxford, Clarendon Press, G. Schwarzenberger, *A Manual of International Law*, 4th edn, 1960, London,

Vol. 1, p. 158; Sir John Fisher Williams expressed the idea thus: 'the phrase *rebus sic stantibus* is a convenient catch-word: treaty obligations are to remain. The essential 'things' inanimate and animate, material, moral and mental must remain in the condition in which they were when the treaty was concluded.' 'The Permanence of Treaties', *American Journal of International Law, Vol. 22 (1928), p. 89.*

6   Grotius, *De Iure Belli ac pacis*, Lib. II, Chap. XVI, p. 525 – cited by McNair, 'La Terminaison', p. 469.

7   McNair, 'La Terminaison', p. 470; H. Lauterpacht, *The Function of Law in the International Community*, 1933, Oxford, Clarendon Press, p. 270.

8   J. Kluber, *Le Droit des Gens Modernes de l'Europe*, (1874), cited in the commentary to Article 28 of the Harvard Draft Convention of the Law of Treaties (hereinafter will be referred to as the Harvard Project), published as a Supplement to the *American Journal of International Law*, Vol. 29, No.4 (1935), p. 1098. For the opinions of other writers like H. Wheaton, F. Wharton, Sir R. Phillimore, J. Westlake, F. Despargnet, de Louter, P. Fauchille, A. Werth-Rengdanz, ibid., pp. 1099–1100.

9   Oppenheim, *International Law*, p. 939.

10   Fisher Williams, 'The Permanence of Treaties', p. 89.

11   Schwarzenberger, *Manual of International Law*, 3rd edn, Vol. I, p. 543. Schwarzenberger has also this to say: 'In a swiftly changing world, the dynamic principle underlying the clausula (meaning *rebus sic stantibus*) has much to recommend itself' p. 159.

12   C. Rousseau, *Droit International Public*, 4th edn, 1968, Paris, Dallaz, p. 74.

13   D.P. O'Connell, *International Law*, 1965, London, Stevens, Vol. I, p. 297.

14   W. Freidmann, *The Changing Structure of International Law*, 1964, London, Stevenson, p. 300. He says: 'It is equally true that the theory and practice of the western democratic states accepts: (a) to an extent controversial in detail but not in principle, the doctrine of *rebus sic stantibus*, i.e. the principle that a basic change of circumstances may be a legitimate cause of repudiation or non-observance of a treaty commitment; and (b) the over-riding force in extreme circumstances of *Staatraison* i.e. of national policy interests over international obligations.'

15   Ibid., p. 301.

16   Schwarzenberger, *Manual of International Law*, p. 158. For further details, see J.W. Garner, 'The Doctrine of *rebus sic stantibus* and the Termination of Treaties', *American Journal of International Law*, Vol. 22 (1928), pp. 509–10 and *Harvard Project*, pp. 1113–24.

17   William Bishop, *International Law: Cases and Materials*, 1953, New York, pp. 106–2.

18   Cf., Oppenheim, *International Law*, p. 940. See also G. Fitzmaurice, *Second Report on the Law of Treaties* (International Law Commission of the United Nations), A/CN.4/107 (1957), pp. 119–21.

19   *The Canton of Lucerne v. The Canton of Aargau* (1882); *Lepeschkin v. Gosweiler et cie* (1923); *The Canton of Thurgau v. The Canton of St Gallen* (1928); *Hooper v. United States* (1887); *Bremen v. Prussia* (1925); *Rothschild v. Egyptian Government* (1925).

20   Oppenheim, *International Law*, p. 1106. It is to be noted that the Swiss Federal Tribunal in the case decided in 1882 made the following remarks: 'There is no doubt that treaties can be denounced unilaterally . . . if a change of circumstances has intervened which, according to the apparent intention of the parties at the time of the conclusion of the agreement, constitutes an implied condition for its preservation.' (Arrets du Tribunal Federal Suisses, 1882, Vol. VIII), cited by McNair, 'La Terminaison', p. 57.

21 O'Connell, citing the *Russian Indemnity* case and the case of *Nationality Decrees in Tunis and Morocco*, decided by the Permanent Court of International Justice in 1916 and 1923, respectively, *International Law*, p. 299: 'International tribunals, before which the doctrine is more suitably invoked, have in fact been confronted with it on only rare occasions, and while admitting it to be part of international law have not in fact found a fundamental change of circumstances.' See also Oppenheim, *International Law*, p. 940, and Schwarzenberger, 'Treatise', p. 544.

22 H. Lauterpacht, *The Development of International Law by the Permanent Court of International Justice*, (1934), London, Stevens, p. 43. For similar interpretation of the decision, see Friedman, *The Changing Structure of International Law*, p. 300; Schwarzenberger, 'Treatise', p. 545; *Harvard Project*, pp. 1106–10, in which the case was fully reviewed.

23 Article 62. *Fundamental change of circumstances*: (1) A fundamental change of circumstances which has occurred with regard to those existing at the time of the conclusion of a treaty, and which was not foreseen by the parties, may not be invoked as a ground for terminating or withdrawing from the treaty unless: (a) the existence of those circumstances constituted an essential basis of the consent of the parties to be bound by the treaty; and (b) the effect of the change is radically to transform the scope of obligations still to be performed under the treaty; (2) A fundamental change of circumstances may not be invoked as a ground for terminating or withdrawing from a treaty: (a) if the treaty establishes a boundary; or (b) If the fundamental change is the result of a breach by the party invoking it, either of an obligation under the treaty or of any other international obligation owed to any other party to the treaty; (3) If under the foregoing paragraphs a party may invoke a fundamental change of circumstances as a ground for terminating or withdrawing from a treaty, it may also invoke the change as a ground for suspending the operation of the treaty.

24 Article 19: 'The Assembly may from time to time advise the reconsideration by Members of the League of treaties which have become inapplicable and the consideration of international conditions whose continuance might endanger the peace of the World.'

25 Schwarzenberger, 'Treaties', p. 545; Garner, 'The Doctrine', p. 511. For further details on this point, see McNair, 'La Terminaison', pp. 477–88, and Georges Scelle, *Théorie Juridique de la Révision des Traités*, 1936, Paris, Sirey, p. 73 *et seq.*

26 Lauterpacht cites also the Roman rule *ad impossibilia nemo tenetur* as a further example of the doctrine in Roman Law. Op. cit., *supra note* 6, p. 272.

27 *Harvard Project*, p. 1111; Fitzmaurice, *Second Report*, p. 12; Georges Scelle, for example said, 'La théorie de l'imprévision n'est rein autre que l'application de la clause rebus sic stantibus aux contrats passés par les particuliers', *Théorie Juridique*, p. 29.

28 Brierly, *The Law of Nations*, p. 337.

29 McNair, 'La Terminaison', p. 474 *et seq.*

30 Lauterpacht.

31 Sir David Hughes Parry, *Sanctity of Contracts in English Law* 1959, London, Stevens, p. 47.

32 Ibid., pp. 50–1. For further details see, for example, S. Williston, *Selection of Cases on the Law of Contracts*, 6th edn, Boston; and B.J.L. Chitty on *Contracts*, 22nd edn, London, Sweet and Maxwell, Vol. 1, in both of which the famous case of *Krell* v *Henry* (103) and the group of similar cases which came to be known as the *Coronation* cases were cited and discussed (pp. 871–7 and 1159–229 respectively).

33   Bruzin, *Essai sur la Notion d'Imprévision et sur son Rôle en Matière Contract-uelle*, 1922, p. 219, cited in the *Harvard Project*, p. 1112

34   J.D. Mitchell, *The Contracts of Public Authorities: A Comparative Study*, 1954, London, G. Bell, p. 190. For further details on this theory, see André de Waline, *Droit Administratif*, 9th ed. 1967, Paris, Sirey, pp. 622–4; *Traite Elé-mentaire de Droit Administratif*, 4th edn., 1967, Paris, Librairie Général de Droit et de Jurisprudence, pp. 326–32; and more particularly de Laubadère, *Contrats Administratifs*, 1956, Paris, Librarie General de Droit et de Jursi-prudence, Vol. III, pp. 71–135.

 In France, like certain other countries, there have been specific legislative enactments embodying the substance of the doctrine of change of circumstances such as the *loi Faillot*, of 21 January 1918, enacted in France after the First World War. Although the French court of Cassation has been very reluctant to apply the theory of *l'imprévision* to private contracts, there are several pro-visions in the French Civil Code tempering the rigour of the contractual obliga-tion in case of non-fulfilment of the obligation for reasons independent of the debtor, such as Articles 1134, 1135, 1148 and 1150. See Lauterpacht, supra note 6, p. 272.

35   supra note 6, p. 272.

36   Ibid., p. 274.

37   Ibid.

38   Ibid., p. 275.

39   L'idée d'imprévision s'instaure plutôt dans la conscience morale que dans la conscience juridique', Bruzin, *Essai*, p. 91.

40   Hans Wehberg, 'Pacta Sunt Servanda', *American Journal of International Law*, Vol. 53 (1959) reprinted in *Selected Readings on Protection by Law of Private Foreign Investment*, 1964, Dallas, p. 52.

41   H. Lauterpacht, *Spinoza and International Law*, *British Yearbook of Inter-national Law*, Vol. 8 (1927), p. 94.

42   Lauterpacht.

43   *Laesio enormis* and its modern derivative, *lesion a posteriori*. For a more detailed review of these and other ideas, see Scelle, *Théorie Juridique* and Fitzmaurice, *Second Report*, pp. 124–8.

44   For a review of its development throughout the ages see Wehberg, 'Pacta Sunt Servanda'.

45   After reviewing the various considerations that are influencing the public in their attitude to the fulfilment of contracts, especially under English law, Professor Hughes Parry observed: 'All this tends to diminish the regard of the promisor for his promise or contractual obligation and it is not without interest that in the United States also the nineteenth century faith in the freedom of contracts is neither universally nor potently felt . . .' (*Sanctity of Contracts*, p. 76).

46   Lauterpacht, *Private Law Sources*, p. 170. See also Brierly, *The Law of Nations*, p. 332.

47   Cf. J. Kunz, 'The Problem of Revision in International Law', *American Journal of International Law*, Vol. 33 (1939), p. 42; and 'The Meaning and Range of the Norm Pacta Sunt Servanda' *American Journal of International Law*, Vol. 39 (1945), p. 197. In one of his judgments, Lord Summer observed that the prin-ciple of frustration, which corresponds to the doctrine of *rebus* under English law, 'is really a device by which the rules as to absolute contracts are reconciled with special exception which justice demand' (*Hirji Matji and others* v. *Cheong Yue Steamship Co. Ltd.*, L.R. 1926, 497, 509, quoted by Williams, 'The Per-manence of Treaties', p. 91.

48   Quoted by Sir Hughes Parry, *Sanctity of Contracts*, p. 74.

INDEX